Lorraine Butterfield

The Journey to Self Love

When Love Turns to Harm

Lorraine Butterfield

Copyright © 2018 Lorraine Butterfield

All Rights Reserved

ISBN: 979-8-6270-2718-0

DEDICATION

For the three most beautiful people in my life
Lauren, Violet & Ruby xxx

For all my friends and family who have stood by me whilst I wrote this story and listened to my frustrations, particularly my Mum and Dad.

For the lovely Jan Hiscock who edited and proof read my book so many times to get me to this point.

To all the people who have crossed my path and have contributed to my journey, my lessons and my enlightenment.

PREFACE

This is the story of Jennifer Smith, an everyday happy-go-lucky girl. Her life takes her on an adventure of twists and turns, going from a happy life into a life of manipulation, abuse, fear and torment.

She had always had a spiritual connection and intuitively knew that her life's purpose was waiting for her but in the meantime had endured good times and bad times. Her happy-go-lucky personality reached out to draw in things that she wanted to manifest. However, in the midst of all this came her biggest lesson by far.

The Law of Attraction is very straight forward if you understand it but if you are not quite on that conscious level it can bring all sorts of things to your door. By the very act of thinking something you can draw it in to you. This was something Jennifer was not completely conscious of and thereby not only drew in experiences of the good but of the bad and the ugly too.

Friendships, relationships, family and foe all feature on this journey. It is a story of strength and willpower. Her lesson being that anything is possible and there is always a way out. Never give up being her biggest motto.

This story is about big life lessons and how Jennifer came through the other side and how the universe kept presenting these lessons until she decided to finally listen. Something we can all do…. Listen more.

CHAPTERS

Chapter One	- The Background	P.6
Chapter Two	- A New Home	P.21
Chapter Three	- New Experiences	P.29
Chapter Four	- The First Marriage	P.39
Chapter Five	- My New Best Friend	P.46
Chapter Six	- Flying High and Then Back to the Ground	P.50
Chapter Seven	- Engaged But Not To Be	P.60
Chapter Eight	- A Chance Meeting	P.78
Chapter Nine	- The Relative Realisation	P.88
Chapter Ten	- My Eyes are Opened	P.95
Chapter Eleven	- The Wedding	P.105
Chapter Twelve	- My First Born	P.109
Chapter Thirteen	- The Emotional Blackmail	P.119
Chapter Fourteen	- Family Life	P.127
Chapter Fifteen	- Our Third Baby Arrives	P.132
Chapter Sixteen	- Our Neighbours	P.138
Chapter Seventeen	- What's Love Got to Do With It	P.143
Chapter Eighteen	- The First Court Order	P.146
Chapter Nineteen	- Another Hearing	P.174
Chapter Twenty	- Be Strong and Carry On	P.206
Chapter Twenty-One	- Social Services Reports	P.212
Chapter Twenty-Two	- Final Hearing & Family Group Conference	P.222
Chapter Twenty-Three	- A Start of a New Romance	P.225
Chapter Twenty-Four	- My Spiritual Revival	P.235
Chapter Twenty-Five	- My Soulmate	P.248
Chapter Twenty-Six	- Home At Last	P.269

Chapter One
The Background

My name is Jennifer Smith. I am just a normal everyday Mum of three children, or so it would seem! I'm not famous or glamorous but I am loving, giving and attractive, slim and petite, very active and sometimes referred to as a firecracker (as I get very excitable). This is a story about my life in the last 30 years or so and how events and life lessons in love and relationships have changed me to become the person I am today. It seems apt to start it here as this is about my relationships and where it all started. It's a story which I hope will reach out too many of you who may have been, are in or will find themselves in this situation and my intention is help you see that there is light at the end of the tunnel and to never give up hope but to heal the journey from abuse and manipulation and make way for the future.

My story starts a little while ago as this what I will refer to as the start of my lessons and learning in the journey of relationships. The learning coming later when the realisation of how I got into the relationships I was in and how I had the strength to walk away.

It was 1989 and I was a young lady of twenty and had not long left college. I was a very petite, curly headed brunette with the darkest brown eyes and a smile that lit up a room. I had headed out into the big wide world, full of enthusiasm and excitement. The world was my oyster and I was determined that I was going to make my mark on it. I had started working in a local Bank in the January in a place called Hereford. Hereford is a City that has so much history and beauty. The Cathedral sits proudly in the centre of the city with the River Wye running alongside it, very majestic and picturesque. There are cobbled streets and twittens and the remains of a city wall, historic landmarks all surrounded by rolling hills and beautiful lush countryside. This was my home and where I grew up, surrounded by family and friends. Everyone knew each other and if they didn't know you, they knew someone who did know you. My Dad was a northerner and had moved to Hereford in his young adult life with his parents. He worked for a local company as a Manager and my Mum was a housewife and occasionally took on casual work. Mum's home was her palace and she never ever stopped cleaning. You could see your reflection in the brass knocker of the front door and many a time, birds flew straight into our windows as the glass was so clean. Mum was a traditional mother and everything she did was for the family, particularly my brother and myself. We were a very close and loving family. We lived in a 1970's three bedroomed semi-detached house in a lovely area of the city on the outskirts. The house was close enough to walk into town but also near countryside, fields and the very famous race course. I had my own room which I had chosen the decor for and always had everything that I had ever wanted. I felt very blessed. School years had been tough years for me as I had very tight curly hair and had worn glasses and this had been used to ridicule me by a small minority of school children and had an effect on how I felt about my appearance. It had knocked my confidence but since leaving school things had changed. I was now an adult and the glasses had been replaced with contact lenses and styling my hair had become easier due to the increase in styling products now at hand and the curls could be controlled. I was earning my own money and felt a sense of self-worth. It had enabled me to purchase my own car and give me an independence I had never had before and it felt good. Working in the local bank was fun for me, as the people were very happy and easy to be with and I enjoyed every moment. Sometimes it really didn't feel like a job as we would laugh a lot and it was a pleasure to be there.

Then along came Finlay.   Little did I know how this was going to change my life and the path that I was to take. He came to deliver my Mum and Dad's new TV!!

His Dad owned a local electrical shop. A very individualistic business that offered TV sales and repairs, amongst other things. It was very much a personal service and most of Hereford used his shop due to the fact that they knew someone would come out if need be to fix any problems. They even did TV rental. Not like the major electrical retailers that we know today, where the personal service doesn't exist to the same level. Mum and Dad had ordered a new TV and Finlay was the person who delivered it. He turned up on a summer's day in a little white van and carried the TV into the lounge. He was a slim build and he had the bluest eyes and blonde wavy hair which fell over his forehead but the type of hair where he could flick his fringe. I just remember walking into the lounge to find this person standing there installing the TV. When he finally raised his head up and turned around he caught my eye. There was a moment of silence and we smiled at each other bashfully and he went bright red. He didn't say a lot and stumbled over his words as he installed the TV and then he left. I could feel my heart excitedly pumping blood around my body and the heat of embarrassment flushing my cheeks. I'd never experienced this feeling before and it felt warm and fuzzy and very lovely.

From then on synchronicities seemed inevitable. I worked in the centre of the city, so parked my car every morning on the outskirts and had a little walk into work. It seemed that every morning he would pass me by in his van and wave. I felt that warm, fussy feeling, every time he waved back and a little bashful blush on my cheeks. One day I told the girls in the office about the meeting and how lovely I thought he was but that he was very shy and so was I. A lovely lady called, Sarah, who was a colleague and friend, took it upon herself to do something about this situation as she couldn't bear the fact that neither of us were being proactive about moving this relationship forward to more than just a morning wave.

"Write him a letter", Sarah said.

"What would I say? I don't think I could, it doesn't feel right for me to approach him," I replied.

I could feel Sarah's frustration as she tried to persuade me to move things forward and I stood like a rhino in mud, not convinced that this was appropriate.

Every day Sarah would try to persuade me to write the letter and one day her frustration got the better of her and, unbeknown to me, she wrote him a letter telling him how much I liked him and it would be very nice if he would call me at work and maybe arrange to meet up. She put the note through his office door. The next day I had the shock of my life when he called. I was so embarrassed and amazed as the lady on switchboard announced to me that he was on the phone. The whole office stood still and gasped and all seemed to look in my direction. They all knew and I knew nothing of this. I could feel the anticipation in the air and my face was burning, my cheeks were flamed coloured and my hands were shaking, that warm, fuzzy feeling taking over again but nerves as well. I picked up the phone to answer the call and he told me that he had received the letter and then asked if I would like to go for a drink on the Friday night. My whole body shook and trembled and a "yes" slipped out of my mouth. That was the start of a very lovely relationship.

Finlay turned up on the Friday evening, again in his little white van and on time too, to take me to a local country pub for a drink. My stomach was doing cartwheels in anticipation of his arrival and how the evening would go and then it started knotting. This was my very first proper date and it seemed very scary. Although both of us were very shy we both chatted and chatted – in fact, that first night was not long enough. I felt as though I was floating and the butterflies were definitely fluttering in my stomach. The evening went so well that we arranged to meet the following week to go out again. He dropped me off before 11pm and drove away. I walked into the lounge and my Mum and Dad were sat, in anticipation, to find out how the evening had gone. I couldn't give them any eye contact as I felt embarrassed.

I Mumbled, "Yeah, it went really well. He seems nice enough".

"Are you seeing him again", my Mum asked.

"Yes, we are going out again next Friday," I replied.

There was silence but I could almost feel an air of disapproval. I shrugged it off and went upstairs to bed. I undressed, walked into the bathroom and threw up. The pre-date nerves of the evening had overcome me.

Every week, Finlay would pick me up in either the work van or his Dad's car. We would speak from time to time on the phone. Finlay would ring at work occasionally in between meeting, as a week where we didn't see each other seemed a very long time. There were no mobile phones then, I just trusted that we were meeting. He wasn't overly pushy and very often we would just meet up and go to a country pub for dinner or drinks or both. We became an item and that meant introductions to his friends and their girlfriends and every weekend became a big social event, with lots of drinking involved.

Finlay and I had lots of fun, very childish innocent fun but fun nonetheless. Very often I would come back to my car and he would have put fake spiders all over the windscreen or written with lipstick all over the windows 'I Love You'. It felt very romantic. Sometimes it was little notes. A lot of the time it was pranks where I would have to spend half an hour trying to get into my car before driving home. It made up for the times he refused to hold my hand in public or show affection whilst in company. Things that I shrugged off as just being him but that hurt deep inside. I repaid the favour one day by getting a friend to ring him up and tell him he was on the local radio quiz and he needed to answer three questions correctly and he would win tickets to a Hereford United match (he loved Hereford United Football Club). He fell for it hook, line and sinker and became very serious when answering the questions. All of the office staff were giggling in the background and when he found out it was a joke he was quietly amused. There was a consequence to this bit of mischief. Finlay had been teasing me about sending a man in uniform to strip for me on my 21st birthday and I was not keen. Finlay knew I liked a man in uniform but he also knew that having someone stripping was just not my thing. I was very naïve and conservative at this stage of my life and, just simply, those sorts of things embarrassed me.

My 21st Birthday arrived and I was at work. There had been lots of cards, flowers, gifts and frivolity. The girls in the office had been joking with me that maybe I would get an extra special gift from Finlay and laughing. I was getting about my business and was bustling about in the upstairs office of the bank.

I then got a call from the downstairs clerk,

"Jennifer, there were two policemen in the customer service area and they needed to speak to you".

I was agog – men in uniform!!

"Ok, I'm coming now. Do they definitely want me?"

"That's what they said," he replied.

After everything that had been said, I was now considering whether Finlay's joked was a reality.. All I could think was that he had arranged this and sent them to my place of work; how embarrassing. I descended the stairs of the bank followed by all the girls in the office, desperate to see what the male strippers might look like. This had never happened at the bank and the experience was new to them as well. There stood two policemen, one was a little portly and my only thought was; I really hope he isn't going to strip off!! The other Policeman was very tall and quite intimidating.

"Are you Jennifer Smith?" asked the taller of the policemen.

"Yes", I replied hesitantly.

"Is there a private room that we could talk to you in?" said the shorter of the two policemen

Oh my god!!!! I was in shock, not only were they going to strip but they wanted to do it in a private room!! Good Grief!! So, the Manager of the branch led the two policemen and myself to a private consultation room. I was now extremely hot and flustered and looked the colour of beetroot. The room door shut and as it did, the portly of the two policemen reached into his inside pocket.

"I hear today is a special day?" he said smiling.

"Yes", I replied with a jittery voice, "It's my 21st Birthday".

"This is for you", and he pulled out………. a birthday card from Finlay.

I don't think I had ever been so relieved in my whole life. A huge sigh of relief raised in my chest. No stripping involved. It was extremely funny and he had got me well and truly. The policemen happened to be friends of his family but it was very well thought out, although the Manager of the branch was not amused as she thought it was something serious. She gave me a stern stare but let the incident go.

Finlay was five years older than me and had his own flat right in the centre of the city and had travelled around India. He seemed very grown up to a young impressionable girl like myself. I had already placed this man on a pedestal, without really knowing whether we were in love or not and our relationship progressed very quickly. We had only been together six months when we decided that I should move into the flat and cohabit. Finlay felt we knew each other well enough and that it would be more convenient to live together. At least when we went out at a weekend we could both come home to the same place.

Although this felt like a good idea to me it turned out to be very traumatic one, as I now had to tell my Mum and Dad that I wanted to move out. As expected, my Mum was not pleased and I knew that this would be the case. She wanted her little girl to have the dream of meeting someone and getting married. Finlay was not her idea of the dream and although she had nothing against him, she was unsure of how committed he really was. I had broached the subject with my parents about moving in with Finlay after three months, which was met with disdain, and now we were back having the same conversation. My Mum felt that he needed to marry me or show some sort of commitment if he wanted me to live with him. I knew my Mum had always been very intuitive and this had upset me that she felt this way, not really knowing what Finlay's intentions were myself. I was determined that this was going to happen and opposition to this made me push harder.

When I did finally decide that it was time to move out, I probably did not execute it in the best way. It had got to the point where it was time for me to grow up and to leave home and I knew no other way. Although, in hindsight, I would have done things differently. It was February time and it was one evening after work so it was dark. I came home with a friend who I worked with and who I had confided in about my plans. She had agreed to help me with the move. I knew that my Dad who worked shifts at that point, would be asleep, so we would have to be very quiet when entering the house. My friend, Valerie, and I snuck up the stairs to my room with a handful of black sacks to fill with clothes and shoes and as much of my personal belongings as possible. As we busily and quietly put items in bags, my intuition, the voices in my head, were telling me that this wasn't the way to do things but, at this point, I could see no other way. My Mum must have heard us moving around.

"Is that you home, Jennifer?" Her voice sounded quite brusque, almost knowing what she was going to find.

My heart beat faster than it had ever done and Valerie and I stood still, as though time itself had stood still. Then Mum ascended the stairs rather hastily and she burst into the room. Caught red handed. We must have looked like two rabbits in the headlights. There was a period of silence. I stayed very calm and cool whilst my Mum proceeded to scream and shout to get an understanding of what was occurring. My Dad woke with all the noise and came to see what was going on. My Dad was always so calm and logical and very softly spoken and tried to calm things down. He took Valerie home and whilst he was gone Mum continued to cross examine me. Upon trying to explain my side of the story and to get across that I felt very strongly about needing and wanting to move out, Mum then decided to grab all the bags that were filled and throw them out through the front door down the driveway.

"Leave and don't come back and I really don't want to speak to you again," with that she turned around and left the room.

I had upset the one person who absolutely and totally loved me and it didn't feel very nice. My heart sank. I did as she wished and I picked up my belongings and got in the car and drove away. It wasn't a good way to start my first real relationship and I knew it but chose to ignore the voices in my head.

With trepidation I would make time to visit my Mum and Dad and brother every week, not knowing what to expect. I would sit and talk to my Dad who would be interested in how I was and my Mum would sit in silence. My younger brother, Mike, would excuse himself from the room as he didn't know what to say. It was not pleasant but they were still my family and I still wanted that connection. All I could do was to try and bridge the gap that I had caused, no matter what that took. Eventually, after several weeks of visiting, Finlay sent my Mum a huge bouquet of flowers and an apology and who knows what changed but things did. My Mum and Dad accepted that I had moved out and that I was now with Finlay. So, visiting home became pleasant and I would either visit with Finlay by my side or on my own and communications had opened up. The barriers had come down but it had knocked my confidence, as I had never been shut out of my family's life before.

Finlay was very shy and so was I, although I could be extrovert on times, especially when I was out socialising, dancing on tables etc... It felt like we knew everyone and everyone knew us when we were out and about. Our relationship seemed very solid although I had to admit that he could be a little too laid back for me, sometimes emotionally detached and a little immature although romantic behind the scenes. It took him quite a while to get used to holding my hand in public or showing any form of emotion towards me. It wasn't becoming to hold hands in public or show affection and that was a reflection of how his Mother and Father had been. His stuff that he carried with him. Although, I persevered with him and although it took him a little while to learn how to be more tactile and be comfortable with it, he eventually seemed to get there. However, he was funny and had a good sense of humour, liked a good time and loved to travel. Our common interests which held us together.

Wow, this all sounds just perfect!! In actual fact this relationship wasn't perfect and unbeknown to me, I had started to lose my identity. I had idolised this person and was now doing all the things I felt he liked. Finlay, he hadn't changed at all. He carried on doing what Finlay did. I had made him 'the one' and I was prepared to change myself to be with him. Very often my intuition would come into play and so many times I ignored the signs. I knew I had a gift and I knew my self-worth but was prepared to forego all of it for a relationship.

One evening Finlay and I left the flat and met up with friends in town for drinks. I had been tea total before having met Finlay, so was having an education in all sorts of alcoholic concoctions, much to Finlay's amusement. The evening was fun as we met up with Finlay's friends who like to have lots of drink and light-hearted banter. This was all new to me and I felt very grown up. Although I worked, I had lost touch with a lot of my school friends and now found my social circle were Finlay's friends. I had totally submerged myself into his life. I was doing the things he wanted to do and going to the places where he was comfortable. This particular pub was a place where he felt comfortable. It was more of a spit and sawdust type of place but it had live music as entertainment. Finlay had decided with his friend and his girlfriend to play a game. He loved to play all sorts of drinking games but this one was different. He decided that we should all go separate ways and see who could get chatted up first!! I laughed but I could feel inside me a certain amount of discomfort and felt my stomach turn. This wasn't my idea of a game and I wasn't comfortable with it. How could I tell him? I couldn't and instead I played along for fear of being the spoil sport. The two boys moved to the other side of the pub and I was left next to his friend's girlfriend talking. My attention not fully on what was being said as I was too busy observing Finlay and his friend in action. They approached two girls and bought them drinks. They laughed and joked. I could not bear this, it felt like betrayal to me. It was torture and all my emotions were boiling; the jealousy, the anger and the humiliation. How was this fun? Finlay caught my eye and smiled wryly at me. Rather than cause a scene I did the only thing I knew how to do, I turned and walked out. Finlay realised he had gone too far and followed me out of the pub. He ran to catch up with me and he grabbed my arm to stop me from moving forward. The tears welling in my eyes as I could no longer hold back how upset I was.

"How could you do that?", I asked him.

"It was just a game", he replied.

"That was no game, our relationship is over. I don't want to play games like that," I sobbed.

"Please don't end it... I never meant it to hurt you," he said as he pulled me into his arms.

This was something he very rarely did. He really does care about me, I thought!

For a while things improved although it felt different. I had started to feel a little insecure and had wondered whether Finlay really did love me but Finlay was on his best behaviour and I needed to trust that this was the case. I decided that I would like to travel and Finlay hadn't travelled for a while so had the bug again. The planning started for a new start in a new country. The idea was that we would learn a language whilst working abroad with the intention of staying there.

We decided on Spain and that was where we were headed. It was just after my 21st birthday. It felt very exciting. I love adventures and had always wanted to travel abroad. My parents were a little shocked when I told them and a little worried but had decided that they couldn't stop their daughter, as they knew that I had a mind of my own and needed to make my own journey in life.

Finlay and I travelled from Hereford to Plymouth to catch a ferry to Santander in my little gold Fiesta car with everything we thought we would need for our travels; a tent and sleeping bags and all the personal possessions we could carry, including a huge selection of music CDs; we both loved music and Finlay had introduced me to Jazz music and whole lot of other diverse music, compared to the Spandau Ballet and Bon Jovi that I had been used to. The first CD he bought me, as they were very new then, vinyl was just going out, was Fleetwood Mac. Finlay had treated me to an evening at the NEC to see them live. Their music had quite an impact on me and throughout my life. I had discovered the importance of lyrics, instead of making up the words. To me now, I understand the lyrics to be the messages that we would get if we tuned into our intuition. Now at this point I was listening to' Tell Me Lies' by Fleetwood Mac, the lyrics of which were:

'If I could turn the page,
In time then I'd rearrange just a day or two
Close my, close my, close my eyes

But I couldn't find a way
So I'll settle for one day to believe in you
Tell me, tell me, tell me lies

No more broken hearts
We're better off apart let's give it a try
Tell me, tell me, tell me lies'

Although I was learning the lyrics of songs, I was not consciously taking in the messages being relayed to me. My team of guides were trying to tell me something and I wasn't listening.

Lorraine Butterfield

We took the 24-hour ferry to Santander. That journey was the worst ever. I felt so ill. Ferries and me just do not mix. It's the rolling sensation and being ungrounded. Finlay tried to convince me to have a drink but not even a drink could steady me. I spent the whole journey lying down on some chairs in the bar area whilst Finlay wondered around to explore the ship. When we arrived in Santander it was very exciting, we drove away from the ferry and we set up the tent in a campsite a stone's throw from the ferry port. However, the stay was short lived and we only managed a couple of days as we found Santander a little unwelcoming. It was time to move on and find somewhere more amenable to tourists trying to learn Spanish. We packed up the car and then spent the next three months, not working as planned, but travelling and sight-seeing. A journey that eventually ended up in us driving over the Picas de Europa (a huge mountain range) and into Portugal. We headed to Estoril where I met with my cousin, Ian. Ian happened to be in Estoril for a wedding and had messaged Finlay whilst in Spain. Finlay and Ian were very good school friends and coincidentally, he happened to be a relative of mine too. Upon meeting up with Ian, Finlay and myself were introduced to the family where Ian had been staying and, of course, Portuguese hospitality meant that we were welcomed with open arms. We even ended up being invited to the wedding at the local church and the after-wedding party – five courses of fish. At the time I found that sort of food was quite off-putting as fish was not my favourite food but the traditional dishes were received with great appreciation. It was a very beautiful wedding.

When the celebrations were over Finlay and I spent a couple of days with Ian catching up on news back home and then it was time to move on. We travelled along the coast in Portugal and made camp in several places and eventually ran very low of money. Whilst visiting Lisbon a beautiful city with so many wonderful sites to see and whilst we were at the top of the Santa Justa Elevator in Lisbon, my car was broken into. We had

had such a wonderful day but when we returned all the valuables had been stolen and, at that point, we decided that with the turn of events it was time to head home. We both had an open return ticket for the ferry and enough money to feed ourselves and fuel the car to get to the ferry port. We rang relatives to let everyone know we were returning to the UK. Finlay contacted his friends in Plymouth to tell them too and to make arrangements as we needed to stay somewhere for the night before heading home to Hereford. The journey home was pretty much the same as on leaving and I felt quite ill. It just so happened that upon boarding the boat we met a lovely couple who chatted for a while and seeing my distress offered us their spare beds in one of the cabins. I was so happy and grateful for their offer. I rolled into one of the basement bunkbeds and slept most of the way. It was a relief not to have to sleep on a chair or the floor. We arrived in Plymouth and I was very relieved to see terra ferma. The one-night stay turned into us making Plymouth our home for the next two and a half years. We landed, met with friends; who put us up for several nights.

Life was about to change again. I had learned so many things and had found my independence, but the independence was also at a cost. I was following the path of someone else, because I loved them but was it my path?

Chapter Two

A New Home

Finlay had made some life changing decisions whilst we were away in Spain and Portugal, one of which was that he didn't want to take over the family business. The other was that, if he wasn't going to take over the shops (his Dad had a couple then), that he needed to decide what career he wanted. He decided that as he was good with computers that a Degree in Computer Studies would suit him. He applied straight away to the local University in Plymouth and was accepted. I was quite happy to be there for him but needed to sort out some work. Although I had only worked in the Bank for a couple of years and had left a few months previously, I decided to walk into the local Bank and told them that I had previously worked for them in Hereford. In those days, it wasn't what you knew, it was who you knew. They rang the Manager at the Hereford branch who was very complementary about me and my work, and I was given a job the next day. Within one week we had found a flat to rent local to the city centre, Finlay was a full time University student and I had a job to keep the money coming in. Everything was perfect for a while.

I joined the administration team in the local Bank and most people were friendly enough but very clicky and kept a very close network. I could feel the energies were different and it certainly wasn't as friendly and comfortable as my last branch. There were only really two people in the office who I felt I connected with; both of whom were from outside the area. This kept me sane enough and they would join me at lunchtimes to wander around the town but I was starting to feel a little lonely and isolated and the only person I really could talk to was Finlay. The job was not really satisfying a need and I felt my energies being drained by the negativity of the people around me but I carried on. This was a good job and well paid.

Finlay decided that he needed to sell the flat he owned in Hereford. It went on the market and it sold very quickly. Some of the money was used to put towards a deposit on a flat six months later. As I was a Bank employee, I managed to secure a mortgage. I had to convince them with facts and figures that buying was more financially beneficial than renting and the argument swung in my favour. This felt good to be able to buy my first property. This was somewhere I could make my own and it would be mine. My spirits lifted and, as if by magic, an opportunity came along that was very rare and I got promoted to work within another area of Plymouth, the Area Office. This felt like a huge step up for me and I was very proud to be selected to work in such an exclusive area of banking. I had felt uncomfortable in the local branch for some time and this was an opportunity for that all to change. The people who worked in the Area Office were much more amenable and friendly and work became enjoyable again. Even the working conditions were brighter and lighter.

My Mum and Dad had now come around to the fact that Finlay and I were together and seemed to be making a life for ourselves. They spent many weekends visiting us and we made the journey back to Hereford every other weekend, to catch up with the family. Part of me missed home but something inside of me knew that it was the people I was missing, not the place. Finlay was getting along with his course, although it appeared he spent a lot of time at home rather than at lectures but he was getting the work done.

My time with Finlay was filled with many happy occasions. He was a jolly person in the right company, easy going and there was no harm in him. The monotony of working and university was broken by travel. We loved our holidays and especially skiing. My income and the savings that Finlay had gave us the opportunity to carry on travelling. In fact, Finlay gave me quite an introduction to skiing. Finlay had taken me to the dry ski slope first, just to get used to wearing ski boots and putting skis on my feet. It had been a successful visit although a little tentative. We decided to travel to Val D'Isere in the French Alps. This was my very first skiing holiday and he took me to the top of a black slope. For anyone who skis they will know that ski slopes are graded by their level of difficulty. Black being extremely hard, followed by red, yellow and blue slopes (generally beginner runs). I froze (as in couldn't move) as I looked down at the immensity of this slope and then something took hold of me. I took a deep breath.

"I either ski this or walk this", said the voice in my head.

I felt myself moving down the slope. Tentative at first and then relaxing more and more as the skis glided over the snow and I swayed from side to side, traversing the mountainside. I could hear nothing but the breeze as I moved faster and faster. It was so exhilarating, the powder of the snow and the ease that I felt gliding over this winter wonderland. When I questioned Finlay later about why he took me down such a difficult slope, Finlay explained that the snow at the top of a black and red run is powder and a lot easier to ski. He was right and I couldn't agree more with him. I took to it like a duck to water. That was the first of many ski-ing holidays and they were incredible. Some of the holidays we took alone but there were a few with friends, Finlay's friends who had become mutual friends.

We stayed in Plymouth for two years and then Finlay was given a work placement in Brighton for one year. I wasn't very keen on staying in Plymouth on my own as I had found making friends extremely difficult, which was unusual as I am outgoing and friendly. Although I loved to be on my own, the only friends that I had made had been with the two people who also came from outside of the area and they had their own families and commitments. So, I decided to follow him over to Brighton,

Sussex. I applied for a transfer to move with work to different offices. Again, fate was working in my favour and I had an interview in offices just outside of Brighton and hey presto, I had secured myself another position. I had set an intention and imagined what it would be like to live somewhere different and it all felt very exciting.

I had visited Brighton for the first time a few weeks previously to look at the flat that Finlay was going to rent. Somehow, I knew that I was going to love living there. The energy felt right and I felt at home.

When Finlay moved to Brighton I still had one month to work at the current offices. So, he moved over first. I still had to find a tenant to take over the flat. Whilst he was away I took it upon myself to find an agent and get a tenant. Finlay moved to a flat in Hove, which he shared with a young man named Jake, who was also doing a work placement at the same offices in Brighton. As I was still living in Plymouth and my heart wasn't really there, I decided to drive over to visit Finlay for the weekend. The strangest thing was he had never given me the address and I had only ever been to Brighton once before. I arrived in this metropolis to suddenly realise that actually, I did not know exactly where he was living or the address and we did not have a mobile phone between us. Finlay obviously realised this too. Whilst I was driving around Brighton, the only thing he could do was to stand outside the flat in the street he was living in the hope that I would go by. Now it may sound like complete madness but it worked. I drove all the way along the seafront to Hove and turned into a road which looked vaguely familiar and there standing on the side of the road was Finlay. It was unbelievable. Telepathy in full swing and the energy fields opening to guide me in.

When I eventually moved across to Sussex, I realised that it was where I was meant to be. It felt as though my purpose was to learn in this wonderful metropolis, a knowledge that can only be gained from life experience.   I moved into the flat that Finlay shared with his work colleague. It was fabulous. There was nowhere quite like Brighton and I could instantly connect with the buzzing energy and excitement that surrounded me. Nowhere had felt like home until now. Although I had moved several jobs now all within banking I decided that there was more. Demographically I felt now this place had something to offer me and life was to take a different turn. Opportunities seemed abound.

Not only did my location move but I regained a new confidence. Finlay had commented on many occasions about my figure and how my legs could be longer, as he felt they were quite chunky and this had impacted on me more than I let on. I am extremely sensitive and the criticism was hurtful and untrue. In fact, I was very slim and petite and not at all chunky. I had started running a little in Plymouth but now found that I had a zest for more exercise perhaps subconsciously aware that I was being judged by the one person I adored. The running toned my body and I felt differently about how I looked. There were so many options available to me. I took myself off to the local leisure centre and found an aerobics class. It felt good to be exercising and I was looking good. I attended classes at least three times a week. In my very first class I was particularly excited to be taking on this new hobby, as aerobics was a new thing not just for me but the country. I entered the hall and paid my money and was directed to go and take a seat on the floor. I sat next to a girl who I tried to chat to. She was very similar looking to myself, small and dark and petite build. She was not particularly friendly and didn't really want to interact. At that point I realised that the people in Brighton are not always the friendliest of people. Not because they are being rude but they are busy getting on with their lives and don't tittle tattle (as my gran would say). This girl eventually would become one of my best friends. Her name was Sally.

In between aerobics, walking along the seafront and working, Finlay and I would play squash together. A game Finlay liked to play to keep fit but I rose to the challenge and learnt how to play too. Again, the endorphins would kick in at the thrill of winning, especially being new to the game.

After a year in Brighton, Finlay went back to Plymouth to finish off his Degree. I had been introduced to one of Finlay's work colleagues and he happened to be renting a bedsit in the centre of town. The accommodation was at the top of a private house. It had been agreed that once he moved out this was perfect accommodation for me to stay in whilst Finlay finished his final year at University. So, I moved to the accommodation in Brighton just by the station for six months with a lovely South African couple, Daphne and Edgar, who were like a Mum and Dad to me. They had retired and were very accommodating. I had made some lovely friends working in my new office and very often on a Friday night we would all meet up and go clubbing. Very convenient that they all lived in Brighton too. Daphne would very often mother me and tell me that I must get a taxi home after a night out, as I was a small build and anyone could attack me. This made me smile but I understood the sentiment. However, very often I found myself walking home after clubbing as the queue at the taxi rank was so long it was quicker to walk. I was also kick boxing at the time and felt as though I could conquer anything. I would very often go out clubbing wearing Doctor Martin boots and leggings. My Dad would very often comment, if I was dressed this way, that I looked like Max Wall. I would ignore the comments as I was feeling very cool and trendy. I was starting to grow into the person I wanted to be, doing the things I wanted to do because I enjoyed them and I had no one around to challenge that.

I was still in love with Finlay and when he returned to Plymouth the contact with him became less and less and I found that I was the one making journeys to Plymouth nearly every other weekend and I was the one calling him. I was convinced that if I didn't call him that he would probably never have got in contact. My absence didn't seem to bother him and I felt he didn't care. The point came when I could take no more, as once again my confidence was being battered, I called it off. I desperately hoped that there was something left and that he would argue to keep our relationship going. I was wrong and he seemed to accept at that point the relationship was over. I was very upset and concluded that I obviously had meant nothing to him but decided that I needed to get on with my life and embrace all that it held.

It concerned my Mum and Dad that Finlay was no longer on the scene but they also appreciated that I had made a life for myself in Brighton and although I had considered moving back to Hereford, it didn't feel right and I was very, very happy where I was.

I had accumulated a group of friends within the fitness group and at work and we spent a lot of time going out and exercising together. Work was enjoyable and I loved going from department to department chatting to different people. I was running, doing aerobics and roller skating up and down the seafront. I kept myself very busy and very fit, as well as kick boxing. My life was full of fun again and my soul was being fed with all the exercise that I was doing. It was a great distraction from the broken heart that I was carrying inside. The aerobics instructor was very well known and a bit of a Lothario. He owned lots of property in Brighton and Hove and had become my friend. He would even get me up on stage to teach the classes. He had arranged for a skiing trip over the Christmas period, returning on Boxing Day and that's where Sally and I really became very close as we were the only two girls amongst a group of five on the trip and we stuck together like glue. Sally was quite shocked when I reminded her of the first time that we had met but did laugh at the irony of it. The ski-ing holiday was fantastic although Christmas Day felt a bit odd ski-ing instead of being at home with family. Once I returned on Boxing Day, I got into my car at the airport and drove straight back to Hereford so that I could be with family. My Mum and Dad had delayed Christmas Day for Boxing Day so we could all open presents together. It was a very enjoyable Christmas.

Sally and I spent a lot of our spare time together and became very close. Very often we would be mistaken for sisters and Sally's Mum and Dad were absolutely adorable and became very fond of me as I was of them.

Life for Jennifer Smith had been full of mixed emotions but it was now looking up. She had money, her own place to live, good friends, fun and excitement and life was really good. Her heart had been broken by someone she had trusted and there had been disappointment that Finlay had not fought to save their relationship, but she had decided it was meant to be. It was time for her to move on and find her path in life.

Chapter Three

New Experiences

I realised that I needed a new challenge in my life and knew that I had the travel bug again. I started to apply to the airlines which made sense, with the urge to travel. So, you can imagine how I felt when I got a job working for a very well-known British Airline as ground staff. You know, checking people into their flights and boarding them at the gates. Seeing famous people trotting through the airport. A step in the right direction. I found them a fabulous company to work for. It was all very exciting and even the experience of wearing a uniform for me raised my confidence. It was in this job that I started to show the spiritual side of me and I became known as 'Mystic Meg'. It was discovered one night on a shift that I could read palms and not only read palms but read people intuitively as well. I had known as a child that I had this skill and had practiced for many years at home and amongst the safety of family members, but I had been too shy to admit to it. It became quite a thing on a work shift, as very often whilst on a check in desk, I would be called and asked to close my desk and return to the allocating area and then asked to read for someone. I didn't mind and found it amusing. My reputation for this skill was spreading far and wide over the airport. Until one day when I did get a bit spooked. I read a gentleman's hand and I didn't like what I saw, the energy around this person was dark and fearful. This scared me as I realised how much responsibility I was carrying for such a skill and how people had expectations and I might not be able to give them what they wanted to hear. I closed down my psychic side and from that point on refused to read anymore palms and concentrated on the human side of me.

During my time as a member of ground staff I also moved house, yet again. The fitness instructor had bought a large house in the area and was looking for someone to take one of the bedsits who could also be trusted to make sure the house was running to everyone's satisfaction. For being in charge, I was offered a discounted rate. I couldn't resist the bargain so told Daphne and Edgar that I was moving on. It was quite a sad moment as they had been like a surrogate mother and father to me and had wanted to look after me but I felt to need to stand on my own feet again. The house had six other tenants and we all got on very well. This was lots of fun and because the other people in the house were from all over the world, it made evening conversations interesting, learning about different cultures and foods. Unfortunately, I only stayed for six months in this accommodation as the owner became a bit too friendly and I felt uncomfortable. Luckily, whilst working as ground staff, I had got very friendly with a lady called Denny and her partner Jim. They had spent most of their lives in Australia and then had come back to this country but their hearts were in Byron Bay on the surf. They had a house in a beautiful village called Lindfield and they were renting one of their rooms out. I jumped at the chance to move in with them. This was an opportunity to be with other shift workers to share lifts with and it meant that the travelling distance to the airport would be shorter. Jim and Denny had their bedroom in the lounge and we shared the dining area, kitchen and bathroom. Both of them were very laid back and very amusing.

Finlay and I had stayed in contact albeit on a platonic level. Whilst I was living with Jim and Denny, Finlay called me, "Hi Lorraine". He said with a hesitant voice.

I wasn't surprised to hear from him but his voice sounded different. "Hi Finlay, how are you?"

"I'm good but I was wondering if I could come over and visit you?"

I was a little taken aback and not sure what the implications of this visit would be. "Why do you want to come and visit me? I thought it was all over between us?"

"Well, I have done a lot of thinking and I feel that we have been together for a long time and it's a bit strange without you and maybe we should try again."

My heart started to beat faster and faster and a mixture of emotions welled up inside my stomach. I couldn't work out if I was happy, sad, indifferent, overwhelmed or shocked.

"Umm, well I suppose we could talk. When were you thinking of coming over?"

"This weekend?" Finlay answered with an air of hope in his voice.

I could hear how excited he was at the prospect of us reuniting but I wasn't sure I felt the same. "Ok", I agreed.

Finlay arrived and stayed for the weekend. Upon lots of talking, walking and negotiation, we decided that we would try again to get our relationship back on track. Jim and Denny agreed that Finlay could move into my room with me. Finlay went back and organised renting out the flat again and within a short time, he had found a job locally and we were a couple again.

He admitted that he had realised that he wasn't very forthcoming with his emotions and that he missed me and that he loved me. I had taken him back but part of me had found a new life and it was a compromise again to have him living with me. My routine was thrown, I no longer had just myself to please, Finlay needed my time too. It was during this time that he did what a lot of people do, he got down on one knee and proposed. He had always said that he would never get married but our relationship had got to a point where it was make or break and I had told him what I was really thinking; that I was considering walking away. When he proposed I was quite shocked and all that I could do was say, "yes". I considered my decision over and over again and had come to the conclusion that we had been through so much together that this was how relationships were supposed to be and we should be together!! Not only that, but I felt very flattered and a little overwhelmed. This was everything that I had ever wanted but my gut feeling was telling me this wasn't really what we should be doing. I couldn't put my finger on what had changed for me but there had been a shift. He was giving me all the attention that I had always craved from him. Having been the only person that I had had a relationship with and going against my intuition, I agreed to marry Finlay. Finlay and I wandered through the Lanes in Brighton and stopped at an antique shop where I spotted a Sapphire ring surrounded by diamonds. We went inside and the ring fitted perfectly (my fingers are very small, so it's always a miracle when a ring fits). The ring was mine and we were now planning how and when we would get married. It was now official and it was all meant to be!

Within a month of the marriage proposal I became very ill. It started with stomach ache and sickness. I was floored and couldn't get out of bed. I had never felt so ill in my life. It then developed into me bleeding from every orifice you can imagine; bottom, nose, blood in my vomit, urine and stools. This went on for several days and eventually Finlay decided that the doctor would have to be called in. He was a lovely local doctor and he came to the house as I was not able to walk due to weakness and the pain in my stomach. He decided that I had developed colic and that the best way forward was to take all the dairy out of my diet and refer me for some tests. I was already vegetarian at this point, it meant I would now be on a bland vegan diet. My weight had dropped considerably from 8.5 stone to 6.3 stone. I looked very thin and fragile. With massive weight loss, I was also at risk of losing bone mass. Therefore, my illness was accompanied by hospital appointments, endoscopies and dexa scans (for bone mass assessment). Although the sickness and cramps passed and I did become well very quickly, the weight stayed off for quite a considerable time. I just had to carry on working and life got back to normal with the occasional follow up hospital appointment to keep an eye on my progress.

Then my life really turned around. I had always wanted to be cabin crew and recruitment for this role was very sporadic. When the opportunity arose, I applied and was over the moon when I received a letter to say that I had an interview. I put the blip of my illness behind me and everything was falling into place. Sally had also decided she had had enough of the banking business that she worked in and had applied for Cabin Crew and was flying at this point. We decided to do a trip together, as I could get staff standby tickets. Sally had a Bermuda trip coming up. She got herself a ticket and a week later we were jetting off to Bermuda. Due to the Economy and Club Class being full, I managed to sit in First Class, a super luxury. As I was travelling with a crew member and was also a member of staff it meant that I was allowed to travel on the crew bus the other side which took us to the hotel. I found everyone so lovely and helpful and I got lots of pointers from the crew members in preparation for my interview and how to get through the process. Although Bermuda is not very big Sally and I found it very beautiful. We had an amazing three days. The beaches were white sand and the water was so clear. We cycled around the island and one evening, whilst sat in an Italian restaurant waiting to be served darkness fell upon the restaurant. A huge cruise liner had pulled into dock and now completely blocked our view of the sea. When our meal was finished and we left the restaurant, we stood by the side of this huge achievement of engineering. Looking up we almost fell backwards at the vastness of this vessel. It was a very surreal moment. The holiday was very relaxing and the opportunity to experience different cultures and Bermuda was very exciting. The men really do wear Bermuda shorts and long socks and the island is incredibly friendly. This trip had given me the insight that I needed to realise that this was the life that I wanted.

When we got back to the UK it was all systems go. The interview process is the most gruelling (almost an assault course) and consisted of several interviews. I had always worked for Banks and financial services institutions but it had always been my dream to fly and get paid to see the world. Even though I was told by a career's officer at school, at the tender age of 16, that I should think of another career, maybe secretarial or hairdressing, as there was no possibility of getting an airline job!! I had learnt, through my experiences so far, never ever listen to someone who tells you something is not possible, everything is possible. There are so many wonders to be had. I was a dreamer but I knew that if you have a dream, it may come true. The interviews consisted of an initial assessment to see if you are intelligent enough to work for the company. I sat and took an online test at the head office at Heathrow and was then advised that they would let me know if I would be picked for the next round of interviews. The next day I got a phone call to advise that I had qualified and I was asked to attend the next interview the following week. The interview that followed was on a one-to-one basis where the interviewee is looking for all the "buzz" words they called them then. I had been told that certain words scored points on the interview process and was given examples such as, "team player", "communication", "attention to detail", etc.... I made sure that I used them within the explanations to the answers. The wait for the next stage was a little longer. However, I received a phone call and was advised that I had been successful. The excitement was uncontainable, my heart was pounding and the thought that my dream was coming true just made me glow. But I was advised that I would have to pass the medical before a final offer was made. The medical consisted basically of height/weight ratios and eyesight and hearing. Funnily enough to fly you used to have to be 5'2" and I knew that I was 5'1.5" but the nurse that was measuring me was using a very old-fashioned rule and when she questioned my height, I told her that their height chart must be wrong and she agreed! So, after completing all these rigorous assessments there was no guarantee that the position would be offered out. All I could think about was whether I was going to get the job? I believed that I had done enough and sure enough, I had. It was then on to the eight-week training course. I was advised that the course was quite long as there was so much information to take in, such as safety equipment to learn and its uses and being able to serve in first class using silver service. I attended the course and everyone was so lovely. Every day felt exciting and I really connected with all the other trainees. Excitedly, near the end of the course, everyone received their rosters. The rosters were only planned 28 days in advance and everyone was very enthusiastic to see where our first trips were taking us to and whether they had been chosen for long haul (Worldwide) or short haul (European destinations). Everyone had been chosen to fly long haul. The air was buzzing. The next question on my mind was, "where will I fly to first?" My friend on the course had got Dallas, would we be flying together? It was Miami, in fact during my time as cabin crew I spent quite a bit of time in Dallas and got known by several crew members as 'Debbie Does Dallas' as I had come to get to know all the highlights of the City! Such as the grassy knoll and the book depository, of course!! Wow, this was fab. Life couldn't get any better I was now working with my bestie for the same company however, our paths didn't cross whilst on flying duty.

My time with the airline was filled with many wonderful adventures, of which Finlay joined me. He came to Africa with me and we flew to Victoria Falls, then Brazil and we flew up to Iguazu Falls on the Brazilian, Paraguay border. Our most memorable experience ever though was the chance that I got to go on Concorde and fly to New York. It was 1997. I was truly grateful for this experience especially bearing in mind shortly after this trip in 2003 Concorde decommissioned. I had seen Concorde on several occasions when I had flown out of

Heathrow and had even considered transferring to short haul to qualify as a Concorde cabin crew member. When I saw that there was a deal on Hotline (a last-minute flight deal company used for staff) I couldn't believe my luck. They were offering tickets on Concorde and returning subsonic for £500 so I acted quickly and got myself two tickets. It was a very exciting time. Finlay and I arrived at Heathrow and I could feel myself smiling so much I could burst. We waited in the departure area and Concorde pulled up to the jetty. It looked so small and once we boarded I was so amazed at how small Concorde actually was inside as well. The grey leather interior was very plush and the seating was very comfortable but it felt quite compact. The crew knew that I was a member of staff and approached me to let me know that they were aware of this. If going on Concorde wasn't enough, we got some extra special treatment of a bottle of Champagne to accompany us on our journey and even a visit up to the cockpit to meet the Captain, First Officer and Engineer. I had to admire how they worked in such a confined space. During the flight there was a loud bang and the Captain announced the aircraft had hit Mac 2. We were now going faster than the speed of sound. Incredible experience. I grinned at Finlay with that 'cat that got the cream' expression. I had been to New York several times before but never on Concorde. I felt very privileged to show Finlay all the sites, even climbing to the top of twin towers which sadly no longer exists. Being at the top of the Empire State building was definitely my favourite moment due to the fact that I love the movie 'Sleepless in Seattle' with Meg Ryan and the final bit of the movie had been filmed there. An old romantic, it couldn't get any better. Coming back on a 747 felt a bit slow. It had taken two and a half hours to get to New York and seven and a half getting home. However, a truly special experience.

The more you do in this life the more you realise what you think you are missing out on but sometimes what you have is all that you need. I went away 3-4 times a month to most amazing beautiful places. The first time the airline flew to Baku in

Azerbaijan, I was so excited. It was the first time that tourists (well crew and oil workers) were permitted to fly into the country. This war-torn country had very architecturally beautiful buildings that were looking very tired. I compared it to Russia, even though I had never been to Russia. The crew stayed in quite a plush hotel in the centre of Baku and it even had a Casino. As far as I was aware, it was the only hotel there. It seemed very unusual to me for Baku to have a Casino, as most of the locals were extremely poor, although, it was rumoured that Russian mafia lived and ruled within Baku. At the centre of Baku were the old silk Markets, it felt very romantic to me. It could have been a scene out of an Arabian movie. The buildings were low built with beautiful arches that surrounded a square. I could feel how the energy would have been in years gone by when traders would travel far and wide to bring the best silks to sell. When the people smiled, they were genuine smiles and their teeth were almost all gold. I had asked in the hotel about why so many people had gold teeth and had been told that, apparently, when the war had started the locals hid any wealth that they had. Therefore, the best way to hide their gold was to have it put into their teeth to keep it safe. Walking around I witnessed the men sitting around playing chess in the park. The women and children were the workers in Baku. Whilst walking through the park a wedding party passed me by. It was like watching something from the Smirnoff advert I had remembered from days gone by. The bride wore a very large white dress and the skirt looked as though it had three or four steps from her waist and make up that was completely overdone. I gazed on in awe as this beautiful bride joyfully and gracefully moved passed her with her family as an entourage, happy chatter and joyful laughter sang out. I thought about how my marriage to Finlay would be. The happiness that it brings when two people who love each other celebrate that special connection and how happy we were going to be.

Baku is on the Caspian Sea and obviously, a stroll along the seafront was a must for me as I loved being by the water. I felt very comfortable near water and it always made me feel so calm and relaxed. Although the sea in Baku was not quite as I imagined. There was slick oil floating on the water and on the horizons, are the mighty oil refineries pumping away. The smell was not the seaside smell that I had been used to but that of rotten fish. On the second day of this trip I had encouraged two crew members to come out walking with me and whilst walking along the seafront we met a man who offered us the opportunity to go out on a ferry boat and have a trip around the bay. Never one to miss an opportunity, I jumped at the chance. My colleagues looked at me in disbelief, laughed and joined me. The boat was so old and rusty and we were all quite relieved when the journey was over. I was surprised we lived to tell the tale but it was an experience and one which I would never forget. Whilst on the boat I got to see a beautiful house that had been derelict for quite some time. The building had been decorated with gold but the door had been barred with iron gates which were highly padlocked. I was told by a local that it was Rockefeller's old house and that when he had moved out it had been boarded up and that is the way it had stayed. I was sure it must have been a jewel in the crown many years previous.

I had everything I could hope for, a man in my life who wanted to marry me, my dream career and money. There was nothing more I could have hoped for or wanted. I felt strong, confident, independent, I knew what I wanted. So why was it about to change?

Chapter Four

The First Marriage

Finlay and I decided that we couldn't carry on sharing the house with Jim and Denny and, as we were getting married, we needed to get our own home. We decided that, as we had rented out the flat in Plymouth again, we could afford to buy a new house on an estate in Burgess Hill. Sally and her partner had also moved to Burgess Hill. I loved that we could arrange to meet up and go for a workout at the gym or just have coffee. Happy times for me. Finlay came on a lot of my trips abroad and got to travel quite extensively and we saw some amazing sights.

We had also decided that as we had been together for nine years, that a big wedding would not suit Finlay, as he was so shy. I felt strange as I had always wanted the big white wedding but there was something of a 'get out clause' with a small wedding. Again, my intuition was kicking in and I wasn't listening.

"Could we not get married in a church in Hereford?" I asked tentatively.

"I'm not really religious and I don't think it would be right. I don't really want all the fuss. People watching us and having to walk down an aisle. It's just not me and it's not want I want to do. It has to be something small or I can't go through with the wedding and I'd rather go away and then there doesn't have to be a big fuss," he replied in a nonchalant manner.

My heart felt heavy with disappointment and almost rejection. It was his way or no way. This had not been how I had wanted to marry but I was going along with it to placate the person who I felt would be my life partner, 'The One'. It was decided that it would be easier and less fuss if we went away and married abroad. At that point getting married abroad wasn't as common as it is today. Las Vegas was the easiest and cheapest option. I booked a flight to Las Vegas, accommodation and wedding arrangements through the same company. This even included hairdresser, limousine and all the wedding chapel arrangements – easy peasey. My parents were not amused that it was in Las Vegas and didn't see the need to marry abroad when we could get married in the UK, where it was more accessible. They decided that they were not going to attend. I was upset as all I had ever hoped for was that I would marry and make my parents proud and have my Dad walk me down the aisle. This wasn't going the way it should and it didn't feel comfortable. I went off on a trip to Rio and whilst I was there I rang my parents to try and persuade them otherwise but to no avail. They had their reasons and I respected that. Everything felt wrong but "it can't be", I told myself. I had been through thick and thin with this man, we had been apart and come back together.

It was the summer of 1998 and we took our last trip as singletons. Finlay and I boarded a flight to Los Angeles, accompanied by Finlay's mother. She was the only relative to attend. Upon arrival we weaved our way through Los Angeles airport to find the transferring flight to Las Vegas. I felt more nervous than I had ever felt before not helped by Finlay who constantly reminded me that he said that he would never get married.

In my head the whole way I had a song in my head, Aerosmith's 'I don't want to miss a thing'

The lyrics being:

I could stay awake just to hear you breathing
Watch you smile while you are sleeping
While you're far away dreaming

Lorraine Butterfield

**I could spend my life in this sweet surrender
I could stay lost in this moment forever
Every moment spent with you is a moment I treasure**

**Don't want to close my eyes
I don't want to fall asleep
'Cause I miss you baby
And I don't want to miss a thing
'Cause even when I dream of you
The sweetest dream will never do
I'd still miss you baby
And I don't want to miss a thing**

**Lying close to you felling your heart beating
And I'm wondering what you're dreaming
Wondering if it's me you're seeing
Then I kiss your eyes
And thank god we're together
I just want to stay with you in this moment forever
Forever and ever**

The second verse was how I wanted to feel about Finlay. I am a romantic. Was this romantic? Was this what I wanted? Was he the one I wanted forever and ever?

A car was waiting to take us to the hotel when we arrived in Las Vegas and everyone was very welcoming. I was in a daze the whole time. Everything had been taken care of and it was just a matter of turning up. The day we arrived it was a matter of settling into the room. Then the following morning it was all happening. This was my wedding day. The hotel had arranged a hairdresser to come in. She put my hair up into a curly bun and surrounded my hair with gypsophila. The white Scarlett bouquet and button hole were delivered and I put on my wedding dress. It was a beautiful red dress to the knee. It hugged my tiny body to the waist and then three layers of organza skirt floated around me. I put on my white shoes. I looked like a beautiful, delicate doll. This was it. I was getting married. Bouquet in hand Finlay escorted me to the limousine. A photographer was on hand to take lots of photos. Then on to get married in the Little White Wedding Chapel on the Strip. A very memorable day. The service took no longer than 5-10 mins and Finlay's Mum witnessed the service. My stomach turned and I knew that I was doing the wrong thing but I chose to ignore my gut feeling yet again. It had all gone too far to change my mind. I had been through thick and thin with this man and that's what you do when you are in a relationship and if you can overcome all of these things then it is meant to be. Well, that was my belief at that point and what I kept telling myself over and over again. Having been brought up on the proviso that you make things work whatever the situation (there's that belief again). When the service was over it was back to the hotel to meet up with Finlay's relatives who lived in Arizona. His Aunt had baked a wedding cake which had come as a huge surprise for me. The family all ate together. Then it was time to say goodbye to everyone. The rest of the evening we spent relaxing in the hotel, playing on the slot machines. It was a wonderful experience even though I knew that I had done the wrong thing for me. A few days later we flew home and back to reality.

The months following the wedding became very interesting. Now that we were married it felt as though something in our relationship had been lost. Very often I would come home from a trip in the early morning burst into the house, excited to be home and see my new husband to find him rushing out the door with just enough time to say "hello" and "goodbye". The cupboards would be almost bare. There would be no bread or milk or butter and all I wanted was some toast and a cuppa before heading up the stairs to get some sleep. Very often Finlay would forget that I was due back on a certain day and would look surprised as I walked through the door.

"Oh, how come you are back today? I didn't think you were back for another day or so." Finlay's eyes almost looking like a rabbit in the headlights.

"My roster is on the wall, Finlay. Have you got time for a cuppa?"

"No, sorry, got to leave. I'm off to work. See you later." And with that he left the house. No questions to how my trip went or to ask how I was. It all felt a bit emotionless.

His dirty clothes were strewn across the bedroom floor as he hadn't done any washing. It felt all very tiresome and I felt uncared for. There were no romantic gestures. I was worth more than this.

It was six months later when the realisation kicked in and I knew that I really had done the wrong thing by getting married. I was on a flight to Rio and I was working in First Class. I met a man who was in charge of the flight. He was tall, dark and very, very handsome with a charismatic personality. Rio is a sixteen hour trip so you spend a lot of time with the people you are working with. This man was very charming and romantic and I realised that there was more to relationships than just friendship. There was a spark between us that I could not explain or ignore other than to say that an exchange of energy was taking place. An exchange that I had not felt ever with Finlay. He was funny and made me laugh and the attention was very flattering. I realised that with Finlay I was the one constantly giving and not receiving. There has to be that spark and that spark had gone out long ago. My head had been turned by the chemistry between myself and another member of crew and although nothing happened, it had made a mark on my heart. It also made me appreciate that there are men out there who can give attention, love, compliments and their heart. I suddenly realised how important all these things were. Being a very loving, giving, person I now knew that that is how I would like my ideal partner to be. But for some reason I had a belief that Finlay was enough because he liked me and he was someone to be with and having a husband made you acceptable.

So, with a heavy heart, I returned home in the realisation that I could not carry on in this relationship and that my wings felt clipped. The compromise was too great and I now needed to fly on my own personal journey. He was more upset than I could ever have imagined as he had thought that we would be together for life. Which is understandable, after taking vows but it was not to be. The only thing I could hold on to were all the happy memories that we had made together but my heart had let go. He begged me to change her mind but I could no longer see our future together. Our bond was still strong as we had been through so much and we decided that we would stay friends.

The divorce was painless really. We agreed unreasonable terms. I even sat with Finlay one day to ask him if he would be upset if I put certain things under the list of unreasonable terms. It was very amicable. I moved out of the house that we had bought and moved in with my friend Julie, who I had met through the airline. She was my saviour at that point. Finlay would still come and visit me once a week, sometimes more. He had decided to stay in the marital home and we agreed that, as part of the financial agreement, he would pay me a lump sum of money that represented my share of the house that we owned together. Finlay lived in hope that I would change my mind. He'd suddenly grasped how he had taken advantage of the one thing he really did love instead of looking after me.

My time as a cabin crew member was filled with wonderful adventures and this is where I met Julie. She was very attractive, around 5'7" with lovely red hair in the perfect bob and green eyes. Julie was a very intense person but I found her open and friendly and we hit it off straight away, in fact we both lived in Sussex and quite close by, which is unheard of in flying as most crew members live all over the country and the world. My reputation on the ground as' Mystic Meg' had proceeded me and when I met Julie she very quickly realised who I was having heard from other members of staff about me. Julie and I were working on board the aircraft. It was a short shuttle flight from Pheonix to Las Vegas, where the crew just operated but did not leave the aircraft until the return to base in Pheonix. This is where I first met Julie. All the crew were sitting on the plane in first class having a meal after the passengers had disembarked and I was reading palms for people. Julie approached me as she had realised who I was and we sat together and chatted for the whole break. That was the beginning of a very lovely friendship.

I am a great believer that good friends are very few and far between. I had always been surrounded by people I would consider acquaintances but true friends that will stand by your side whatever, (whether they agree with you or not) I could count on one hand. I believed Julie to be one of these people, and for a while she was but I was to be proved wrong and my belief that everything happens for a reason was to be proved right.

Chapter Five

My New Best Friend

I had been known over the years to dabble in tarot cards which started at the tender age of 16 and I had frequently visited a lady who read Angel Cards for me every six months. The guidance that I had received had been absolutely correct and I had been advised that my relationship with Finlay would not last but chose to ignore it. I also knew for years that I had healing hands but kept this very close to my chest, mainly for fear of being judged as a witch. However different I felt I wanted to hide behind a mask, my Mrs Normal mask. This part of me was shut down as I was struggling to acknowledge my gifts. Even reading palms on the flight in Pheonix was very difficult for me to do. It would mean being different and I didn't want to be different. I just wanted to be liked and fit in.

I was brought up with good morals and a Christian faith which has been my saviour on many an occasion. Julie found this all very interesting. She had come from a broken home, where her Dad was an addict. My life intrigued her. We bonded and became the best of friends although with differing rosters getting together with other crew members/friends was always difficult. Luckily, I was a friendly person who had surrounded herself with many people. However, on so many occasions, I felt that I could be surrounded by people and yet still feel very alone in this world. Even as the life and soul of the party, I found that everyone wanted to be me or was envious of my lifestyle and yet I was still trying to discover who I was and what my purpose on this earth was going to be. I also attracted a lot of people who felt that intruding into my life was acceptable and for a long time I let them do this. Overstepping boundaries. Some of that purpose had been answered for me but there was still this inquisitive side that believed that this was not it.

Julie and I became best buddies and we saw each other through some pretty good, exciting times and through some bad ones as well. The end of my marriage to Finlay was one of these occasions. When I moved into Julie's house, our rosters were not compatible which meant we weren't always at home at the same time and that suited both of us as we needed our own space. The house was a large three-bedroom detached house and gave me the space I needed to think about what accommodation I would need and where I needed to be living. In the meantime, it also became a place where Julie's friends became my friends and my friends became Julie's friends and very often there would be dinner parties and gatherings and all in all it was a very happy time.

Julie, Sally and I would often sit in Julie's house on many occasions and put the world to rights, with a large glass of pinot in our hands, of course darling! I found that the only outlet was to talk and talk and talk and then I felt that I had dealt with the issue or that's what I thought at the time. Talking definitely did help but it didn't necessarily get to the route of why things actually happened and how I had got to this point in my life. I stayed with Julie for approximately two months and I then used the lump sum that Finlay had paid me to secure a deposit on a house in Brighton. It was a lovely two bedroomed mid-terraced house and had lots of original features. I loved the old Victorian fire place and the wooden floors that had been sanded and polished beautifully. The stairs rose a level to a mid landing where the bathroom was positioned. From the mid-landing were some more stairs which led to another landing. A step to the right took me into the second bedroom and a step forward took me into the main bedroom. A very large room again with polished floors and a beautifully well-maintained fireplace, an added feature. The kitchen was a long galley kitchen and there was a back door to the garden. Although not particularly large, it was enough for me to manage and it had a shed. My Dad had always told me that I had to have a shed, as a garden wasn't a garden without a shed. I was over the moon when the deal was secured and moved out of Julie's home. Again, I had found my little place of peace in the world and was still flying visiting the most amazing destinations and exploring all of them. North America, South America, lots of the African countries, Middle East, Mediterranean islands, Caribbean, the new Russian states and I loved it. I had everything I had ever wanted again and life settled down.

Although I had found where I wanted to be. Finlay had not. Every Friday night Finlay would roll up in the early hours of the morning to my new home wanting to come in, as he had missed his train home with nowhere else to go (and it was an excuse to see me) and I would let him in and he could sleep his hangover off on the sofa. He did this on a regular basis until one day, my brother, Mike, had come to stay. Finlay was not expecting to see someone else open the door. Mike answered the door and Finlay looked quite shocked and a little shameful. Finlay asked where I was. He told Finlay that I was away on a trip and so it wouldn't be appropriate for him to decide to let Finlay stay and funnily enough he stopped calling after that. He eventually got himself a job in South Africa and I was very pleased for him and also a little relieved as I had felt his desperation to rekindle our relationship and that was something I was not prepared to do. However, when he did move out to Cape Town, I did take a flight out to see him upon his request. He wanted to know if maybe being in a different country would change things. I know a part of me was swept away by the romance of living in a different country but also, I knew that I was still trying to please him and, in a way, he still was manipulating me by telling me his sob story of how much he missed me. He just wanted one more chance to see if it could work again but there was nothing there, I knew in my heart as soon as I landed and saw him that it could not work. I had done enough now and this had to stop. This connection with this man was not doing me or him any good.

I returned home to my house, dream job and knew life was abundant and perfect but a change was coming and little did I know what was to follow. My relationship really was over and it was time for both of us to move on. After being in such a perfect place the change that came was not quite what I was expecting.

Chapter Six

Flying High and Then Back to the Ground

I had some amazing times whilst flying and I always felt that I was a very lucky person. I had travelled to places only people could dream of and I had done things that I will always hold dear to my heart.

I was coming home one morning from a flight. It had landed in the early hours of the morning. I owned a little red Mazda MX5. I loved my sporty convertible. I had always wanted one and I was living the dream; flying to wonderful destinations and driving my little sports car back home to my new house. This particular day I was flying down the M25 at approximately 90 miles (oops – a little over the speed limit). I had always put my airline uniform hat on the rear parcel shelf. A habit I had adopted very early on in flying to keep its shape and stop it getting squished. There I was singing away to my music, which was twice as loud as it should have been; shooting home in my little dream car. All of a sudden, I felt I was being watched. I turned my head to the right and driving besides me was a police car. My heart started to sink. Four policemen all looked at me, smiled and the policeman in the passenger side flapped his hand up and down and told me to slow down. I smiled, waved and eased up on the accelerator, expecting to be pulled over. Then, all of a sudden, they all waved at me, laughed and sped off. I had never been so relieved in all my life and I hadn't been pulled over. I grinned from ear-to-ear all the way home. How lucky was I? And that is how I felt about my life in general. I was very blessed and very lucky. At this point in my life I believed in me and my self-worth and my ability to manifest whatever I wanted, although I did not completely understand how it was all working. All the time unaware of how I was creating my own existence.

I came home one day from a flight and realised that flying no longer held the passion for me that I had once had. A lot of crew were not enjoying their job and that was very obvious and also, being sensitive, it was affecting me. My empathic nature was picking up on all the negativity and every flight seemed to be full of crew who had had enough of flying but were directing their feelings towards everyone else. I wanted to meet my Mr Right and if I was really to meet someone special and have children and live happily ever after, it wasn't going to happen on the airline. My reasoning behind this was that a lot of people think that whilst you are flying you are just partying and sleeping around. That was totally not true but there was a stigma there. Also, unless you are in airline, understanding the work is quite difficult for a partner and the times spent away from home can have an effect. That was my thought process and of course I was never going to attract anyone with that belief running through me. After a lot of deliberation, I resigned and took a job as a receptionist to get me by until I knew what I wanted to do. I had asked the company for part time work or a ground job but it was coming up to the Millennium and they needed all crew on board as flights were fully booked. The reception job was back in Burgess Hill and I worked alongside another girl who was and remains one of my best friends. Her name is Debbie. I had a strong sense that things were for a reason and I was right. Debbie came along at the perfect time. Debbie is what I would call a soul mate friend. We had a perfect understanding of each other and our lives were almost in parallel to each other. Debbie's life map running about 6-12 months ahead of mine but very similar – spooky but reassuring.

My airline job had quite a considerable pay package so when I left, I knew that my house would have to go as I would not be able to carry on paying the mortgage with the job I had acquired. I knew that things needed to change and with a little sadness in my heart, I sold my house in Brighton. It made me quite a lot of money with the rise in house prices. Finlay at this point had come back from South Africa and had started work in offices in Brighton but had no sooner stepped back into the country and was redeployed to South Africa on a secondment. He still owned our marital home and in order for him to keep the house safe, he asked me if I would house sit for him. That's exactly what I did. I moved back into our marital home and my place of work was around the corner. Perfect!!

Whilst working as a receptionist at this small firm with my best friend, I suddenly discovered something that I didn't realise that I had and that was sex appeal. Actually, it was self-esteem but I did not recognise it at that point. I realised my worth. I joined this company as a receptionist and I had never ever received so much male attention. I found this very flattering for the ego. But I was not a bad girl. I had always been friendly and sometimes, in fact, most of the time, men took this the wrong way and then I would end up in a situation of having to explain what being friendly was and that did not mean being available to have affairs. Having so much attention though can be very damaging and I found myself caught up in a small-town mentality and losing the vision of where I was heading in life. The company were very big on socialising and putting on social events and it was very easy to get carried along with big drinking binges of a weekend or sometimes midweek. I was still going to the gym and running a lot. I played squash with a team from the company and this would be followed by an opportunity to have a drink. I was working, exercising and playing hard. Although I was physically fit and looked slim and toned, I wasn't putting my emotional and spiritual health first. I was drowning in a life that wasn't what I wanted or needed.

My vision was to meet someone to have and to hold for ever in harmony, with four children and two dogs. But unfortunately, my vision was being hijacked by married men who had the family and wanted the dream; The mistress and one party after another. I never succumbed to this but was very close. Hence, I also ended up dating people that perhaps I would never have dated and having a string of very meaningless relationships that all ended in disaster and heartache for me. Then my self-esteem took a plummet and the belief system started to follow. I was not the sort of person who gave myself without it being wholly. Therefore, in my head I had fallen in love with all of these people and it had made the break-ups even harder. I often appeased myself with the fact that if I didn't trust to love how would I ever know if it was real love. But actually, love is a two-way thing and you have to receive as well as give. This was something that was still alien to me.

Whilst working as a receptionist, the travel bug had taken a grip of me again and I decided to go on a holiday to Greece (Lindos to be precise) with a female friend from work. The holiday was much needed and very relaxing and fun. My friend had lived and worked in Greece previously and introduced me to lots of lovely local people. One of the people that I connected with was a man called, John, he had done nothing in recent years except travel. He spent the whole of this holiday following me around with puppy dog eyes. He had the most amazing piercing blue eyes but he was rather large. I was very dubious as I wasn't used to the overwhelming one on one personal attention he was giving me. We swapped contact information but nothing ever happened between us. When I returned to England, John would send me a weekly email telling whereabouts in the world he was and what he was up to trying to entice me to join him. This appealed to my desire to travel and one day I messaged him back asking where in the world he was. He had travelled to Thailand and was on an island called Koh Lanta. Without a second thought I decided that I needed to travel and this was ideal. I booked my leave at work for the following week, I booked a ticket to Bangkok, with an onward flight to Krabbe. I had arranged with John that he would meet me in Krabbe and arrange transport to Koh Lanta and that would mean we could travel together across land. This was all very exciting and spontaneous and the fire in my soul was alive again.

I flew out to Bangkok on Garuda Airlines, which was different to the airline that I had worked for, but they got me there. I landed in Bangkok airport and not having much time to look around headed straight for the next boarding gate for my connecting flight. My flight to Krabbe was approximately half an hour, on a smallish plane. I landed in Krabbe very excited and then very hesitant, in case no one was there to meet me. The temperature had risen and I could feel the warm Thai heat and sure as eggs are eggs, John was there to meet me when I arrived. I was a little surprised at John's appearance since the last time I had seen him was in Lindos. He had changed considerably and for the better. He had been working out and was no longer the sunburnt John that I had met in Lindos. He was very toned, bronzed and he had the biggest, whitest, cheesiest smile ever. We hugged and kissed and he took my bags over to the 4x4 he had borrowed from a friend. He drove us into Krabbe to our accommodation for the night. It was a basic room but it had all the facilities that we needed and was very clean and very oriental. That night in Krabbe there was a festival on so we took the opportunity to embrace the atmosphere and walked around gazing in awe at all the people dressed up singing and dancing. The energy was amazing and the company seemed pretty amazing too. Before sunrise the next morning John took me up into the mountains to a Buddhist monastery where I got to look around and pray and eat with the monks. The offering was only of rice in a wooden bowl but I felt incredibly honoured to be sitting and eating with such private enlightened individuals. The monks then granted permission for John and I to wander around and see the mountainside cave homes that they had made. It was incredible, spiritual and exciting and I felt alive again. Nothing could ever compare to that experience, it felt very intimate and privileged. We left there to head to Koh Lanta taking the ferry. John drove straight to my accommodation. It was a beach hut next to the bar right by the edge of the sea. There were several other beach huts placed nearby but all of them were very private. It had a four-poster bed with organza drapes around it and fresh flowers on her bed. It was the most beautiful place. The little balcony was idyllic and by the water's edge and the sea was crystal clear. It even had a shower in the beach hut but it was cold water, of course. Not that it bothered me with it being 34 degrees, a cold shower was very welcome.

We went to the beach bar and John introduced me to the people who worked there, as this was where I could get my breakfast every day. He then introduced me to a few people who were staying in the other beach huts around the beach. Some of them were staying that week but were moving on to travel the world, others would be there a little longer. I was in my element, this was another adventure. I met a lovely Canadian couple and some girls from Switzerland and Oslo. All of whom were at the end of a year-long worldwide travel. We really connected well as a group, which was good really; as John managed to fall out with me on day two and we didn't really speak for the rest of the holiday. He had got a little upset one evening when I had stayed up drinking with the group and we had called at his beach hut to lure him out to join us. He had an early morning dive the next morning so was not amused as we had woken him up. Luckily, I had made friends with a Canadian couple and some other ladies who were travelling and we did lots of lovely things together such as riding elephants, visiting the local town by hitching a ride in the back of trucks and just hanging out. We spent the nights dancing and singing. It was fabulous apart from the person who had invited me was no longer in my radar. My last day came very quickly and I was very sad to leave but actually I now wanted to go home. Even though we had not really spoken much John turned up in the 4 x 4 to take me back to Krabbe, in order that I could catch my flight back to Bangkok. John and I spoke on the way back.

"I can't believe I'm taking you back to the airport already". He was a little sheepish.

"No, but I have had a lovely time and it has been wonderful to experience the different culture and the monastery was amazing."

"I'm sorry that I haven't been around more. Maybe you will come out and see me again somewhere else on my travels? Or maybe you would consider travelling with me?". He beamed a smile at me and I smiled back.

"Thank you, John, and however much I would love to travel, I am looking forward to going home. I will keep in touch though."

"Yes, for sure. I totally understand". There was almost a sadness in his voice.

We exchanged gifts. I gave him a ring that I had on my finger which had three adjoining dolphins on it and he gave me a friendship bracelet. We kissed and said our goodbyes and that was the last time we saw each other. We kept in touch although not as regularly as it had been and occasionally John sends an email.

My flight from Krabbe to Bangkok went without a hitch. Things weren't quite running to plan, however, when I got to Bangkok. The flight had been delayed and everyone who was booked to fly were being put in hotel accommodation. My airline experience and my intuition were kicking in, and I knew there was something more to this situation than a flight delay. I rang my brother in the UK and found that Garuda had gone bankrupt and were not putting any more flights on. There must have been a thousand people in this hotel as several flights had now been cancelled. So, Jennifer to the rescue. As soon as I arrived in the hotel I got on the phone and contacted the Embassy to advise that we had been put in hotel accommodation with no means of getting home. A representative of the Embassy came to the hotel to meet with me. I gathered as many of the passengers as I could to give them the news. The representative from the Embassy reassured everyone that they would find a way to get them home. The Embassy advised me that this would take some time but I could be their point of contact. So, what do you do when you have a few hours to spare? I decided to hop into a cab and go to downtown Bangkok and explore the wonders of the city. Can you believe, synchronicity again, I was walking through the market in Bangkok and all of a sudden, I heard my name being called. As I turned around, I could see in the distance, leaning out of an Irish bar door, the Canadian couple that I had got to know in Koh Lanta. So, I smiled my huge big smile at the coincidence and went over and joined them for a drink. We spent the evening exploring Bangkok, it certainly was an eye opener. They introduced me to the wonders of Pat Pong and although it felt as though I had experienced the culture, I also felt very sad and very uncomfortable witnessing the dancers doing incredible things with ping pong balls. They looked dead behind the eyes. Their souls had been removed all for money. But I also appreciated that this was a way of life for them and not necessarily a choice.

After a very eventful evening we ended up in MacDonald's in downtown Bangkok, from where I caught a cab back to the hotel. The following morning the hotel staff tried to get everyone to check out and leave their rooms. I rallied everyone around and told them not to leave their room until they knew they were on a flight. It was quite funny as I had got to know a few people quite well and they cheered, "go, Jennifer, go" at this rebellious stance. This annoyed the hotel staff but actioned them to contact the Embassy again and three hours later they had managed to lease two aircraft from Thai Airways which meant everyone could get home. Hooray I was on my way home. Because of the incident at the hotel, I had become quite well known by the other passengers and I did get asked out on a date by another passenger who gave me his business card but it never came to anything. I very often compared my life to Bridget Jones and this was a very 'Bridget' moment.

Eventually, I decided that working as a receptionist wasn't challenging enough and I ended up doing a short stint as customer service engineer to pacify my thirst for knowledge but it wasn't my life's calling. There had to be something more so I decided that the financial world was waiting for me again. I jumped ship and off back to the world finance but this time IFA's (Independent Financial Adviser) and para-planner. Time had moved on and although Finlay still kept in touch from South Africa it was very infrequent. I had also met someone. He was a friend to start with and we had ended up dating. He was a very lovely young man. Tall, dark and very, very handsome. He was fun to be with and loved life to the full and we just had a year of so much laughter. He was a very intelligent professional man but had a wonderful outlook on life. I took this relationship across with me to the new job. It sadly failed very painfully for both of us. He was 10 years younger than me and although age was not a barrier for us, we were at different points in our lives. He was not ready at that point to take the relationship any further and I was ready to settle down again. When our relationship ended I took it very badly. I fought every day to hide the tears that welled in my eyes. My heart was definitely broken and it would take some healing. I had lost something very special but deep down I knew it would not last forever. It was a deep knowing. I needed to concentrate on my career and I knew deep in my heart of hearts that we had loved each other but it was not meant to be. This felt as though it had been some sort of lesson for me and if I had been paying attention, it was teaching me how love should be. Where two people give in the relationship and it isn't all one sided.

It was time for me again. Where was that girl with the confidence and the big smile? I needed to unlock her but I knew that a great healing was taking place and that I would not appear straight away. It took a while and eventually the old

Jennifer reappeared. I felt that a change of location with my job helped and gave me a different focus.

Yet again, I had been through heartache and yet again, I needed to come back to who I was. To find me. This seemed to be a recurring pattern. A lesson coming along followed by a period of regaining my true self. A true self which I needed to hold on to and not let slip through my fingers to please others. Why was I drawing in these experiences? I could not see the pattern that was forming for me, that I was creating and so moved forward towards another lesson. The universe was trying to teach me but I was not listening.

Chapter Seven

Engaged but Not To Be

I enjoyed my new job and I did find it very challenging and there was always something new to learn. The office where I worked was at the back of two shops, a Building Society and a Shoe shop and the access to all three were through the same door. All the office and shop staff all got along. In fact, it suited me as I very much enjoyed moving from office to office and catching up on a chat with the staff during my break time. The Manager in the one branch was to become very significant in my life but I was unaware of this at the time. In fact, at that point in my life, I considered him to be one of the most boring people ever!!!!!

The job I had was varied and well paid. There was an office romance going on and sometimes the atmosphere was a little tense but I just got on with my work. I got invited to an office launch in the Building Society where a lot of local businesses had been invited along. It was there that I met a man who chatted to me for hours not only about my job role but about my fitness and running. His interest seemed a little intense at the time but I was going to find out why the next day when he contacted me and asked me if I would be interesting in working for him. He dangled the carrot of a higher basic wage and commission on top and that was it. I had been officially poached from the company I was working for by another IFA. I did feel very flattered. In this job, I have to say that I did a lot of learning and training and became a mortgage adviser. It was a more varied role and I enjoyed it as I was learning, running the office and getting to interact with clients. I got to be in charge of the office as the owner of the company still had a manual system and with business getting busier he needed it computerised. This was my speciality, organising and setting up my own computerised systems and filing systems. This was well within my remit and gave me a sense of authority. Although my career had now taken off again, I could not say the same about my love life.

It seemed as though it was constantly in tatters. My relationship self-esteem was very low. When my previous relationship had ended it took my confidence too. I didn't believe I would meet anyone like my last partner and because I believed it, the universe delivered exactly what I was thinking. I decided that I needed to focus on what I really wanted and again, decided that as I was earning quite a lot of money, that I would like to get back on the property ladder and have my own home again. The wheels were set in motion and what I wished for came true, I made it happen.

I bought a little flat locally. It needed a lot of work but it was mine and I loved it. It was on the ground floor of a block of four but only had one flat above and two flats on the opposite corridor. It was very unloved and had no kitchen and a hole in the bath. I looked beyond all that. It was a space, a space to make my own and no sooner had completion happened, I got to work. My Dad knew a man who could fit a kitchen but it would mean him travelling and staying a couple of nights to be able to do it. We agreed a price and he arrived the day that I completed the purchase and the kitchen was delivered the next morning. In one weekend a new kitchen had been installed. Then to the bathroom. Again, the bathroom was ordered, delivered and installed all in one day. Whilst all this plumbing work was going on, I had a paintbrush in my hand and my little brother to help me. The doorways were not in very good condition so a carpenter was called in and I decided that all the door surrounds and doors would be replaced. In no time at all new carpets were being laid and the flat looked completely different. It was my little place of peace again and I had made my mark on it.

I settled in and then joined the local leisure centre so I could keep my fitness going. Something that had become part of my every day routine. I would get up early in the morning and be at the gym for 6am. It was enough time to exercise, shower and head off to work. I loved the gym and the people there were particularly friendly. There would be lots of banter with like-minded people with a great sense of humour. I love to laugh and joke and this is where I connected with someone new.

He was older than me, had a good job, smart and into fitness like myself. He was a runner, just like myself. Running has always been my salvation on so many occasions when I needed to clear my mind and process the bad thoughts and the good ones! We were very similar in looks, he had dark hair and dark eyes. He laughed a lot at me and the things that I would say or do. I knew that he had never met anyone quite like me. He reminded me on so many occasions of how different I was. I am honest, upfront, loving, giving and happy. This intrigued him. He was the Manager of the Building Society where I had worked in the office behind previously. His name was Matthew. He adored me and this was something very different for me. He said that I had the most incredible energy and that I could make anyone smile. I had had men chase me and then not make the effort but I had never been with someone so attentive and loving and just wanting to do things for me. He even made me my pack lunches for work and bought me flowers every week; always on a Friday, as he knew I loved flowers. All of this seemed like a dream to me. All of my adult life I had been looking for this man and he was here, now. It was as though I was living in a bubble. He wanted to look after me, or so I thought. He had been married twice, the first time him and is wife had parted after the birth of their child. They had agreed that he would walk away and have no contact with the child. He had then met someone else very quickly and had remarried. He had had his own issues with his ex-wife and had suffered from depression at one point. Something that was not evident now. I had given him an extra zest for life. Alarm bells should have been ringing but I was ignoring them again!!

The weekends would be full of fun activities and we would go out all day cycling and talk about the children we were going to have and what names we would call them. All the time we talked about our future together. Then he took me on a very special romantic holiday to Fiscardo on Rhodes Island. It has to be one of the most romantic bays that I had ever visited. It was small and there was a scattering of houses around the bay with a few eateries. The hills provided a beautiful backdrop and the sun always seemed to glisten on the sea. When walking hand in hand around the bay every evening time seemed to stand still. Matthew and I could not take our eyes off each other. My heart was ready to burst. Then one evening after dinner Matthew took me to the edge of the promenade and he got down on one knee and proposed. It was totally unexpected. The ring he presented to me was platinum with a single diamond which he had arranged to have secretly made for me. Without even thinking I gave him his answer, "yes".

As soon as we got back home we headed to Hereford to see my parents. I kept my ring in the box as we wanted to surprise my Mum and Dad. He asked me not to tell them straight away as there was something else he needed to do. I held my surprise for a little longer and whilst I was talking to my Mum in the kitchen, he asked my Dad's permission for my hand in marriage. Unheard of in this day and age. My parents were over the moon. It was a very happy day. He produced a bottle of champagne and we celebrated with bubbles and a meal out.

Matthew did have a condition that he broached with me that I stop the very minimal contact that I had with my ex-husband. Finlay wasn't in constant contact but on the odd occasion he would call me for a chat. Sometimes when I was at the top of a hill walking with Matthew and he would screw his face up in disapproval as I answered the call. I agreed to this and text Finlay to tell him my circumstances. He was very understanding and the contact stopped for a very long time. His other condition was that I leave the job I was in, working for the IFA as he did not like my boss. I agreed to this as well and I applied for an administration job in financial services for another company with less money but less stress and hours. The job was not particularly challenging, although, I did make another very good friend there. The office was very small and the people in the office had a lovely energy, although manly sales people occupied the building and so most of the time it was only the administration staff present. I sat one side of the office with my mortgage team and another lady, called Vicky sat the other side of the office with her Insurance team. Vicky was a northerner with a very strong accent and a wicked sense of humour. Vicky and I got along like a house on fire and spent a lot of time laughing, particularly when the boss was out, which was a lot of the time. Vicky became a very good friend and was to become a huge support through the highs and lows of my ever-changing life.

When I changed jobs, Matthew decided that I needed to change my car too. He bought me a new car to replace my sports car. It was a little grey Volkswagen Golf – a much more suitable family car. It wasn't the sports car that I loved but I understood the practicality of it and the fact that we were now planning our future together.

The wedding plans were being put in place and a Christmas wedding was planned. It had been my wish and everything I had hoped for. I love Christmas and to have a wedding at that time of year felt very exciting. A venue had been booked and the deposit had been paid. I invited my Mum and Dad down. A wedding dress had to be picked and who better to help than my own Mum. This is how a wedding should be planned. My Mum and Dad were over the moon to be included this time. I excitedly drove my Mum to the wedding dress shop. I had picked a gown but it had to be altered as I was very small and the design I had picked was a little big on me. I had picked out a strapless bodice which had been intricately decorated with pearls and sequins. The skirt was organza layers which flowed down to my feet. The dress was beautiful and finished off by a fur cape. The perfect dress for the occasion.

In the meantime, things were changing in our home. Matthew was buying my clothes, the ones that he wanted to see me in. He was trying to tell me what friends he thought I should mix with and telling me that drinking with Julie was not good for me and that we should be exercising instead. All were very valid points, but I was mystified as I went every morning to the gym, was running three times a week and cycling approximately 30-50 miles at the weekends. I felt that drinking wine once a week was not doing any harm. I could not see what was happening and I certainly could not see what the future was to hold, other than he was my future.

Woo hoo… my happy ever after at last, yes? No!!!! This man decided two months before the wedding to stop communicating with me. I would come home from work and he would do all he could to avoid having a conversation with me. I was so upset. My head whirled constantly over the events that had taken place in the previous weeks and months to try and understand what was actually happening. Things started to get really strange and then one evening after work when we were both home he made an announcement.

"I've decided that we should go away for a short break together." He was very matter of fact when he delivered this news.

"Okay, that sounds like a really good idea. Where shall we go?" I was a little unnerved but felt that maybe things were turning around and perhaps a break away would do us good.

"I've booked for us to go to Devon for four days. There is one thing though," he paused and with a pensive look on his face, "when we are away we are not to talk about weddings, children or our relationship." He looked away and I could not gauge eye contact with him.

I had a mixture of emotions running through my body. There was the thought process that we needed to clear the air and maybe a trip away would do this and then there was the dread. What was really going on and what could he not tell me. Why couldn't we talk about our future. It all seemed so odd.

"Okay, I'll do my best but you know me," I nervously giggled but I couldn't even ask him why there were conditions.

We drove down to Devon and the air felt a little lighter. However, it turned out to be the most difficult four days ever. I loved this man to the moon and back and I couldn't talk about the most important day of our lives. We spent the days walking and eating and talking about nothing in particular. My throat felt as though it was closing and my heart was heavy. My mind went into overdrive and the wait almost was unbearable. But, I waited patiently, or as patiently as I could be, and on the car journey home the temptation was too much.

"What is happening with us?" I could feel the lump in my throat as I asked the question and tears in my eyes but tried to keep upbeat.

He turned on me quite fiercely, "You couldn't wait could you. You had to bring the subject of 'us' up!"

"All I want to know is what I have done wrong," I could feel my bottom lip quivering as I asked the question and the tears ready to fall in plenty.

"You haven't done anything wrong. I don't know what is wrong. I need space. I can't think and I don't know how I feel anymore," his voice was angry and defensive.

"Are we still getting married?" It was the question I had been desperate to ask and afraid to hear the answer to.

"I don't know and I don't want to talk about it," he said.

That was the end of the conversation and we spoke no more on the very, very long journey home. Perhaps silence would provoke him to say something first but it didn't. He wasn't prepared to tell me and this was a horrible moment in my life. I knew that what I thought was going to happen may not be what was going to happen and that scared me. I had already mapped out in my head how our future was going to look and he had taken the map and scrunched it up in front of me with no rhyme or reason.

Upon our return home, the communication between us became more and more scarce and his avoidance tactics were obvious. When he came home it was for a very short time and he headed out again to play badminton or go to a gym class. I had this awful feeling in the pit of my stomach and I didn't want to admit what my intuition was telling me. It was all over. My brain couldn't comprehend what was happening, especially with all the lovely things that had happened such as the marriage proposal and romantic gestures but my heart was sinking and it knew the truth.

One night I came home and he decided he was going to a fitness class. I was quite happy about this as the atmosphere had been very tense. I asked him if he could tell me what the problem was and whether we could talk about the problem that we obviously had, as the wedding was getting closer. He went out and told me that we would speak later. When later arrived, I persisted with the line of questioning.

"Matthew, what is really going on with us. This is agony. I need to know where I stand."

I was sat on the top of the stairs and he was changing in the bedroom. This way I could ask this question without looking at him and reading the expression on his face. He came out of the bedroom,

"I don't know what to say. I don't know what is going on."

His refusal to look at me and tell me the truth frustrated me and with that frustration my hands hit the floor of the landing so hard the pain seared through my hands and up my arms. My teeth were gritted and the hugest sob came out of my mouth from my heart. My heart was breaking. All I wanted was him to be honest with me and talk to me. He looked shocked. My hands swelled considerably and the bruising was like I'd never seen before. He clammed up on me even more,

"I don't like temper and I'm not sure that this is the appropriate time to say any more. You need to calm down," his body was shaking and he moved away from me.

I sobbed and sobbed and my hands were throbbing with pain. That was just so insulting as I had never had a temper in my life. I had been so patient waiting to see what my future with him held, if any. I took it upon myself to make a decision. I took a deep breath to compose myself,

"I'm moving out for a short time to give you time to think about what you do want. I cannot stay here the way things are." I was calm and brought myself to a place of peace and dignity. Although I said it, deep down I was hoping he would beg me to stay but he didn't. He just agreed that it was the best thing at that point and then he broke down in tears. I held him in my arms for a few seconds and then something told me to let go. I released my arms and got on with the task in hand.

I packed my bags that night and messaged Julie who was more than happy to accommodate me. When I arrived, I broke down in tears and tried to explain what had happened. I carried on going to work although in a daze and pretended all was well. Vicky had already guessed but didn't say a word. She knew that when I was ready I would break the news but I needed to know for sure exactly what was happening. A few days went by and there had been no communication from him. I came back from work and shortly after arriving back a delivery came. Matthew's car pulled up outside and he walked towards the house with the hugest bouquet of flowers. My heart skipped a beat and I was so happy to see him. The message on the card read,

'To my angel sent from heaven to be by my side always'.

He came inside and we hugged and kissed and chatted briefly. I thanked him for the flowers and then he asked if we could meet up and go for a meal. I thought it was all back on – it was all just a huge mistake and he had had cold feet but it was going to be alright.

He came the following night and picked me up and took me out to a local country pub. We had pleasant chit chat for a while. I kept looking at him but he avoided my eyes. Our main meal arrived and whilst we were looking down eating he broke the news to me.

"It's over Jennifer," almost Mumbling the words under his breathe.

"Sorry?" had I heard him correctly?

"It's over. Me, you, it's over. I can't get married and I don't want to. Things aren't right."

I was speechless and my lip had started to quiver. I didn't want to embarrass myself in public but I had been stabbed in the heart and I wanted to release the biggest sob. I tried to eat more but my appetite had disappeared and I couldn't look up. I excused myself from the table and headed straight to the toilets. He placed his head in his hands almost knowing that he had picked the wrong moment. I locked myself in a cubicle and cried and cried. The release felt good but I needed to get myself together to face the outside world again, so I tried to repair my make-up stained face in the hope that no one would know how upset I was. He couldn't even explain to me why it was over which was the hardest part for me.

"I want to leave please," I said as I arrived back at the table.

"But you haven't eaten your food."

"I'm not hungry anymore. I just would like to leave please." I had put my metal plated armour on and the Ice Queen was now in the room.

"Okay, I'll just pay the bill and we can leave." He looked very nervous and unsure of how I was going to react.

I said nothing more on the car journey home but make up stained tears fell again and I stared blankly out of the side window so as not to have eye contact with him. When we arrived at Julie's house, I got out of the car and refused to even say goodbye to him and got into the house as quickly as possible. He drove away.

Julie was flabbergasted when I returned and told her the news. Especially after delivering such beautiful flowers with such a special message. How could this be? But it was. We broke up and I took myself back to Julie's to work out what my plan was going to be. It was the weirdest break up ever. I had moved house several times but I did have my flat that I owned that I had rented out and the tenancy had not expired yet so Julie was there to put me up and look after me during this very painful breakup and six weeks later I was able to move back to my flat. I told Vicky at work what had happened and she threw her arms around me and told me he didn't deserve me. From that day on she watched over me to make sure I was coping and everyone else in the office seemed to tip toe around me, until I could talk to them about it. I carried on as though nothing had happened but I was working in my own little bubble so as not to think about anything in particular apart from work. Matthew and I had very little communication but I did have a lot of my belongings still there and I had asked him if they could remain there until I moved back to the flat. When I turned up at his house to collect my belongings, he had gone out. My brother and a friend had agreed to come with me and when we entered the house - It was the strangest thing but he had packed all of my stuff into boxes and labelled it?! It almost said to me that he didn't want me in the house any longer than I needed to be and, in his head, he had packed me up and moved me out of his life. It didn't take long to remove the boxes and when I left I pulled the door to and posted the key through the letterbox. It was definitely over. I walked away with grace and dignity. My self-esteem well and truly flattened, my heart broken and my head completely mashed. I suddenly had a realisation that you can do nothing about these situations and however painful they may be, wasting time and energy on something you cannot change is pointless. But, you must cry and release that sadness as, after all, it is an energy and suppressing feelings is not good either. We just have to be more accepting of our feelings which is easier said than done. This was the first time I really let go of a relationship. I never called him or chased him or tried to reason with him, I let go completely. Mentally there was no closure due to there being no rhyme or reason so that was quite difficult to deal with.

I did struggle with this break up as he wanted to look after me and nobody had ever done that before. After eight weeks of being apart Matthew contacted me out of the blue. We had had no contact in-between and we met for a meal. I did what I do and got excited in the hope that we were going to reconcile. We sat down and ordered and caught up on our daily lives. Our meal arrived and we started to eat. Everything seemed lovely and then,

"You know that you were the reason we split up."

I looked up in amazement at this statement, "What do you mean?"

"Well, you were so possessive and jealous and I couldn't do anything without you being by my side. It was stifling." I could see in his eyes that he actually believed what he was saying to me.

"and your temper was the final straw for me." He looked down at his food to carry on eating.

He was using this meal as an opportunity to try and blame the break up all on me.
I was devastated. He was throwing all his stuff at me and I was totally unaware of what he was actually doing. He had torn me apart in public again. I begged him not to talk like that,

"Please don't say these things. That is so untrue. I am not jealous or possessive. I've never stopped you doing anything. You always wanted me by your side and I was willing to please you. All I ever wanted was for us to get back together. I was hoping that you were going to tell me we could try again." I could actually feel myself almost begging this man for another chance.

"It's just not going to happen. It's over and that is that." He was cold and unfeeling and any amount of begging I might want to do was going to fall on deaf ears.

My meal was very unappealing and again, I asked him if we could leave. He paid the bill and drove me home. I asked him in and he obliged. We walked into the hallway and floods of tears cascaded down my face again. He held me close and I held him so tight I never wanted to let him go.

"I'm so sorry," he whispered.

I looked up and we looked into each other's eyes. My body jerked and our lips met. We were kissing. He pulled away.

"I need to leave," he became jumpy and nervous.

"You wanted to kiss me. Why do you want to leave? You still love me, don't you?" I could feel almost a feeling of satisfaction. I now knew he loved me but why was he trying to leave.

"I need to leave," he repeated again and with that he turned to leave. As he opened the door he stopped, "I will always want to know how you are and whether you are safe." Then he left.

I stood in disbelief at what had just happened. What had just happened?

I went over in my head everything that had been discussed that night. Jealous? Possessive? Things which I am not and have never been. In fact, I was the one who had had to cut ties with people due to his insecurities. Sometimes when people cannot look at their own stuff they throw it at you because they know no other way of dealing with it but this is something I had no comprehension of at the time. It is still very hurtful all the same. This time was no exception and not acceptable. Whatever the situation of a relationship breakup, blame is never a good game to play. There are two people in a relationship. I did however feel that he had pushed all of the blame on me and brushed me aside. My heart broke yet again and all the healing I had done was undone in a flash. When you truly love someone, you don't just stop loving them and the unloving is a process.

My work colleagues had been amazing and very supportive and Vicky and I spent more and more time together. Another colleague had suggested to me that I put my running to good use and maybe enter a race. I had never considered ever entering a race. I ran because I loved the freedom to just be in the moment and look at the scenery. I took up the challenge and for the first time in my life I was going to do a half marathon. The thought terrified me but excited me as well and it gave me a focus for my energy having to plan my eating and training. My training started straight away and then the day of the race came.

My brother, Mike, drove me to the race, as I wasn't sure if I could run 13 miles. This was a weight off my mind, as I knew that he would be there for when I finished. It was a lovely early morning in Spring. The weather was dry and mild and perfect conditions for running roads and countryside. There were lots of people milling around, running up and down and stretching. It was all I could do to stand still, I was so nervous. I knew very little about pacing myself or what time I was running per mile. I knew I needed to run this to my best ability. My heart was racing and my legs turned to jelly and the start gun was fired. I was off. I tried to calm myself and get my legs back to normal and not be pulled along by the other runners, some of whom were particularly quick. My mind went into persuading me that I was out for a leisurely run and I would be taking in different scenery and I needed to enjoy it. I spoke to several people on my way around who were lovely. I talked to a group of runners who were running for a local running club. We ran a considerable part of the run together until we got to mile 10 and then my pace started to slow up and they ran on ahead but not before convincing me that maybe joining a club might be a good idea. This was incredible. I felt incredible. I was enjoying every moment of this experience and I still felt good. As I neared the 12 mile mark the runners were more spread out and I could only see one or two people in front of me. I seemed to have quite a few people going by me. My pace was definitely easing but I knew I needed to keep going. I was almost at the 13 mile mark and my legs didn't want to run any further, they were heavy and I just wanted to stop. A girl who had been just behind me grabbed my arm, "you can do this, we have less than half a mile to go and I can see the finish," she said and with that she held on to me and pulled me along. I smiled gratefully at her and the adrenaline kicked in. My legs powered up again and she let go, "come on you can do this," she said with determination for me and her. I gritted my teeth and almost felt as though I closed my eyes to find the strength to get to that finish line. My arms raised in the air and a medal around my neck. I had done it, I ran 13.2 miles and I was shattered but exalted. The tears flowed from my eyes and heart felt sobs rang out. Mike approached me and hugged me, "I'm so proud of you Sis". He handed me some food I had brought with me and I sat for a while to recover. The bug had got me and I knew that I wanted to run another race. It took me away from everything that was going on in my life and it gave me so much pleasure.

Moving back to my flat was a rude awakening and I realised that my salary could barely cover the bills, never mind eating and socialising. A time to make another career jump back into financial services as an adviser. I believe I am one of life's survivors (another belief) and that will probably be the case until I can win the lottery (although I bet this is most people's dream). I needed something to focus on other than the hurt and this job gave me a chance to throw myself into my career again. Not to ignore the pain, but to ease it and focus my attention somewhere else until I couldn't feel the pain anymore. The family car that I had now acquired did not suit me or my personality so I decided that needed to go as well. I got myself a little sports car again to tune back in to the old Jennifer; the fun loving, sporty, happy person.

At this point I also lost my friend, Sally, as a friend. She had married a year earlier to her long-term partner – a beautiful wedding I might add, where I was bridesmaid. Sally had become pregnant. I had spent the months after the break-up going out and dating an undesirable person and I am still not sure to this day why I dated him. He had a drug habit and was not even fun to be with but he paid me attention and yet again I fell for it. I was searching for any attention I could get. I had told Sally about him and at that point she distanced herself. I now have clarity, having my own children and understand why that sort of influence would not be welcome. However, I was not the one taking drugs or participating (in fact, I don't need drugs being very high on life). Sally had her baby unbeknown to me and I found out via a friend a week or so later. She had been kept in hospital, as the baby was born very early and had had to have major surgery to survive. I sent flowers but I heard nothing from her and decided to call and visit one day and that was the last contact we had. Her barriers had gone up and probably her hormones were all over the place. Something, at that point I couldn't understand and I felt I had done something wrong. Probably my perception of the situation but it felt uncomfortable. I think I was so preoccupied with my life that I felt I was quite selfish at this point. It was a sad moment but maybe she came along for a reason or a season and not a lifetime.

My new job had given me a purpose again and I felt important at work, although my offices for work were in a beautiful town called Arundel, which was quite a long drive. If you have never been, you should go, the castle is amazing, and Selsey – not such a beautiful town but lovely all the same and there is only one road in and one road out but the people I worked with were amazing. It was difficult to get clientele as these two towns are extremely different. Arundel has a large amount of wealth and very few people who want or can afford to get on the property ladder and Selsey has a large proportion of foreign field workers who are brought in to do the harvests for the salad produce and then there are the local fishermen. I gave it my all and as I said, I worked with some very funny, amazing people.

I dated a couple of people but nobody of any importance. I had lots of nights out with friends, particularly Julie and it was on one of these nights out that I met the person who was to become husband number two. My life was about to take a turn again at a point where I had regained the real me. The Jennifer who just loved life.

Chapter Eight

A Chance Meeting

We had been out drinking and eating and then needed a taxi back. I was with Julie and a few girlies who were ex-crew. All amazing people and a lot of fun I might like to add. Julie, myself and another friend managed to get a taxi and two other friends went up the road to try and get their taxi. They tried to get in a taxi that was waiting for someone else and he agreed to share with them so they could get home. They, during the very short five-minute journey, proceeded to cross examine him about whether he was single and decided that he would be a very good match for me. Amazing what people think when they've had a few pinots. They told him that he should meet me and proceeded to arrange a blind date for me. When their cab turned up at Julie's house, they called me out and introduced me to this dark silhouette in the taxi. I remember not being very impressed as I felt I wasn't ready for a new relationship. Something my gut was telling me but I was ignoring. I smiled pleasantly at the shadowy figure in the car and he handed me his business card which I took and he drove off. I couldn't really see what he looked like as it was too dark and all a bit of a whirlwind. We got back into the house with lots of laughter and chatter going one. When they told me how they had cross examined him I felt awful. I took it upon myself to ring him to apologise and that it where this story begins.

The next part of my life has been the most painful, heart-breaking rollercoaster ride. I have hit the lowest of lows and plodded through them like an ice queen. I didn't know that it was going to be this way and this part of my story unravels in layers all that I had built up over several years.

Against the odds, I decided to meet for a blind date with this man. I actually could not tell you what he looked like but I thought I would give him an opportunity to see if he was my Prince Charming. He turned up to pick me up and he had a lovely Mercedes convertible, it was immaculate and so polished that it gleamed. He obviously took pride in his appearance and not just his personal appearance, which was a plus for me. He was not like the men I had dated in the past and, that may sound crass, but I do appear to have a type and he certainly was not my type. He was 6'2" and very broad, not into fitness although his job was physical. I was drawn to his hands when he placed them on the steering wheel, they were the size of shovels. It was more his attitude that struck me. He appeared to be what I would call a gentle giant. He was very confident in his approach and also very smartly dressed. I am very small and petite so he did seem like a monster to me.

We drove out to a local restaurant where he had booked a table. We sat and chatted generally about our jobs and the hobbies we liked. He seemed a genuine guy and family orientated. I was determined not to talk about my ex fiancé as, I was aware that living in the same town, it was more than likely that he would know him. I was right, in fact he knew him very well which came to light at a later date.

The thing that he did though, which in hindsight is very clever, is that he made me feel very sorry for him. He had a very turbulent relationship with a girl and she had been extremely violent towards him. Difficult to understand when you see his size but believable. You see he was playing to my sympathetic ear and he told me all these horror stories of how she would get drunk and come back and hit him and he would try and lock her out and she had kicked the door down. She had had several children by several different men and he was left every night to babysit them whilst she went out drinking. It was very difficult for me to understand not being that sort of a person. I certainly could not understand how she could have left her children with him whilst she went out drinking every night. He went on to say that he had had a restraining order against her and it all sounded very horrible and at this point alarm bells should have been ringing but my intuition was definitely not working properly. Actually, I was ignoring it, more to the point. I was still unsure of him but I had swallowed the whole story, hook, line and sinker.

He then told me all about his ex-wife and how they had been childhood sweethearts and how their friendship was very platonic but because they had been together for so long they just ended up getting married. But obviously, all was not well and she had cheated on him and spent a long time during their marriage siphoning off thousands of pounds before producing divorce papers and to add insult to injury, she had been into their family home and removed all the furniture from the house. His Mum and Dad had come to the rescue and helped him buy her out of the house that he had bought. Poor boy, I thought, what terrible things happen to people!

We had an enjoyable evening but a part of me was not sure about him. He didn't set my world on fire or trigger those flutters in my stomach. He dropped me back home and asked if we could meet again. I smiled politely and told him to contact me but I wasn't sure whether I wanted to meet him again. I found it difficult to say a straight out "no". I am not cruel and didn't want to hurt his feelings. For about eight weeks he continually texted me and came around for coffee. I felt no physical bond with him and, therefore, was reluctant to take our relationship to that level. He was persistent and I suppose I was enjoying the attention although in my heart of hearts I can remember wishing he was my ex fiancé. It was just at this point that he decided one Sunday morning to pick me up and he took me over to meet his parents so that we could take their dog, a spaniel called Maggie, for a walk. His parents seemed lovely and they lived in this chocolate box cottage in the middle of the countryside. It was idyllic. His Dad worked for the council and was very high up as well as being very funny and amusing and his Mum was a freelance book-keeper. They were both very well spoken and well-dressed and very welcoming. I was a bit overwhelmed by how lovely they appeared. We then popped around to his cottage around the corner. It was beautiful and immaculate inside and I could see my dream future unfolding in front of me. I'd never met a man that had good taste and vision and was so tidy. It was everything I had ever dreamed of and this man wanted somebody to be with him for life and he wanted children, or that is what he said. I was welcomed into the family and his Dad treated me like a daughter, although he had two daughters of his own. The family was a little dysfunctional and his sister in Manchester had not spoken to his parents for years due to them not being able to see eye to eye and his sister, who was local, was married and seemed friendly enough. Her husband was also very friendly and actually we got on like a house on fire. We all started going out as a big family for meals and very often we would have his parents round for dinner and vice versa. There were always lots of homemade goodies to eat such as jams and cakes and fresh picked fruit from the orchard. It had a very homely feel to it and I felt comfortable with this environment.

Dave and I would spend the weeks working and the weekends socialising in a local bar in town. My journey to work meant that getting home was late and eating was late. His business permitted him the privilege of getting home at 5pm. It was a matter of eight weeks when he suggested that I rent my flat out and move in with him. I loved the idea of living in a cottage and I jumped at the chance. The cottage was a typical Sussex build semi-detached house and had a beautiful large garden which was laid out to lawn and borders. It was perfectly landscaped and at the bottom the garden was a fenced off orchard with apple and plum trees. The neighbours both sides seemed very pleasant. I happily moved in but not all was as rosy as I initially had thought. I felt a little spoilt at first as Dave would prepare dinner so that I could eat when I got in. He would wash and load the dishwasher and little things so that I didn't have to do them. One day, on a day off in the week, he had a delivery of mail and his policy was that, now that I lived with him I could open all the mail. This was a job he didn't like doing so was quite happy to pass this responsibility to me. However, this responsibility came with a realisation. I discovered that he had lots of red letter bills waiting on his doormat and had not a clue as he hadn't read his mail for months. As the rent on my property was paying my mortgage, I took it upon myself to pay off all the bills so that we could start afresh and set up direct debits so that this situation would not arise again. In a way, this gave me a little bit of power and authority in his home and I think I quite revelled on this. My Mum and Dad had been down to visit and stay and had been made very welcome and were pleased that I had found someone that I was going to settle down with. It was all about image for me at this point. Dave had a certain presence in the area and reputation and was well thought of and so was his family. This impressed my Mum and Dad and to be honest, it was what drew me into the situation.

I very often struggled with the intimate moments. I was very small and Dave was a particularly large built person and however much I tried, I couldn't overcome my disapproval of his physical image and yet I stayed with him. I believe a part of me felt protected by that image and maybe even safe.

Our Friday evenings mainly consisted of visiting the wine bar in town and meeting up with other business colleagues that Dave knew and I would invite friends of mine along. We realised very early on that we had some mutual friends and that brought us together as a group. The strangest thing started to happen at this wine bar though. Matthew, who I was engaged to previously started socialising there on a Friday night too with his friend. We would be all very polite to each other and Dave would shake his hand and pass the time of day with him. All evening though he would stand somewhere where he was near to me. Every time I turned around, there he would be. The words in my head that played over and over again were the words he wrote on my card on the flowers he sent me about 'being his angel sent from heaven to be by his side always' and some of his final words in our parting conversation where he had told me that he would always want to know how I was and know that I was safe. This was a very peculiar situation and not particularly comfortable for me. It almost had a feeling of mental torture to it. I sometimes wonder if in some sort of angelic form, he was trying to warn me. I still had feelings for him but he was with someone else (a friend of his whom he had known for years who had grown up children) and I was now with Dave. A part of me felt that I wanted to make him jealous to make him want me back but that situation did not arise and my circumstances changed very quickly.

After one of these renowned nights out, I awoke on a Saturday morning at the cottage. Dave was chatting about the night before and then all of a sudden, he proposed to me. I could feel and still feel to this day the shock ripple through me.

"Well, what do you think? Shall we get married? It makes sense. You live here now and we are together."

I held my breath and didn't want to answer.

"Yes, ok let's do it," I really wanted to say no as my stomach was churning and not in a good way but something inside me said that it was the right thing to do (maybe guilt that I loved him in a different way and a lack of understanding on my part of what I was feeling).

I agreed to marry him. Why? Although, I did not realise it, Dave was very persistent but also very manipulative. He would feel sorry for himself and me, being the person that I am, an empath so very sensitive and a people pleaser, would not want to disappoint him and would try to make him feel good about himself. My self-esteem at this point was very low and I believe that I felt that I didn't have any other options. My ex had moved on and I hadn't found anyone else that seemed to even come close. It was someone to be with and although I did not have the same affection for him, he idolised me.

At the end of the day, I have realised that my personality is that of someone who wishes to please, which isn't always a good thing. Dave obviously knew this, if not purposely, as he is one of those (another belief) people who prey on people like me and I was being the perfect willing victim.

The bizarre thing is that I went back to the shop where my ex fiancé had got my engagement ring from and I part exchanged it for another (bad omen really). My ex fiancé had picked the design of my ring himself and surprised me and I was now picking my own ring. I am a little old fashioned and I felt that this was the man's job. His response to this was that he would not know what he was looking for and it would be better to pick something I liked. Oddly enough I then paid for the ring? Why would I do this when I don't actually want to marry him? Because I wanted to please him and he had a lot of debt at this point and there was no way he could have afforded the £2,500 ring that I chose. Being very financially conscious, I did not want him to accumulate any more debt and I wanted us to start our future with a clean slate. I had rented my flat and used my salary to help clear his debts and get him set up on the straight and narrow. I was being carried along by a series of events and I didn't seem to be able to stop them. He was being exceptionally kind, cooking my tea as I worked a long way away and I was always late home and, in a way, needy of my attention. But he managed to do all the things that I found I was grateful for (sometimes he put the washing machine on/empty the dishwasher) and that all sounds good but there are always underlying reasons for actions, or there was in this case.

We announced to the world we were getting married, which was met with a little hesitancy on my parents' part but they were pleased. Dave's parents were over the moon. His sister was not too enamoured when she learnt the date of the wedding, apparently, she had got married around the same date we had chosen only several years earlier. We weren't in control the date, as it was down to when the venue could book us in. We had picked a local venue, which meant all the family could attend and there would be no issues with where to stay for the night, as it had hotel accommodation as well. I had a beautiful wedding dress it was a tight-fitting bodice with organza skirt and I was so petite at that stage it looked magnificent. Actually, it was the dress I was going to wear to marry my ex fiancé. Oh, dear, writing it all down makes you realise how really doomed this all looks. I knew every time I looked at this dress that all it did was remind me of the wedding that never happened.

Underlying all that was going on, was my six-monthly visits to a gynaecologist. I had fully recovered from my illness in my late 20's when I had started to suffer some very severe bleeding. The colic that I mentioned earlier and my weight loss. After many hospital appointments and tests, I was diagnosed eventually with a lactose intolerance. I was put on a very bland, wheat free diet and when I came to have an endoscopy they found blistering but no sign of coeliac disease, which of course they wouldn't as I had not eaten wheat for 3 months. During all the tests that were carried out I had been put forward for a dexa scan to check my bone density to see if it had been affected and sure enough it was discovered that my bone density was very low and I needed calcium supplements and I would require scans from time to time to monitor this. I was now very high risk of osteoporosis. The Lactose intolerance is a strange thing and covers all sorts of misdemeanors such as the fact the pill is filled out with lactose. The actual ingredients are too small to see and the lactose, when added, makes it big enough to be tablet form. Therefore, when I tried to take it, I suffered from terrible pains and constant bleeding, so I was advised to avoid it as the build-up of lactose was having an effect. However, the point I am trying to make is, I was also suffering with menstrual cycles of seven to ten days which I had been suffering for years and a lot of women will know that this also affects ovulation, but I was totally unaware of this. I had been put on the pill injection to overcome the short cycles and stop my periods and then I had to be removed from this injection as there were concerns as to its effect on my bone density. I could not take the pill due to the build-up of lactose making me bleed again. In actual fact, I was healthy as could be but they still needed to keep an eye on me. I would not even think about what was going on until another appointment cropped up.

With all that in mind I am now rolling along in this relationship that I'm not sure I should be in and my six-month check arose. Not thinking too much about it I turned up at the hospital and did all the height/weight measurements with the nurse. I then went in to see the consultant for a general chat about my wellbeing. We had got to know each other quite well by this point and he knew I was into my fitness. I then asked a question regarding the shortness of my menstrual cycles and what sort of contraception he would advise as I was very limited at this point.

"I wouldn't worry about contraception. You've had children anyway, haven't you?" He was still writing as he spoke. "With the shortness of your cycles there is no way you could conceive as they are not long enough to ovulate." He was very matter of fact.

"No, I haven't got any children." A lump rose up in my throat.

"Oh, well," he tried to clear his throat.

"Does that mean I won't ever have children?"

"The likelihood of you having children is non-existent." He said it as though he was telling me he had run out of carrier bags.

There was no emotion. Maybe he had said it to so many women that he had lost touch with the consequence of such a statement but it felt cold and unfeeling.

I was absolutely devastated. I could feel a searing pain through my heart and my eyes welling with tears. My dream of the cottage, husband, four children and two dogs had just been taken away from me and now I faced a life of possibly working for the rest of my life, childless and not sure if I wanted to be with this man that I had agreed to marry.

I went home and rang Dave and told him my news I was devastated and in floods of tears. He was understanding and suddenly I felt I needed this man in my life and I must love him as he was so understanding. In actual fact, his reaction made me feel as though he felt a sense of relief. I went for a run to clear my head (running is my salvation) and got myself completely lost. I must have run 10 miles and eventually recognised where I was but I was still a good three miles away from home and headed towards the in-laws.

My in-laws gave me a drink and I told them my news. They weren't quite sure how to react and told me that they were sorry. My father in law drove me back home.

I spent all day pondering this information overload. I made a promise to myself that things are for a reason and I am meant for some other work in this world. Now you are all looking back to page one of this book because it says I am a mother of three children. Yes, that is true and I will come to that now.

Jennifer Smith now had more thinking to do. Where was her life going and how were things meant to be? Was it her destiny not to have children? Was her destiny with Dave?

Chapter Nine

The Relative Realisation

You see, Dave (husband no 2) has two sisters and the younger one who lived locally had been married a couple of years and was desperate for children. She and her husband were even on the verge of going through IVF. I do feel for people who really want children and will make exceptional parents.

We were all summoned to a gathering at the in-law's house one evening and it was then that Dave's sister announced that she was pregnant and it had happened naturally without intervention. I was extremely pleased for her and congratulated them both. She turned her nose up as if to show she was better than me. I found this very hurtful. I said nothing but I had just been told that I couldn't have children but I would never dampen the mood of anyone else's pleasure. Children are a blessing.

I had this sudden realisation that the family I was now involved with wasn't all that it seemed. Firstly, the reaction when we told Dave's sister when the wedding was going to be was met with disdain and then her snobbish behaviour about being pregnant. Something was not right. I also knew that she had a bit of an issue with Dave's birthday. Dave was born the day before his sister only four years later. This had griped with her for many years and had obviously embroiled her in jealousy. Dave constantly celebrating his birthday before her. I had always wondered why they hadn't used it as an opportunity to celebrate together. It is rather special to have a situation such as they have.

However, the tables were about to turn. Two weeks later Dave and I had news of our own. I had been feeling very, very sick and I had very low blood pressure. It was all I could do to get up in the mornings. I thought maybe the bad news had hit me harder than I thought. It wasn't like me to feel so low as I am an early riser and always full of beans. I managed to get in the car and get to work but I felt so ill. The office was quiet and I sat for a while staring into space. A voice in my head said, "Jennifer, you're pregnant." I felt myself jolt and grabbed my bag and coat and headed to the local pharmacy. I bought a pregnancy test. I asked if anyone minded if I left the office and so to the long journey home. So many questions in my head. What if I was pregnant? What if I'm not? How do I feel about it? I pulled into the drive at home and ran into the house. I threw my coat and bag down and delved into the bottom of the bag. My fingers were all over the place. I was trying to open the packet and read instructions at the same time. My whole body shook. I told myself to stay calm. I completely mucked up the first test and it read that it was not working properly. Luckily there were two tests in the pack. I opened the second one and this time patiently followed the instructions. Low and behold, the person who could not have children, was pregnant. I was over the moon and got in the car and drove over to Dave, who was at his mother and father's house mowing their lawn. He looked at me and he just knew. I told my parents on the phone, as I knew that this was something they had hoped for and they knew how upset I was at the Gynaecologist's diagnosis. They were a little shocked that I was pregnant understandably, but pleased. So, we agreed to tell his Mum and Dad the same night. We took them for a Chinese meal and whilst we were in conversation Dave announced that there would be the patter of little feet soon. They were thrilled but a little concerned as to how Dave's sister would take the news as it might overshadow her pregnancy? This is something that I struggled to understand as I was looking forward to having someone to discuss pregnancy things with. However, it was their wish that we were not to announce our pregnancy until after Dave's Mum's birthday in a week's time. Therefore, I decided to honour their wish.

When Love Turns To Harm

Have you ever been in one of those very surreal moments were everything is going on around you and you are viewing from inside a bubble. I have and this meal was one of them. It was the following week and we were all attending Dave's Mums party. It was being held at a lovely venue out in the countryside. I decided to drive, as I could not drink. We all welcomed each other and did the pleasantries. Dave's sister found that odd that I had driven but I told her that I was having to drive a long distance to work the next day, which wasn't untrue, so it was better that I didn't drink. With the distance I was covering, I couldn't afford to be even the slightest bit hung over or drink at all. The meal was at an exclusive restaurant (or posh pub, if you will), which was nice, and as the night went on Dave's Dad got merrier and merrier and his conversation became more and more suggestive to the fact that I was also pregnant. Dave kicked his Dad under the table. It was their wish that his sister didn't find out. Eventually, as the evening drew to a close, Dave's sister asked me outright if I was pregnant. To respect the wishes of Dave's parents, I denied this. Well, actually, I avoided the question altogether. I do not like lying to anyone and this felt really awkward, especially as I had been put in such a difficult situation. I didn't want to upset his Mum on her Birthday but I didn't want to lie either. I laughed off the accusation and felt myself go crimson in shame.

I would have just preferred to have told everyone the truth, it would have made life so much easier. I believe this one particular night started another series of events which occurred whilst I was in this relationship. When I did confirm the news to Dave's sister she was very off with me and, in fact, very jealous and could not even bring herself to talk to me when we met up on the rare occasions that we did. This made life very awkward. Jealousy is a very dangerous and consuming thing and not pleasant at all. It was made worse by her husband who was desperately over compensating for her weird behaviour. Everyone was aware of the situation but nobody wanted to say anything. Well, except Dave. But not to his sister.

Lorraine Butterfield

Dave is a character that rants on and on about things to everybody except the person who he should say it to. The situation, was to say, extremely embarrassing. Dave would fly off the handle with his Mum and Dad about the situation and they would make excuses about hormones and tell him not to say anything as she was pregnant. All of which I understand but please, these were supposed to be happy days. His constant ranting at the situation would bring my mood down and I struggled to lift the energy but I tried. I was always trying with him to stop his constant complaining and inflate his ego by agreeing with him just as a pacifier so that I didn't have to listen to it over and over again. He would drain me of energy to the point of exhaustion and in fact, I was glad when he and I went to work just for the silence and a break.

Anyway, this news changed a lot of things and it meant that the wedding plans were put on hold and the venue was cancelled and the dress that I was due to wear would be no good in my circumstances. Probably all for the best. We decided the best thing to do was to delay the wedding until after the baby had been born and I think part of me felt a sense of relief. But the relations were still rumbling in the background and things weren't quite as they seemed.

I had hoped that the initial shock of our news would have settled and that life could return to normal (or as normal as it had been). I was wrong and one day we had all and by all, I mean Dave, myself, his sister and husband, been invited to his parents for Sunday roast. This was a regular occurrence and in return I cooked for Dave's Mum and Dad nearly every other Sunday. So, I always made sure we returned the favour. It is just the way I am even though I was pregnant and not really enjoying food at that time. On this particular Sunday, we were sat in the lounge having a discussion about baby products. Actually, both Dave and myself are quite thorough when we wanted to buy something so it will come as no surprise to find that upon trying to choose prams, cots etc…. a lot of research was done by myself and especially car seats. We are both fanatical about safety. Although Dave is somewhat of a snob and there was an element of the more you paid the better the product, which isn't always the case. He had his good points though; Dave always made sure that the car I had was new and road worthy but I do think a little of that was the snob in him to be fair. Our cars weren't just a car; it was a car with extras, lots of extras and top of the range!!!! Anyway, back to the Sunday roast. So, we are sat in the lounge with Dave's sister and husband and generally chatting and I mention about car seats. Well, you know that expression a 'bulldog sucking a lemon' – yes, that is how his sister looked and she stormed out of the room. I think deep down, and being a middle child, she wanted all the attention of having a baby to herself. Quite selfish but understandable, I suppose. I wouldn't know as I am not that way inclined. But it is uncomfortable being in a room with a person who cannot even look at you or talk to you when you have not done anything wrong. I never told her that I was told that I would never have children and maybe if she had understood that, then things may have been different. But, you shouldn't have to explain yourself to people. Even if you don't feel it, you can try and get on with people. Anyway, this behaviour went on throughout the whole pregnancy. Every time I entered a room, she moved herself into a different room. I don't remember having a conversation with her about anything in particular throughout our pregnancies.

At 29 weeks pregnant I was rushed to hospital. Dave and I had been out drinking (I was on soft drinks) with friends. We got home about 10.30pm and I got dressed for bed, went to the toilet, as you do, and streams of blood flooded into the toilet.

"Dave, Dave… I'm bleeding," I called him, my voice shaking with fear and I wasn't able to move.

He came rushing in and saw the mess I was in and started to panic.

"Get me the phone, Dave," I could see how panic stricken he was.

He ran out of the bathroom and returned with the phone and he handed it to me. I rang for an ambulance, I will reiterate "I" as Dave was a panicking wreck.

"Ambulance please," my voice quivering as the tears started and shock kicked in.

I still amaze myself at how I can take control when I need too. The Operator answered the call and subjected me to a series of questions to ascertain my situation, "how much blood is there, a tablespoon or a teaspoon."

"A bucket full".

The ambulance was with us in 2 minutes. In fact, one of the paramedics was an old colleague of mine from my reception days at the telecoms company. She walked into the room and said, "how are you?" and then retorted with, "silly question, wasn't it".

The paramedics were brilliant and I was rushed to the local hospital. I could feel the adrenaline rushing through my body and a real fear now creeping in as to what was going to happen next.

When I got to the hospital, I was placed in a side room of the maternity ward. I had a team of three doctors who greeted me and proceeded to examine me. All were very concerned with the volume of blood I was losing. I was then visited by the Registrar. He advised me that he wanted to perform a caesarean. I was still in shock and I just wanted what was best for the baby. His decision was over-ruled by a Senior Registrar as the baby was not considered to be in distress.

My stay lasted three days in hospital under observation and eventually the bleeding subsided. Apparently, I had a second sack in which there would have been Olivia (my firstborn's) twin. But this never formed properly and eventually it fills with blood and then leaves the body. Isn't the body such a wonderful, clever design. I was so relieved to be going home and so glad that baby and I were going to be okay. My Mum and Dad had made their way down and were very concerned that I would have to deliver a premature baby. Dave's parents dealt with it differently. Dave's Mum didn't tell Dave's sister that I had been rushed into hospital and may have the baby early, as she did not want to upset her. Bizarre. She was not aware of anything happening and that is the way they wanted to keep it.

I have to say that Mum and Dad have been the most supportive, protective parents ever and that without them, my life today would not be as it is. They have and will always be there for me should I need them and maybe I don't always take the time to thank them enough.

Having now been through another major life event and come out the other side, things were coming together and life was getting back on an even keel for Jennifer. She had the dream home, a family who were very supportive and a baby on the way. This is what she had wanted. It wasn't all perfect but it wasn't bad, or so she thought. Again, changes were afoot but who would have known that they were going to take the course that they did.

Chapter Ten

My Eyes are Opened

Three days later, I came out of hospital and had to take things a little bit easier, although at that point I had problems with my employer, as they were refusing to pay me as I could not drive to my offices to carry out my work due to my low blood pressure and the risk of me fainting at the wheel of the car. I had offered to work in a local office, which they refused to do. Therefore, I was then in dispute with them and when they stopped paying me completely I threatened to take them to tribunal for unfair treatment. They eventually took it to senior management and agreed to settle out of court. Not the sort of thing you need to be dealing with when you are pregnant.

So, whilst I was unable to work, I needed to do something. Dave's Mum was a book-keeper for several businesses, including Dave's and asked if I wanted to help her out. Every day I would pop down to her offices and help out with invoicing or writing the books up. Having a business can be very stressful, as a lot of people will know. Dave's business was no exception. Cash flow always an issue and constantly trying to keep everyone happy. I know his Mum frustrated him as she always took so long to do everything, but she was just thorough and old school.

One morning I decided to go and help out. I was approaching the office and could hear raised voices. I opened the office door and stood in silence at the most horrendous sight I have witnessed. Dave and his Mum going hammer and tongs at each other. I seemed to be in some sort of time warp or bubble as I watched the scene playing out around me. They were discussing (if you can call it that) money and she was telling him that he did not have the money to buy some machinery for his business. He had obviously promised the seller that he would buy this equipment and was screaming at her asking why she had not told him the financial situation. In my head I was answering this question with 'I imagine the answer to that would be because of his reaction'. I don't think in my short life that I have ever heard anyone speak to their parents the way he was or use such abusive language. He threw things around; anything he could lay his hands on was thrown across the room aimed towards his Mum. I jumped in reaction to the crashing obstacles. His temper in full flow he turned to retreat and stormed out of the office past me. All I could do was stand still. I could feel his energy whisk past me and I wanted no part of it. I was horrified, shaking, scared, frozen in the moment. I had never seen temper like it. The blood must have all drained from my face.

Dave's Mum approached me and just said, "Jennifer, I will understand if you just want to walk away now".

This was actually the point at which I should have walked away but I didn't. I didn't know what to think. I was going to sort this out though because that is what I do. I am a pacifier, I thought I could handle Dave, bring him to his senses, get him to apologise to his Mum. How wrong was I. I made his Mum a cup of tea and she tried to explain the situation to me. I stayed for a while but I couldn't concentrate so I went back home to do some housework. Maybe I could figure out how to handle this a different way.

Later at home, when things had calmed down, Dave came in. He was still annoyed but not as angry.

"How are you feeling?" I was very nervous.

"I'm okay now I'm home," his reply was very stilted.

"Why were you speaking to your Mum that way and why did you get so angry." I would not dream of speaking to my Mum and Dad in such a derogatory manner.

Very cunningly he explained the situation, "I'm just so frustrated. My Mum is always trying to hold me back. I want to make this business a success and to do that I need this equipment. Financially it makes sense. All I want to do is make the business bigger and better so that we can be more secure."

He was frustrated and he justified his behaviour and do you know, I believed what he said. Actually, I think I wanted to believe what he said, after all, I was having his baby. He kept going over and over the situation ranting on and on and I could feel the energy draining away from me but I held a sympathetic and understanding ear. In all honesty, I was just making sure the situation calmed down and he had talked it out until he had justified himself and could let it go. I was not totally convinced about how he had justified himself and I was hoping that this reaction of temper had been a one-off but I was soon to find out that this had been going on for a long time and more frequently than I realised. I have never lived with temper. My parents are the most loving, giving people and I don't remember voices ever being raised or if they were, it was not very regularly. I can also say that all my partners in life have been pretty easy going and may have been frustrated but never displayed acts of temper tantrum. So, this was a whole new ball game for me.

Now that I had witnessed the first outburst from him, the outbursts towards his Mum became more frequent and then the outbursts became focused upon me and my behaviour. I could feel his temper before he arrived. My stomach would turn when I knew he was on the way. I always knew when he was on the way as he was in constant contact with me. He would ring several times a day to find out what I was doing and where I was. He would ring to say he was on the way home and

I could tell by the type of conversation that we had as to what mood he was in. A lot of the time he would be ranting about a job he hadn't got or he would complain about the men that worked for him. My body felt as though I was bracing myself for his arrival. My mind was working overtime to work out a way to bring the energy down to a calmer level. Mentally I was drained and although he probably was not aware of it, he was manipulating the situation, so I would make sure things were done before he got home. Very often he would arrive with a face like thunder and bright red and doors would be slammed and he walked as if he was charging along. It was as though a whirlwind had arrived at the house. If I hadn't got his dinner on the table by the time he got home, he would go berserk. It was like it was the end of the world. He would shout, swear and throw things across the room and get very up close and in my face and growl at me. It was all very intimidating. I would quiver inside but I never answered back. I stood my ground like I was defying him and he wasn't quite sure how to react so would charge out of the house again and up the garden to the outbuilding that he had as an office. He wanted me to react and I would not give him the satisfaction. Actually, it was more that my whole body could not move. I was frozen to the spot. The fear had kicked in and I think I knew deep down that if I answered back I would get more than shouted at. Sometimes when he had had one of his shouting tantrums I would refuse to make his lunch for the next day. I wasn't going to be treated like that and then run around after him. He would suddenly be all apologetic and try to hug and kiss me. I couldn't respond as he wanted as I felt emotionless, dead inside. This cycle continued, day to day and month to month.

At this point, I was heavily pregnant with Olivia and very aware that the baby would also be aware of the atmosphere and how I was feeling. I can honestly say that Olivia, particularly, was affected by the behaviour and still to this day, has times when her past is playing a part in her future.

Lorraine Butterfield

My life consisted of keeping a house immaculate, cooking, ironing, gardening, cleaning cars (inside and out), cleaning windows and helping his Mum with the books, as well as preparing to have a baby and oh yes, dealing with my work tribunal. The fun loving, independent Jennifer was nowhere to be seen. I was shattered mentally and physically but I put a smile on my face and carried on. Dave would come home in a mood and then later on apologise for his behaviour and take me out for a meal to make up for his behaviour. Or, his worst trait was to apologise and then want to have sex. My stomach would turn. How could he be and say such cruel things and then want to kiss and cuddle. My heart and head wanted to run away but the body let him take me, just so as not to have another temper outburst.

The apologies were not enough; I had lost the trust. Things would be good for a few weeks, if that, and I would feel comfortable with him again and then it would start again. As soon as I felt relaxed with him he took it upon himself to scold me in some way. I started to feel that it was all my fault and if I did everything I could he may not lose his temper. However, the problem I had was that it could be anything, there was no identifiable trigger. It was almost as if he just enjoyed trying to antagonise me to see if I would react. As I said, I am a pacifist and I do not rise to being baited. At this point in our relationship I was walking on eggshells. Do you know, I felt sorry for his Mum and Dad and they almost looked to me to solve the problem - him. I was a relief to them. Whenever there was something his Mum needed to tell Dave and she didn't want to, she would tell me to break the news to him. So now the backlash was at me. It is quite sad that they were not strong enough to put their foot down with him and sad that they felt it was down to me to sort him out.

So here I am, I am eight months' pregnant. It was a Saturday morning and Dave and I decided to go shopping at a mall in a local town and we parked in the multi-storey car park. Dave handed me the car park ticket as we entered under the barrier. I took the ticket and I thought that I had put it straight into my purse. We did the shopping we needed to do. When we came to leave the mall, I could not find the ticket to put in the machine. You know how it is pregnant, forgetful, these things happen, don't they? My goodness, I was so embarrassed as he spurted a tirade of abuse at me. I remember him saying to me, "you are a stupid cow", and then proceeded to push me.

I was shaken and in tears and thoroughly embarrassed. I felt cheap and horrible but not strong enough to respond to him or challenge him in any way or form. We could almost have been in one of the popular soap operas that portray these things. I was in shock and trembling, I tried to stop myself from crying and I pressed the button on the ticket machine to speak to an assistant. I explained the situation to a very lovely man who I gave our registration to and he advised that when we got to the barrier he would lift it up and let us out without paying today. I had been publicly humiliated by a man that was supposed to love me. I am pretty sure that there are CCTV cameras at the ticket machines and I am pretty sure the man on the ticket machine assistance had witnessed what had happened. He was my guardian angel on that day at that point as I couldn't have coped with anything more than had already occurred. The fact that we had free parking was a bonus and something we should have laughed about. I remember sitting in the car in silence, leaning on the window holding back the sobbing tears that wanted to flood. He never stopped ranting on at me, even though we had ended up with free parking. I had done something wrong and he didn't want me to forget it. I avoided him for the rest of the day, telling him that I had things to get on with and he left to go and do some work. I was glad of the reprieve. When he got home later, it was as though nothing had happened and it was never mentioned again. He would calm down and over a period of time would regain my trust only to undo it repeatedly.

Lorraine Butterfield

Fear is a lonely place. But this is where I found myself trapped in a world where, from the outside, we looked like the perfect family but the pain on the inside was almost unbearable. My only outlet was to tell my friend Julie what had happened and she would sympathise and offer me a place to stay but I never took her up on it, as I did not want Dave to know that I was telling her what had been happening behind closed doors. That to me would have fuelled the fire and I didn't want to do that with a baby on the way. To the outside world, he appeared shy, smart and well spoken, a good businessman and polite. How could he be the monster that I was a witness to? But a monster to me he was.

Dave would over-compensate in other ways for his abhorrent behaviour. For example, when we knew that Olivia was on the way he converted an outbuilding in the garden into a garden room for my Mum and Dad to stay in. It had a bedroom/living area and a shower room and a little breakfast bar to make tea/coffee on. I paid for the conversion works with the money I was getting from work/rent. It was a little home away from home for them and they felt they weren't intruding in the house and could have their space when they needed. Dad could sit and watch his TV when he wanted to and no-one minded. It was actually a blessing and a relief for me when my Mum and Dad came to stay. Everything seemed easier, Dave was more relaxed and life seemed better.

I was still in touch with Julie and Vicky and would try to get together as often as was possible. They kept me connected to the outside world and although I could not reveal to them all that was going on, I felt a sense of relief to be with them. Dave would want to know if we were meeting and where we were meeting and very often would ring when we met to make sure I was where I said I was. The other relief that I got in my world with Dave was going to pregnancy yoga. I couldn't run anymore and I needed to do something to keep me going. Once a week on a Tuesday evening I would go and do my yoga. I am a friendly person and I got to meet some lovely people and yet again, I made and I am still friends with a lovely lady called Anabelle. She was also someone that helped me remain sane. Anabelle is an Essex girl but had moved to Sussex when she had met her husband. She now lives back in Essex and we still have contact, although not as much as we would like. Anabelle is friendly, outgoing and larger than life personality wise and her family are the friendliest loveliest people you will ever meet. She is also very laid back and loves life. So, we would go to yoga and I think I would spend most of my time at yoga laughing. She is a proper Essex girl with a great sense of humour. We became very close friends and would meet up in the week and have a coffee and cake. She was always suspicious of Dave but actually couldn't put her finger on why, so never said anything to me. Occasionally, she would ask me if I was alright and ask for reassurance but would never dream of interrogating me. I put on a good show that everything was hunky dorey. Even deciding that the wedding should go ahead.

Rather than have a big wedding we spent the money to go away on a holiday to Gran Canaria as we had not even been away together. In fact, Dave hadn't really been abroad at all. My thirst for travel was gripping me. It was a sort of honeymoon before the wedding if you like, as after the wedding I was going to be busy with baby and it would have been too stressful to try and travel abroad with a baby, for me anyway. Our accommodation was all inclusive in a Platinum rated hotel. Our flights were from Stansted and all went well. Dave's Dad took us to the airport so that we wouldn't have to worry about parking. All went smoothly. Our transfer the other side took us to the hotel. Beautiful hotel but in the middle of nowhere right on a private beach in a bay. There was nowhere to walk to and if you wanted to sight see it involved hiring a car. It felt quite claustrophobic to be restricted. The whole idea of going away was to not drive, as I had been doing lots of driving when working and just be able to do walks and relax was what I was looking forward to. I was quite heavily pregnant so I didn't want to lie in the sun all day. This was not my style anyway, I like to be active. I decided that we just needed to make the best of it. The room was lovely. The following day when we got up we decided we would go to the pool and try and read and swim. When we sat by the pool initially it was very quiet and relaxing. Then, all of a sudden, the rumbling sound of diggers and heavy machinery started over in the valley. Dave, was not impressed. He spent every day at work with the sounds of heavy machinery and he hadn't come away on holiday to listen to it all day. That was it for him and I could feel the temperature rising and I don't mean the temperature of the sun. Off he went to the reception to find our representative for the holiday. He was not impressed and having spent a lot of money on the holiday, it was not acceptable to have to put up with the building site opposite. I was feeling uncomfortable with the whole situation. It wasn't ideal but the hotel was very nice and the accommodation was air conditioned which was a lovely reprieve for me in my condition. I just wanted an easy life as life at home was always one drama after another. Dave made such a fuss that they decided to move us on day two to the centre of Gran Canaria to an apartment. It wasn't air conditioned but it was right in the hub of things. There were shops and a beach and lots of things to see and do. Dave was hot and bothered and wasn't coping with the heat particularly well and on day three my body decided to break out in prickly heat. Possibly because I was pregnant and uncomfortable. I went to see a doctor whilst I was there and they advised me to stay in the cool. Enough was enough for Dave. He declared that it wasn't a holiday and it would be easier to go home. So that is what we did. I was in no position to argue with him, nor wanted to. It was obvious the whole time we were away that he really wasn't enjoying it and nothing seemed right. We arranged to come home on earlier flights. That was the end of our first and last holiday abroad together.

I tried to get some perspective on this situation. I am struggling to be at home in the company of this man and we cannot even have a holiday together. Everything feels too difficult and I no longer have any energy to stand up for myself. What is happening to me? Where is the happy-go-lucky Jennifer who gets everything that she could ever want! This was not part of the dream and more changes were heading towards Jennifer but could she deal with what was to come?

Chapter Eleven

The Wedding

Dave and I had planned to have quite a large wedding and we had booked a venue for the November. I mentioned earlier that this was met with disdain by his sister as she had got married several years earlier in the November. I believe also that there had been some huge uproar about Dave taking his then girlfriend to the wedding, in case she created a scene, as she was quite a disruptive personality and that had had an impact on the relationship between Dawn, his sister, and Dave and it had torn the family apart. Apparently, she was very good at getting drunk and then they would argue and even fight!!!

Dawn felt we should not get married around the same time as she did and, for her, she got her wish. Due to me being pregnant we had decided to postpone the wedding until a more suitable time when I could possibly fit back into my dress and be more able to enjoy the day.

As the months got nearer to the birth of our first child, the religious part of me took hold. I felt that I could not bring our first child into this world without being married first. There seemed to be this constant voice in the back of my head telling me to just get married. I spoke to Dave and arranged for us to register to marry. I then spoke to a venue in a local area that I thought would be suitable – Horsham Museum. They could fit us in on a Saturday in March, which happened to be Easter weekend that year. We then had to decide who we would invite. I decided as I was then heavily pregnant and bursting to full that I couldn't cope with too many people. I also think that knowing what I knew about our life, I didn't want to make a big thing of our wedding. So, obviously both sets of parents were invited along with my brother, Michael, Dave's sister and brother-in-law, Dave's Aunty and Uncle from away and my friend, Julie and Dave's friend Keith with his young son, Jack. We then arranged to go to a very nice hotel for a quiet meal afterwards and have photos taken by Dave's Dad who was a keen photographer and very good at it.

Do you know, you can plan the biggest wedding and the smallest wedding and still have people disagree about something. I do wonder what all the fuss is about sometimes. Needless to say, Dave's sister said that they would not be attending the wedding, as she was very close to giving birth. I was very disappointed that she could not get over herself for one day. It wasn't a long ceremony or a long day and it was near to their home and the hospital she would have to attend if she went into labour. I know she was close to giving birth but so was I and I was the one getting married! Dave's Dad made a huge fuss of her and tried to persuade her to attend. They refutably said they would still not attend. So, Dave had another chance to constantly complain about her attitude. I just couldn't give a damn and to be fair, if she was like that, I preferred her to stay away. My energy levels were being depleted and I needed all my energy to keep my baby safe and well.

I needed a wedding dress and therefore, I planned a shopping trip. I went to Bluewater with Julie. Have you ever tried to get something to fit an eight-month pregnant bride? Near on impossible or it was a few years ago. We must have walked into every high street shop there was and department store to no avail. Eventually, in one of them, just as my feet were about to explode with tiredness, there at the back were a few clothes that were on offer as they must have been left over from the Christmas. I searched through the rail and found a cream dress. It had very thin straps that crossed at the back and a seam that crossed over on the front with sequins on. The hem was zig-zag and it was a size 14. I took it to the changing room, hoping it would fit as my feet could not take any more walking. It fitted perfectly over my bump. I already had a little cream fur wrap to go over the top and cream shoes. So, I took my £35 bargain to the counter. I wonder how many people can say that they paid £35 for their wedding dress? I was very relieved as Julie, bless her heart, loves to shop and was more than happy to trudge miles but I was now ready to go home. My feet were sore and my ankles swollen. I sat for a while in the shopping mall until Julie was ready to leave and then we headed back. I sat in the car completely dazed and exhausted. I was amazed at how much it had worn me out but I was now ready for the big day.

The day of the wedding. Dave had stayed with his parents and my parents were staying with me. I got dressed and it was very relaxing. My brother turned up to drive me to the venue. Dave's Dad rang Dave's sister again and had quite a long chat to her and said how bad it looked that she was not attending. She was still adamant that it would not be good for her to attend. However, when we turned up to the venue they were there. I almost wished they hadn't turned up when I saw them as you could tell it was begrudgingly and they hadn't really dressed up. It really did feel like it had been a huge effort. I was actually quite annoyed that they had turned up at all, as they had declined the invitation. After all, I knew how she really felt and that she had been coerced to attend. It was our special day and Dave's family spent their time fussing over her. Give me strength was all I could think. I'm not a horrible person and I do not like ill feeling but I could feel how she felt and I didn't need to feel that on what was supposed to be a special day. Needless to say, that she did not give birth for another five days.

The weather on the day was glorious and we couldn't have asked for better. My friend, Vicky, who I worked with turned up at the museum to see me and wish me luck with her little girl. I felt awful not inviting all these people but we were keeping it small and trying to keep the cost down. Vicky, I have to say has been through some very traumatic times of her own and has been with me on the rollercoaster ride.

The ceremony was a registry office service and is very short and sweet and then the witnesses come forward to sign to say they have witnessed the marriage. My brother and Julie were the witnesses on the day.

We had some photos taken, by Dave's Dad, a keen amateur photographer, at the museum and then it was all off to the Hotel for more photos and a meal. Dave's sister looked like she was sucking on a lemon most of the time and could hardly make eye contact or a conversation with me. Uncomfortable!!

I have to say the photographs were super and the meal was pretty good and Dave's Dad and my Dad offered to cover the bill, so even better. It was all back then to the in-laws for the cake and more photos. The day ended around 6pm. My feet were aching and my back was aching and I just wanted to sit down and not move. But it was odd, no party. I love a good party. I am fun loving girl and I like to dance and sing and jump around, always have done. I'm Jennifer. So, I felt a little deflated. I love having people around me and I like people to have a good time and enjoy themselves and that part of the day was missing, although I think most people found it an enjoyable wedding. But I was married and I was now able to receive a child into this world and not have a sense of guilt that is inbuilt in me by my good Christian morals.

Chapter Twelve

My First Born

Olivia, my eldest daughter, arrived in the month of April at 38 weeks and she was the most adorable baby. I went into labour in the middle of the night. Dave is a heavy sleeper and is almost impossible to wake. I felt the contractions building and lay for an hour timing them. Eventually, I got up and made a phone call to the maternity ward. The contractions were close enough that I could go in. I tried to wake Dave in between putting my clothes on. He wasn't stirring. I shouted in his ear "I'm in labour". Within seconds he was sat upright in bed wondering what on earth was going on. "I'm in labour," I repeated again. Dave jumped out of bed in a daze and dressed. My bag was already packed and we drove to the hospital which was five minutes down the road. By the time we arrived the contractions were so strong that I struggled to get out of the car. Hospital staff approached me with a wheelchair and I was taken to the maternity ward. I wanted a pool birth so I undressed and got straight into the pool with two midwives attending. Dave then arrived after parking the car. I knew I wanted a natural birth. I was breathing through the contractions and very calm and all was well and then the contractions stopped. I was asked to move out of the pool which I was reluctant to do. My breathing had been so controlled that I had stopped the contractions. The midwives were actually very impressed but it posed a problem as I was 9cm dilated and needed to deliver. I was asked to get onto a bed and as I climbed up I threw up. I was given an injection to bring on the contractions again and Olivia was born. I cannot explain the warmth of emotion that took over the day she was born. The love is unconditional and exclusive. Dave was very supportive and even though this was totally out of his comfort zone he managed well. My instinct to protect and love her unconditionally instantly kicked in. Dave was a very proud father although he was never particularly hands-on. Part of that, I believe, was because he was so big that he didn't know how to handle something so small and delicate. However, he could not cope with baby sick and would lose his temper if Olivia was sick on his t-shirt and would have to change straight away. Olivia would be instantly shoved into my arms and his look of disgust was hurtful. We all know babies get a little sick with the milk sometimes and it isn't pleasant but we have to accept these things and not lose our tempers.

As soon as I had Olivia my Mum and Dad were down to visit and stay and came to the hospital to see her. My Dad and Mum were very emotional. At that point, my Dad struggled to stop shaking, as he had suffered with very poor health for several years and was lucky to still be with us. I stayed in hospital two nights with Olivia, as she was my first born. It's not like that these days I know, but those were the rules then. I remember having her at 9.30 am and walking down the corridor of the hospital the next day to go to the toilet and hearing someone calling my name at the top of their Essex voice. I looked to the right and there in the next ward is my friend, Anabelle, who had just had her baby the following day. I was wearing a pink dressing gown at the time and she said, "I thought I recognised that pink blob walking down the ward". She always made me giggle. Anabelle had had a little boy, Jack, the following day and Olivia and Jack are still friends to this day and birthday buddies. Anabelle and I spent our first 48 hours of motherhood feeding babies in the nursery and keeping each other company through the night. It was so lovely to have a close friend to be with at this initial stage and I am sure it was divinely planned. We laughed through the tiredness and sat in motherhood bliss.

The most emotional moment of Olivia's birth was the day I took her home. Dave came to get me and it is all very nerve wracking getting a new baby in the car seat and a little stressful if you happen to be with a stress head. We got home and my

Mum and Dad were so excited. I took Olivia out of her car seat and my Dad was sat on the sofa. I asked if he wanted to hold her. He was very hesitant as he shook so badly with his illness. I placed her in his arms and he cried. But I think it gave him the strength and determination to get better (well, I like to believe that anyway). Although his health is not perfect, he is still here to this day when all the odds were against him. There's nothing like a new life to inject a new jest into your own life and give you a purpose. My Mum just adored Olivia and couldn't wait to cradle her in her arms.

I have never been so inundated with presents as when Olivia was born. Because she was our first baby and Dave is a businessman, we had presents from all over the county from family and friends. It was lovely. I had never had so many visitors. Everyone seemed to want to be part of this very special occasion. I enjoyed every minute as I loved to entertain people and it gave me a different focus.

Dave's sister had had her baby, a boy, at the end of March and therefore, the competition was over with who was going to give birth first. Not a competition on my part, I might add. I am very glad that we had had a girl as life for the children would have been unbearable if we had both had little boys. The constant comparison was a little wearing. It had already started with how much they weigh and when they feed, how long they are etc.

Every occasion when we met up with in-laws and sister in law, it felt like a competition and then afterwards, Dave would rant on and on and on about their car seats or the way they do things and how it wasn't the correct way. Of course, we were much more superior in his eyes, especially with his loving fatherly care that he provided. It wears you down into submission until you can no longer reply to their constant injustice of the world, you just agree and go along with everything they say.

Like I said earlier, my bad days with Dave were helped with the respite that my Mum and Dad provided when they came to stay. They probably did not realise it at that point, but I feel that they knew (without knowing) that it gave me a break. He would never have shown to them his true colours as it would have spoilt the image that they held of him. It was the first time that I had lived somewhere where my Mum and Dad had some living accommodation. It was nice because they had their own space and were not in the house with us but joined us for meals and TV and could retire to bed as and when they wanted. My Dad has been particularly ill in his later life and had suffered two heart attacks, diabetes, blindness in one eye and loss of hearing. His medication is endless. It seemed to me that having grandchildren relit the fire for him.

Dave's Mum and Dad were very much on the scene also and we probably saw them every day. They would just wander into our house as we would their house. Although this is lovely a lot of the time, there are some times when you don't want to come into your kitchen and find your father in law making a cuppa, especially after just having a baby and breast feeding. Every decision we made was made with their approval/disapproval. They became so involved and I believe at the time I felt at least they may be on my side so having them around was easier than not having them around. Dave could not cope very well if he hadn't seen them for a while and they were all very involved with his business.

Our baby had arrived and I was still alive and well. The next thing on Dave's agenda was how long before we could have intercourse again? As many new Mums will agree, this is not the first thing on your mind. In fact, you feel fat, unattractive, tired and sore. I had stitches with Olivia so it was very uncomfortable but as soon as the six weeks were up I gave in to the constant pestering. It felt like a process. There were no feelings or romance involved. It was a means to an end. That is how it felt and it shouldn't be like that and when Olivia was 10 weeks old, I found out I was pregnant again. I was over the moon. I knew that I wanted more than one child but it was just a bit quicker than I had anticipated. I had been blessed with another little being in my body.

My body had not recovered from my first pregnancy and it had not reverted back to normal. I had gone from 7 1/2 stone to 9 1/2 stone with Olivia and not having had chance to get rid of my baby weight. I just looked six months pregnant even from the beginning of my second pregnancy.

At this point Dave's tempers were getting more frequent. The stretches in between becoming days rather than weeks. He would lose his temper over silly things, things I wouldn't expect him to lose his temper over. If I wasn't paying him attention generally. It became unbearable to live in the house. I couldn't do right for doing wrong. I felt this immense pressure to please him, even if it didn't please me. If I didn't clean every day, he assumed I was sitting drinking tea and talking all day. I was like a headless chicken trying to make everything nice so that we had peace in the house. I was expected to jump up and make him tea when he walked in and fuss over him.

One day, I was sat feeding Olivia. Olivia took 45 minutes to feed and then after half an hour wanted more. I felt very relaxed dealing with her and loved being a Mum. My Mum and Dad were busying around me and we were chatting. Dave came in like a tornado, so we all knew he was in a bad mood, the atmosphere changes immediately, you could feel the tension. His energy was particularly intense.

"Jennifer, I need you to send an e-mail," his voice was demanding.

"I can't at the moment, I'm just feeding Olivia."

"I don't care what you are doing. Take that baby and put her down and send my e-mail." There was no negotiation in his voice and his face was red and angry.

I took Olivia away from my breast and placed her in the Moses basket and typed his e-mail for him. My Mum looked on in disbelief. Now, many a woman would have told him to go to hell, but not me because I knew, deep down, even if I did not say it, that if I didn't do as I was told I would pay for it later. Once somebody has that control over you it gets worse and the requests become demands and the timescale becomes instant and the demands become more. You could never say, "I'll do it in a minute". I also understand now that Law of Attraction teaches us that what we fear we draw in but I certainly was not even thinking about Law of Attraction at this point.

With my second pregnancy, I developed a problem with my pelvis and it made going up and down stairs very difficult and I would have to rest a lot during the later stages of the pregnancy. Men who are aggressive are strange. They will look like they are protecting you when you are out and as soon as you are home will turn on you and blame you for the smallest of things. Psychologically they wear you down over a period of time. So many occasions, I have stood blaming myself for something that actually was not my fault.

I had decided that as we now had a family and were married that I would sell my property so that I could make an investment into our home. At this point, Dave had persuaded me that we needed buy a caravan so that we could have fairly cheap family holidays and it could be as and when we liked them to be. He couldn't resist spending money. If we had it, and even when we didn't have it, he would spend it. We invested in a caravan and then we borrowed some more money on our mortgage because, to pull the caravan, we had to have a bigger car. Not just any car though, top of the range Audi Q7 with all the extras. A lovely car, I might add but pricey and perhaps extravagant. Dave did like to spend money and I spent a lot of energy juggling money to make sure that we could afford all we had. In fact, I actually don't know how we afforded things but I made sure that we did. Handling money with someone that likes to spend it can be mind blowing. His excuse was always that it was for the family. But you know, it wasn't. It was to show off and to try and satisfy a need. Dave was someone searching for something he didn't have and the only way he thought he could satisfy himself was with personal possessions. We all know that personal possessions cannot fill that emotional void. I was his prize wife and the children trophies in the cabinet.

Our first holiday we took Olivia away at 8 weeks old on our own. This was a novelty as we hadn't been away on our own, apart from our disastrous holiday in Gran Canaria. It was hard work and took some planning but also enjoyable to be able to get away from everything and everyone. It was only for a long weekend to try out the new caravan and car and that was probably long enough.

I spent a lot of my spare time with my friend Anabelle over the coming weeks and months. We would make a point of meeting up every week for a bun and cuppa. Anabelle is definitely not a possessions girl but they have a lovely home and what they need but she has a respectful, loving relationship and they are extremely happy. What I didn't clock onto early in our relationship was that Dave would check to make sure I was where I said I was. It is only looking back that I realised that he was making sure that I was telling him the truth. He obviously had a trust issue. Very often when I was with Anabelle or anyone that I was meeting with, he would ring and have an excuse to ring me, usually that he needed some information or he couldn't remember something. Of course, I had not realised that this was his way of finding out that I was doing exactly what I said I was doing and keeping a track of my movements.

I would go around to see Julie to have a drink of tea and catch up and he would either make noises about coming with me or drop me off so he could pick me up. Another good way of knowing where I was. He would get upset if he wasn't invited along as he wanted to know what we were talking about, although he would say that it was nice to have a night without me. All of these things were starting the get worse.

"I'm going to see Debbie today. It's her day off and it would be good to catch up." I smiled at Dave but knew what was coming.

"Why do you need to go and see Debbie? Why can't she come here? Are you planning to get some tips off her?" He was anxious and I could tell he was feeling insecure as Debbie was splitting from her husband.

"What sort of tips would I be getting from her?" I was almost humouring him as I got this line of questioning every time I wanted to meet with friends, whoever they were.

"You're probably trying to work out how to leave me." He stared at me with a stern face and he was being serious.

I laughed off the accusation with a nervousness not quite sure of what was coming next.

"You go and enjoy yourself and I am sure you will have a lot of things in common to discuss. Don't get any funny ideas about leaving me though," and with that he left for work.

Debbie was in the midst of her break up and things were very tense. We talked for hours and drank coffee. I was very happy to be there for her and support her. She had always been there when I needed a shoulder to cry on. Then, I got a phone call.

"How's your day going?" It was Dave.

"Yes, it's lovely to catch up with Debbie. We are having a lovely time, thank you."
"How is she?"

"She's fine." I was now a little uncomfortable as Debbie was staring straight at me inquisitively. I smiled at her, "Are you okay?"

"Yes, just wondering what time you will be back as I could do with you sending an e-mail for me and making some phone calls."

"Okay, well I'll be back by the time you get home from work and we can talk about it then."

"So, have you prepared the dinner then?" His tone was sharp.

"Yes, dinner is prepared and will be ready for when you get in."

"Okay, have a good day. See you later."

I screwed my face up and could feel my eyes squinting, "thank you, bye." What was that all about?

Debbie laughed, "he's obviously checking up on you."

"Yes," I said laughing but I knew she had hit the nail on the head.

The insecurities just built and built. He would lie in bed and question me about whether I was going to leave him and what sort of things I discussed with my friends. This would go on until the early hours of the morning until he got the answer and reassurance that he needed. Not only that but whilst I was upstairs putting Olivia to bed, he would be checking to see what text messages I got and what phone calls I had made on the mobile and the landlines and would even admit that he had been doing it.

I hid what was going on very well with a smile, my mask, and carried on as if this was not going on and I suppose it was all for show. I had the house, car, money, and family status. How could I not want to carry on living like this. Life was stressful but I had decided that this is how life becomes when you have children and responsibilities!!

This was not how I wanted my life to be. I loved that I had a baby and I was overjoyed that I was pregnant again but I needed to be trusted and I needed to live my life in peace and harmony. I'm not saying that there are not challenges in life but I was not living, I was existing and I was trying to show to the world a person that I was not. I put myself in a bubble of illusion. My own little world where I ignored all that was happening and pretended that everything was just great. It was the only way I could move forward until the next challenge and I knew that I could not give up. I am strong and I need to be strong for everyone, especially my children.

The only pleasure that Jennifer got was being a mother but it distracted her from the fact that she was not living life the way it should be. Jennifer's journey was taking twists and turns she had not expected or could have ever anticipated.

Chapter Thirteen

My Second Born

I was over the moon that I was pregnant again, as being a mother suited me and it was very quick but I was older so it was good to get the pregnancies over fairly quickly. I am also a bit of an earth mother and felt that this is what I was brought on this earth to do, mother children. It was a little harder the second time around and very tiring, having a baby and carrying one but I coped extremely well. When you want something enough, nothing can hold you back. I still kept an orderly house and garden and cooked and washed, cleaned the cars inside and out etc

Again, Dave's sister was not too enthralled that I was pregnant but I had to try and remove myself from the negative energy, as it was draining. I built almost an imaginary wall around me and whenever she was mentioned my imaginary wall would rise up and it felt as though I could hear what was said but not absorb the energy of the words. Dave would revel in the fact that we had another baby on the way and that his sister was not in that position. I couldn't even think of things in those terms. My priority was my new born and the baby in my belly. My Mum and Dad would pop down every 4-6 weeks for a week or maybe two and help me out. As I think I said before, the relief that they provided in just having an emotional crutch was crucial. I think they could tell that the stresses that Dave put on me were starting to wear me down but they just thought that it was the normal stress of having babies/work balance that was in play. Although, they were aware that Dave was a very hands-off Dad and he was very pleased for my Mum and Dad to come along and take over, even just to make a cup of tea, so he was not expected to do anything.

During my second pregnancy, I spent a lot of time sat with Olivia reading, playing, teaching her to walk and talk, weaning her onto solids, all the stuff us Mums do without thinking about what wonderful natural teachers we are. Pat on the back to all us Mums, we do a fabulous job. I was suffering with Symphysis Pubis Dysfunction and so my pelvis bones were not in alignment and it was very painful to walk up and down stairs or do anything to be fair. Anabelle was superb, she would come to my home for our cake and cuppa in the latter stages of my pregnancy, as I was struggling to get about, drive or anything. She was my light relief. Julie would come and visit too to see Olivia but mainly to catch up on the gossip. We did like a good gossip, not about people just about life in general. She would be telling me about her latest beau and where she had been on her trips around the world, and I would tell her about my sore pelvis and Olivia's development. I also had made friends with a lady called Penny and her partner turned out to be someone Dave knew through work. Again, Penny has been a good friend, although we don't get together very often, she is still very much in the background but there if I needed her. Penny would also visit with her son, Ali, so that Olivia had a friend to play with.

My pregnancy proceeded pretty much as normal with a sore pelvis and Olivia's first birthday was approaching. I was now a massive 14 stone and feeling so big, well big for me after having only ever been 7 1/2 to 8 1/2 stone. Out of the blue I got a phone call as Dave's sister's little boy was approaching his 1st birthday and she was inviting us to tea. I had her on the loud speaker on my phone whilst sat at the kitchen table. My Mum was sat opposite having tea with me. Then she came out with the most extraordinary thing that I have ever heard.

"Hi Jennifer, it's Dawn here. How are you?" She sounded very cheery.

"Hi Dawn, I'm fine thank you. How are you?"

"I'm good thank you. It's Daniel's birthday coming up soon so we thought we would have a tea party at our house to celebrate if you'd like to come along," she sounded upbeat and cheerful.

"Sounds good. Olivia would love that. We will be there," I sounded a little surprised at how pleasant she was being.

Then she continued and her voice changed, "Also, as it's his birthday, it would be really good if you didn't give birth on that day."

There was a stony silence. I looked at my Mum, eyes wide open in disbelief. My Mum looked at me in the same manner, "Sorry what did you just say?" I could feel an inquisitive smile creeping across my face.

"It would be really good if you didn't have your baby on Daniel's birthday. It would be better if they celebrated on different days." I could now hear a tone of desperation.

I laughed out loud in the realisation that she was being serious. I took a deep breath and replied in a calm manner, "I can do nothing about when my baby is born. They come when they want too."

"Yes, I know but it would be better if it was separate," her voice got quieter as she spoke.

"Right, well as I said, I can't tell my baby when to come. Anyway, thank you for the invitation and we will see you at the tea party," I took charge of the call so as not to have a further discussion.

"Yes, okay, bye," I could hear her embarrassment.

Amazingly insecure, how can anyone be that jealous or is it envy? Mum and I sat across the table almost perplexed at what we had just heard.

"Did she just say that?" I quizzically asked Mum.

"Umm, yes," then we both giggled at the obscurity of it.

We went to the party and it was pleasant but all subjects of babies were avoided so a little awkward. I put up my imaginary wall to protect me from any negativity and I was relieved to come away. Whatever this situation was, it was strange. Needless to say, Daniel's birthday came and went and I was still pregnant.

Three days before Olivia's birthday I decided to go to bed in the late morning as I was exhausted. I never slept in the day, I wasn't allowed to, there were too many things to do to make sure the ship ran smoothly and remember, Dave was making sure I was pulling my weight! But on this day, my Mum insisted so I waddled up the stairs to my room. Whilst I was resting, my Mum and Dad had a little altercation with Dave's Dad. Dave's Mum and Dad were very much around Dave and as a family, we did a lot together. They very often spent the evening with us or us with them. However, they thought that his house was their house and would just stroll in. Most of the time, this did not bother me but to some it may be a little strange and intrusive. Dave's Dad decided he would turn up to see how I was as I was five days over my due date. My Mum explained that I was in bed and he proceeded to go up the stairs. My Dad stopped him and asked him where he thought he was going to and reiterated that I was in bed and he was not going to disturb me. He left apparently with a bit of a strop on. They never saw eye to eye after that point.

I got up, unaware of all the toing's and froing's, it was late afternoon and I suddenly felt my contractions building. I called

Dave, "I'm in labour. Can you come and take me to the hospital?" He came straight home and within an hour I was headed to the local labour ward. I was in labour for about seven hours. I had been in a birthing pool with Olivia but the midwife couldn't allow me in the pool on this occasion, as I was bleeding very heavily. I was taken to a side room to be examined. My midwife for delivery was the lovely lady that was my midwife throughout the term of my pregnancy and apparently, it is unheard of that they get to deliver their babies, so this was a very special moment for both of us. Once the examination was over, I was left to my own devices. Dave was in the room with me and the only respite I could get from the contractions was to move around. I stood up for the most part of that seven hours. Dave was in the room all the time and the mess was quite something but he helped the nurse with clearing up the blood, it was quite some bleed. He didn't like mess. I was also insistent that I have no pain relief. I was insistent that the birth be natural, just like Olivia had been. The time was moving on and I knew that the blood was getting more. The Obstetrician on the day decided that it would be wise to break my waters just to check that it was not the baby that was bleeding. He got me to get onto the bed and then re-entered the room with what I can only describe as a knitting needle to pierce the amniotic sack. I certainly felt the water sack break and the contraction that followed was so intense that I thought the baby was going to shoot across the room. The waters were clear and the contractions continued. I got back off the bed and walked around, I leaned and eventually I had to sit down, as I was exhausted. I eventually got back on the bed just to rest. My midwife, her name was Anouk, monitored me but did not interfere. She left the room to make a coffee and just as she did the head crowned. The temptation to push overcame me. "Get the Midwife, I'm going to deliver!!" I shouted at Dave. Panic struck him and he ran faster than I ever seen him run to get Anouk. She entered the room just in time to hold Verity's head in her hands. She was the spitting image of Olivia. I held her in my arms overwhelmed with love and crying. The midwife asked what I was naming her. I said, "Louisa", but within two minutes I had changed my mind. "Stop", I said, "her name is Verity". Verity had been frowned upon by Dave's Mum. Her Aunty Verity had helped bring her up and she felt it wasn't appropriate. Although I still really don't know why. But, my little girl was now a Verity. She was born at 11.30pm. I fed her and put her down and managed to get some sleep myself on the ward. Dave left to get home, tell everyone the news (I knew my mum and dad would wait up until they had heard some news) and get some sleep. I was alone and the ward was quiet. I peered into her cot and saw her tiny fingers and her little scrunched up face and I was awestruck. It was the same feeling I had had with Olivia. You can never take that feeling away. The birth of a child is the most incredibly special moment and it doesn't matter how many children you have the feeling is still as strong. My Mum was over the moon although she had thought that Verity was going to be a Louisa so took her a little while to adapt to change of name.

I was a second-time round mum so I was allowed to leave hospital within hours of delivering. I had managed to have a shower and some breakfast but I had missed Olivia and couldn't wait to introduce her to her baby sister. Dave came to pick me up. I was tired and needed a change of clothes but I couldn't wait to see Olivia's reaction to our new baby. I entered the house with Verity in her car seat. Olivia was standing at this point and getting around but not quite walking on her own. Olivia peered in at Verity and Verity started to cry. Olivia was scared and started to cry too. I pulled Olivia close to me until she stopped crying and introduced her to her baby sister. They are very close and hopefully they will always be close.

I decided on that day that I did not want any more children. I knew things between Dave and I were not ideal and I had more than enough to cope with. I had my two beautiful girls and that fulfilled me.

I had been home from hospital one day and held Olivia's first birthday party. I invited all the relatives and Julie, Anabelle and Jack. I don't really remember a lot but I put on food and Dave's Mum made a cake. My brother came along and he was in awe of the girls. He has always wanted children himself but sadly never had that opportunity. My friend Anabelle took charge of entertaining people, as she could see how tired I was. She is very amusing to listen to and could tell a few funny tales. Then Dave decided to discuss, in a very loud voice, the matter of my weight gain.

"Look at her, she reckons she's going to be a size 8 again! There's no chance of that!" His manner was mocking. I was upset but too tired to even respond to his cutting remark.

It was a terrible thing to say to someone who had just come out of hospital having had a second baby. I could see Annabelle in front of me as she bit her lip. I knew she wanted to reply to him but she felt it wasn't the time or the place. She smiled at me and then sat with me.

"You are very beautiful as you are," she said softly to me as she placed a comforting arm around me. I smiled a grateful smile. I wasn't going to let him get me down but I didn't have the energy to fight him or stand my ground. Actually, now I am a size 8/10 so he did get that wrong, not that I did that for him, I've just very slowly returned to my natural sizing plus I exercise and eat well.

My friends and my family helped me to stay strong and although they may not have realised what was happening behind closed doors, they were there.

I am now in a situation with two very young babies, feeding, changing, playing, potty training, cleaning, ironing, cooking but I was happy when it was me, the babies and my family in my little bubble. I wanted to be a Mum and I wanted my house to be a home but I was struggling with the expectation that Dave placed on me and the unknown mood swings, the constant ear bashings and my submissions to his way of thinking, although it wasn't what I thought, his tempers where he threw things and slammed doors and stormed off in his van wheel spinning as he went. I was pacifying, I was doing a good job, I was being the person I wanted to be? No, I was being a Mum but I was being someone I didn't recognise. You know, even my friends would probably now testify that actually I wasn't being who they knew me to be but we all have busy lives and sometimes, even if we notice these things, we don't act upon them. We do not have the right to intrude in anyone's life unless that person gives you the permission to give an opinion. I wasn't ready to let people in to what was really going on but it wasn't what I had wished and hoped for. I just knew that I needed to stay strong for my babies and do the best job I could in that moment. Jennifer was going to succeed whatever the cost and she knew her strength of mind was her biggest asset but things were going to change yet again.

Chapter Fourteen

The Emotional Blackmail

Things got really bad one night and events were starting to play out in some sort of real life drama.

We were sat watching one of the TV soaps and he loved to watch them, in fact he couldn't miss just one episode. It was his relaxation. The girls were asleep. He liked me to sit right beside him and I always obeyed.

"You don't love me," he suddenly said, out of the blue.

"What do you mean? I must do or I wouldn't still be here," I'm not sure I was convinced of my answer.

This was a game he played every now and then. It was a test to see where the land lay and I played along just so we could have a peaceful night. I realised he was feeling left out.

"I'm not important. It is all about the girls now, I don't even come into the equation. As long as the girls are okay, it's all you care about."

Absolutely blinding accusation bearing in mind that the house was immaculate, so was the garden and the children and he had everything he needed when he came home. I almost fawned over him when he came home from work so that the temper would not rise. But I knew that what he was referring to was the love connection. I was loving and giving towards him but I didn't feel in love with him. I loved my children unconditionally and that is not something I could say about him. He had done and said too many things for me to feel that way. He was frustrated and his frustration was now boiling over.

"That is not true. I am always here for you and I always make sure the home is lovely and your dinner is on the table. I bend over backwards to make sure I get things done for you," I felt very strong and able to express myself.

He was doing the poor me act and I tried to calm him by putting my arm through his arm but he started to get very angry he pushed me away.

"You don't love me and I'm leaving you. I don't want to be with you either," he was angry and his face was red and taught. He stood up with purpose and went to leave the lounge.

I burst into tears, I had just had a baby and couldn't cope with this, not now, although I didn't like what he did I had got used to our situation.

"Please don't go. I do love you but life is very busy and the girls are babies and they need me first. They are helpless and without me they cannot feed themselves or go to the toilet," I was pleading with him not to go.

He stormed upstairs and I waited in the lounge in anticipation of what was going to happen next. I stood up, I sat down. Do I go upstairs? Do I stay here? What's the safest thing to do? I knew how things could explode and I wasn't sure if I wanted to be in the firing line. Maybe if I just stayed downstairs he would cool off and calm down. A little time passed and he came back downstairs with a bag of clothes and shoes and a sleeping bag.

"Where are you going?" he ignored me. "What are you doing and where are you going?" I asked again.

"I'm leaving you and I'm not coming back." He gritted his teeth and his face came close to mine. I was too scared to move or speak. "You don't care about me and you don't need to worry about me. Things will be taken care of and you and the girls will be fine when I'm found dead. Life's not worth living." His voice was menacing and threatening all in one.

I broke down in tears, "No, don't do this. It's not right". I reached out to hug him and he grabbed my hands and pushed me away. "Get off me you bitch," he shouted at me. He turned his back and he stormed out of the house. He was an unstoppable force that could not be reasoned with. He drove so quickly off the drive.

I was tired and emotional and this was mentally all too much to bear. I was working on automatic and I could cope with most things, but not these emotional outbursts. I panicked and rang his Mum and Dad and told them that he had left me and I didn't know where he had gone but that he had threatened to kill himself. They came around within minutes and sat with me. They tried to contact him but he would hang up the phone. They were almost angry with me; it was the strangest feeling. They said all the right things but felt that it was my fault. I was in a state of shock and anything they said went in one ear and out the other. In this panic I felt like I needed to sort it all out but I needed some help as this was beyond what I could deal with on my own. I could feel that they didn't have the energy to deal with him either. The physical exhaustion was evident. They had had a couple of years reprieve of these anger outbursts, where the anger had been fired at me and they only saw the aftermath. So, they felt they were now going to be back in the firing line of his temper. I know that they didn't relish the thought of having to deal with him. His energy and 'poor me' act was wearing us all down. We spent time constantly walking on eggshells and trying to pick someone up who just drains you of every bit of energy that you may have. I like to call them energy vampires. They take but cannot give good energy.

After an hour of trying to ring his phone and him hanging up, Dave's Dad went out to find him. He found him camped out at his office that he hired for his business. He brought him home to sort things out. He apologised for his behaviour and we agreed to try and talk things through. We patched up our sham of a marriage for a while and then his temper would get the better of him. I was in bits and ashamed that I was married to such a person. Someone who could be so cruel and demanding and who would show off like a spoilt child. We would go out with friends and he would make out that I was the most wonderful person in the world, that I had been everywhere, done everything and was very articulate and clever but he would treat me as a servant at home, I'd even go as far to say that he considered me to be one of his workers. This irritated me and I felt belittled and unworthy. My self-esteem being chronically beaten. Needless to say, he did this on several occasions knowing that it would get my attention and niggled with me. He was pushing my buttons and he was doing it more and more to get a reaction.

I needed to break free from this situation and the only way I could get any time for me was to start running again. This was my time where I could process and I could find peace and stillness. It was the only part of me I could maintain, the old Jennifer. My runs were short to start with and over time I built them up as I got fitter and slimmer. I waited until my Mum and Dad arrived and then I would get out for an hour or so. Eventually, I decided I needed to join a club again. I did and Dave agreed to babysit the girls with his mother. It was a little scary leaving them with him, as he had never had the girls on his own, but I made sure they were bathed and put in bed before I left and he only had to listen out if they woke. It made life easier. It was my sanity and much needed but it wasn't the answer to our problems.

I was using sticky tape to mend plasterboard. It was just about holding everything together but it wasn't the solution. What was the solution? I didn't have any answers anymore. I was tired, emotional and stressed and I no longer had a voice to express how I was really feeling. Where was my life going?

This is not the perfect family that Jennifer had hoped and wished for. Jennifer is strong and she can do anything but she was suffering in silence. Why?

Chapter Fifteen

Family Life

Our holidays were just a farce. Another way to portray to the world what a perfect family we were when behind the scenes it was a living hell. We would take the caravan away several times a year but again, I was the one packing the caravan, even down to making sure that we had a meal prepared and in the fridge for when we arrived. Usually a large shepherd's pie and a fish pie, all prepared and ready to go in the oven when we arrived. I would then also prepare all the veg so that the meal was just ready to go. Initially, we took Dave's Mum and Dad with us and they would sleep in an extension part of the awning on an airbed. It was a very small space to be with so many but I was almost glad to have someone else there to protect me. On all those occasions and this was a period over about 2-3 years, I was cooking not just for us but for everyone else as well and trying to watch two very young children who really needed my attention. Things are always worse when you are confined to a very small space. The girls were very small so I was conscious of them falling off beds or out of the doorway, whilst cooking and also sometimes having to feed and change nappies. Dave's Mum would make us feel guilty if we went to spend any money so, even if we went out for the day, I would have to do packed lunch for everyone. The children found it difficult to go to sleep as it wasn't their own beds and Dave did not want them up of a night and would complain if they were still awake. I would spend all the holidays either making or preparing food or sitting with the girls so they would sleep and not disturb the adults. This really wasn't a holiday for me. I was nervous and aware that any little thing may trigger a temper outburst. Dave would constantly moan to me that his Mum was useless or incapable and it was all very demeaning and disrespectful and hard to bear. All I could do was build my imaginary wall to protect me and hope that it would be enough. The holidays did provide me with an opportunity to be away from home and I lived in hope that things would get easier or more pleasant.

Caravan holidays could be wonderful if you are not going away with someone who has to get angry about every little thing that they do or is incapable of doing it unless you are doing something for them. And God forbid if we forgot anything. It felt like I was doing all the work whilst we were away and everyone else was enjoying the food and drinking the wine. I never felt as though I ever truly relaxed and if I did get a chance my name would be called to do something or help somewhere.

I was the satellite navigation on these trips and I would worry constantly about making sure we were travelling in the right direction. God forbid if we made a wrong turning. I was very meticulous and watched the roads and signs like a hawk as well as keeping an eye on the girls and being aware of their needs. All mentally draining.

And so, this endless cycle of life went on. Whether we were at home or on holiday, when he lost his temper my first reaction would be to protect the children. His voice would boom through the house and doors would be slammed. When we were on holiday, it was more evident that he didn't care who saw his temper. He would display his feelings of disapproval and everyone could see his energy and feel it and stayed away from us. Olivia was suffering with quite severe night terrors at home where she would rip her room apart and pull her bedding off and then would lie under the bed stiff, crying uncontrollably, shaking, and she could not be touched. I spent endless nights outside her room waiting until she calmed down enough to let me comfort her. These outbursts could last anything from an hour to two hours in the middle of the night. I'm sure it was a reaction to the temper outburst she was experiencing from Daddy but I cannot be entirely sure.

One Summer's day, after Verity was born, I was sitting in the garden and Dave had lost his temper and stormed off. He was getting to the point now where there was a bit of pushing going on and I was always terrified that he would knock one of the children. Verity was asleep in her cot and Olivia was walking around the garden and I sat and cried and cried but I had nowhere to go. I knew at that point I needed to leave. I sat and thought about where I could go and couldn't think of anywhere. My Dad had had two heart attacks in recent years, so I could not expect them to have us and Julie had her own life and I now had children and I couldn't expect her to have us all. I never wanted to be a burden to anyone but actually, I think she would have taken us in but it could not be long term. My sobs became heavier and I let out years of what I had held back. I stared up at the sky and held out my hands, Okay, give me the answer. What do I do?" I then looked at my adorable children, took a deep breath and pulled myself together. "It's all for them," I told myself. For another few years I carried on taking the abuse, living in hell all for the sake of the children. I thought over time I could fix this problem. My solution; to get a family pet and maybe it would change the dynamics.

Dave loved dogs and had always seemed much calmer when he had his Mum and Dad's dog to stay. So, I asked him if he thought a dog was a good idea. He agreed that he would love to have a pet. I also hoped that it would help Olivia with the seizures that she had been suffering. Stroking a dog actually does calm the body of stress. She had been suffering with her eyes glazing over and her body just stiff and shaking. I had asked the Health Visitor and doctor about them but no one could tell me what the cause was and why it was happening. I had never had a chance to video them when they happened so could only explain the symptoms. The girls were now aged 3 and 2 and I felt I could cope with an addition to the family, especially as it was to calm things down. In the November, I presented the girls with their cocker spaniel puppy. Olivia was over the moon and loved her straight away. Verity was not very keen as she is not so enthused about animals and I think was a little scared of this jumping, biting, excited pup. Meg was my dog and I trained her, walked her and fed her. Dave did hardly anything apart from stroke her and occasionally walk her on weekends with us all. He was too busy working. He promised he would help out but he never did. We set her up her own little space in the utility room which was attached to the Kitchen and the stable door would be left open so she could wonder in and out. Olivia thought this was wonderful and I'd very often catch her rolling around the floor with Meg. They were as mad as each other but loved each other too.

Two weeks after getting Meg life was about to get interesting again. I found out I was pregnant with our third child. Much to the delight of Dave who thought it was wonderful that we were going to have more children than his sister. At this point, his sister had had another little boy, which made two. I was excited. I love being pregnant but I now had two little girls aged 3 and 2 and a four-month-old puppy and a very stressed angry husband. Olivia went to nursery and Verity followed not long after her for two mornings a week which gave me a chance to walk Meg on my own. This gave me my 'me time' again. I had stopped running as I was pregnant and I needed this space to collect my thoughts. Then I would take the girls up to the forest every morning to let Meg have a run around. Unfortunately, being a very young puppy, she loved to chase the rabbits and very often I would be stood in the forest with two children who were cold and wanted to go home and no dog to be seen anywhere. Every walk was an adventure and being out in the fresh air gave me a break from home and all it represented. I was getting bigger and so were my responsibilities but I was just about coping or so I thought.

One morning at 6am I was woken by Dave in a foul mood, "You need to get up, get downstairs and clear up the mess that your dog has made!"

I was dazed as I hadn't woken properly, "What's happened?" I could feel my heart sink into my stomach.

"I'm going to work and you will have to sort it out, it's disgusting," and with that he grabbed his work top, headed downstairs and out of the door. I lifted myself to a sitting position. I was eight months pregnant and getting up was getting harder. I went downstairs to the kitchen, it all looked fine. Meg was in a utility room which was to the side of the kitchen. I peered through the glass in the door to see the most horrendous site. She has been sick and had had diarrhoea and it was all over the utility units the floor, the walls. Meg was covered. I tried not to cry in that moment. I took a deep breath and went to the kitchen sink, still in my nighty. I filled a bucked with bleach and water and grabbed some black sacks and rubber gloves. I put the dog outside and started to scrub the walls, floors, units and doors. Her bed was ruined so I bagged it up and put it outside. I had finished cleaning the utility room and went outside to grab Meg. I picked up the hose and scrubbed the dog clean and rinsed her off and left her outside. How I did not vomit I do not know. I stood for ages admiring my work. You would have never have known an hour before what a mess it had been. I then showered by which time the girls had woken to be fed. I still cannot believe that I did that and that he let me clean up such a mess in my condition.

I cannot believe I just did it without argument! I knew my place! I knew that no one else was going to clear up and I needed it to be clean before the girls got up. Why had we got a dog? Was it making things easier? I couldn't let myself think like this. If I thought too much the overwhelm was unbearable. It was easier not to think and keep going. Keep this ship afloat and keep everyone happy. I knew that the more distractions I had, the less I had to be in my head and the less I had time to feel what was really going on.

In essence, Meg had come along at the right time. Walking her was giving me the headspace and exercise I needed. My running had dwindled so I needed some processing time. The Jennifer I was now had children, so processing time was virtually impossible to gain. Being in the fresh air and in nature somehow gave me some clarity.

Chapter Sixteen

Our Third Baby Arrives

On a beautiful sunny Sunday morning in July, I woke and got the girls up as normal. We played in the garden. My Mum and Dad had arrived to stay in preparation for another birth. I took the dog out into the garden to play with her and started to throw her toy around. The next thing I know I had water gushing down my leg. This was a new experience for me, as this was the first pregnancy where my waters have actually broken. I stood for a minute or so as I let the waters run and for me to let it sink in that it was actually my waters that had broken. I went inside and looked at the clock. It's significance being how far apart my contractions were. It was 11am. I walked into the lounge and very calmly announced that my waters had broken. I could see a look of anticipation on my Mum and Dad's faces. I went upstairs and changed and took things really slowly. I almost felt as though I had gone into some form of shock but in a calm and controlled manner. I rang Dave on his mobile and he came home from having been at his parents. Everyone was now on standby and Dave just sat around ready to take me to hospital as and when needed. Everyone seemed to stop what they were doing and I was being watched for the first signs of labour but as the day went on nothing happened. I went all day and nothing happened. Olivia and Verity had played all day and I bathed them and put them to bed as normal and still nothing. I sat down to watch TV with all eyes upon me and although I was looking at the TV I was conscious that I was not actually paying attention to what was on. It got to 11pm and I stood up to go to bed. I got to my feet and stood upright and all of a sudden, my contractions came on but not gentle, oh no, major contractions. I doubled over in pain and gasped, clutching my stomach. Once the contraction had eased, I rang the hospital and they told me to come straight in as they were expecting a 20 minute birth. Dave got me in the car and raced me to the hospital. I was examined and although the contractions were strong I was only 4cm dilated. I walked, I breathed and stood on all fours, anything that would take the pressure of the contractions away. I knew I did not want any medical intervention but I was older and this birth seemed very tiring. At 6.30am out popped baby Scarlett another little pea in the pod. She was very blue when she arrived but she was healthy and alive and that was all that mattered. My beautiful baby number three. I cried tears of joy and love and held her close, just as I had with my previous two beautiful babies and I fed her straight away.

Dave was sat a little way away from the bed and although he had been there, it was obvious that he just wished he was somewhere else. His interaction during the labour was minimal. I felt his energy and just after feeding Scarlett, I handed her to him.

"Would you like to hold her?" I smiled at him and even though I was exhausted I knew that I needed to make him feel included.

"Ok," he said in an unenthused manner. He stood up and approached the bed where I lay and took her from me. Whilst he held her the midwife, nurses and doctors cleaned me up. I asked one of the nurses if she would take a photo of Dave with the baby and she willingly obliged. Then suddenly the room was empty and we were alone.

Dave decided he couldn't stay any longer. He stood up, handed Scarlett back to me and looked straight at me, "It's another girl! I never wanted her. I'm going home, I'm tired!" and with that he left the room.

I went to say something but nothing came out of my mouth. My heart sank into the pit of my stomach. How could anyone be so cruel. I was so upset. There was no one with me and this beautiful bubba. She needed washing and dressing and so did I.

I tried not to cry as my baby needed me. I pulled the cord to get the attention of the midwife. She arrived promptly and helped dress Scarlett. I then had to wait for a team to sew me up again and then I was allowed to go and have a bath. I was in a lot of pain and could hardly walk and I had developed the most massive haemorrhoids. I was put in a private room but was left unattended and had to keep ringing for a nurse as the walking was too much for me. Eventually, after now thinking that I had completely lost my dignity, I had a visit from a uniformed naval doctor. He swept into the room and my mouth almost hit the floor as he was the most handsome man I had ever seen and he was in a room with me. It's a shame I felt like I had been dragged through a hedge backwards and had a bottom like a baboon! I could see the humour in the situation and as he spoke to me, I smiled. He had to examine me and I don't think I have ever felt so embarrassed but I could feel myself trying not to giggle. He agreed that I needed to be treated and gave me some very strong medication to clear them up. He left as quickly as he had arrived. I was discharged that evening. It was the strangest experience though as when I asked the nursing staff about this lovely doctor, none of them were aware of him or who he was. He was my angel sent from heaven in a moment of need as three days later I could walk again without being in pain.

Apparently, on the morning I had Scarlett my Mum said that Dave had walked back in the house and when everyone had asked what I had had, he has answered, "It's another girl and I never wanted her." My Mum and Dad could not believe what they heard. I think they realised then that not all was what it seemed.

Scarlett was a good baby and fed every four hours and went down to sleep when I put her down. Dave came to pick me up and there was very little conversation between us. I got out of the car and saw two little faces peering out of the window in anticipation of our arrival. Olivia and Verity just wanted to hold

Lorraine Butterfield

Scarlett and I got them to sit very quietly as I placed her in Olivia's arms across both of their laps. I took a photo of them sat there grinning from ear to ear, they just wanted to make a fuss of her. She was a real-life baby doll to them. Scarlett was very happy to have them fuss her.

It was one of the first weekends after Scarlett came home. It was a sunny Sunday and it was still a day when we went to the in-laws or they came to us. My Mum and Dad were still with us and we were all sat on the patio. It was summer and we were having a barbeque. The girls had their paddling pool out and their playhouse and were generally running around the garden. Olivia was teasing Meg. She loved to run around the garden with her. I'm sure she thought she was another sister. I went inside to clear the table and the next thing I could hear was Olivia screaming. My heart almost stopped as the scream was piercing. Dave came into the kitchen carrying her to me and there was blood everywhere. I calmly asked Olivia what had happened. She had run away from the dog who decided to run up to her and butt her. Olivia had flown across the patio and smashed her face on the slabs. I was calm on the exterior but a nervous wreck underneath. I sat Olivia on the breakfast bar. My mum arrived and my mother-in-law. I got a damp towel and dabbed her face very gently. The blood was pouring out of her and it wasn't easing up. I cuddled her to keep her calm. Dave left the kitchen and marched outside and what followed was unthinkable. Suddenly, I could see Dave in the garden chasing Meg. His face was red and his lips pursed. He had lost his temper. As he neared Meg, he kicked her and she flew across the garden. I could hear him shouting, "you stupid dog." He picked her up by the scruff of the neck and threw her in an outside room that was his office. Olivia stopped crying and looked at me, "Mummy, is Meg going to be alright?" I reassured her but felt sick inside, "She'll be fine. Mummy will check on her." Shocked silence had fallen on the house. Dave appeared at the kitchen door cursing. I could not deal with his temper and all I could think about was Olivia. Her nose was still bleeding excessively and she was hurt but I wasn't sure how bad it really was. "I think Olivia should go to hospital to be checked out but I need to feed Scarlett." My mum stepped in, "I'll go with Dave to the hospital whilst you feed the baby." I felt a sigh of relief as I trusted my Mum and she had saved me from an argument with Dave over feeding Scarlett. Once they had left, my Dad let Meg out of the office and fussed her but the atmosphere had been dulled by shock.

Olivia arrived home after being at the hospital for two hours. She had been examined and the doctors had decided that she did not have to have stitches but it was obviously very painful. My Mum said that the hospital asked lots of questions just to ensure that it had been an accident. Dave never apologised for what he did to Meg but went on to justify himself. I could not listen.

How had we got to this point, it was all too much. Everyone had witnessed this event but we were all too scared to do anything about it. It was an accident and accidents happen and it wasn't the reaction that I wanted to see. I needed peace in our lives, especially for the children. I didn't want them to be scared of their dad and what sort of example was he setting. It wasn't the way to deal with things. How could I stop this hamster wheel? Why was life so stressful with this man? What did I need to do to make things better? I was tired and there was too much to do to think about the answers to all my questions. I was just being but I didn't feel like a human being. Life just kept presenting more and more stressful situations.

Chapter Seventeen

Our Neighbours

Life rolled on. Dave is very amenable when he wants your business but he can become your worst nightmare if rubbed up the wrong way. Our neighbours would definitely vouch for that. We had a semi-detached cottage and to our right was our side path, our neighbours' side path, divided by a six-foot fence. The neighbour's two boys, aged 6 and 10 would very often scoot up and down the side path and it would echo. One Sunday morning at 6.30am the two boys, were scooting up and down. The noise was terrible and it rumbled right through the whole of the house. I had just got Scarlett back to sleep after a feed at 5am and Olivia and Verity were still sound asleep. I was tired and a little sleep deprived so had hoped to get another hour but the noise was horrendous. Dave woke with the noise, which was unusual as he could sleep through anything. He was not pleased. He got up, got dressed and went outside. He called to these boys and told them in no uncertain terms to stop making a noise, turned and came back inside. It was all quiet again.

The next thing I could hear was excessive knocking at the front door. I looked at Dave and he had his war paint on and his battle face. I cringed as I knew what was coming. He stormed down the stairs. I followed him to the top of the stairs to observe what was going on. The father of the boys was at the door complaining that Dave had frightened his sons and that he needed to have had a word with him not the boys. Then he aggravated Dave by saying, "you want to have a go at someone, then have a go at me" and offered his fists! I hesitated as to whether to go down the stairs and intervene. It got very heated and at one point I did think Dave would hit him but he resisted. So, that was it, they had both got angry and upset each other without any successful conclusion to the argument. I sat on the top of the stairs with my head in my hands. All I could feel was despair and tiredness. Dave and our neighbour never spoke again. He was always pleasant to me and I think to a certain degree he probably felt a little sorry for me. Dave constantly had me running around doing things for him that most men would not expect a woman, let alone a pregnant woman, to do.

Some people found Dave arrogant and they would be right. He was always right and no-one else stood a chance. When we moved to our detached house, he fell out with our neighbours there too.

When Scarlett came along we made a decision to move to a bigger house. We needed the extra bedrooms. A house came up 20 minutes' car ride from where we were living but the house needed work. As we were in the ideal situation, as we had the resources to carry out the work we took the house on. It was also an ideal opportunity to start again and this would be mine and Dave's project instead of having a constant reminder of how his family had helped him do our current abode.

The house was a Tudor style Potten modern timber-built house but it had a fantastic inglenook fireplace. It was spacious and had a good feel to it. The garden was massive and so was the drive. It had four bedrooms and all we needed. Although it needed a lot of work, I fell in love with it. We actually could not live in it for the first 2 weeks of purchase as the kitchen was so dirty that we condemned the oven. Inches of thick grime everywhere and food still in the bottom of the oven. I even found food on the top of the kitchen units.

The day we moved was even more stressful. It had been decided that the girls would stay with Dave's Mum whilst we moved and we would all stay there the night before the move, so we could pack everything, and then we would take the children with us to the new house and my Mum and Dad, who were staying with my brother in Brighton, would meet us there and they could take over looking after the children at the new house.

There was so much work to do, it was difficult to know where to start but it was evident that we would not be able to live in the house straight away and so every night we would head to the in-laws for food and sleep. Within days of moving in we had ripped up flooring and carpets, painted bedrooms and cleaned and cleaned and cleaned. Dave wanted to make the house and garden secure as we had Meg, our dog, and we needed to make sure that she would not get out. Dave went to work on ripping up dead trees down the side of the house much to our neighbours' anguish. He had already got designs on what he needed to do and he wanted to do it as quickly as possible. He knew the right people to help us.

He approached both neighbours to introduce himself and then produced plans of the extension that we were planning to do. Our neighbours on our left were horrified and immediately, put in an eight-page complaint of they he did not want this to go ahead. Our neighbours on the right were not really interested in what we planned to do, as long as they were not affected. Dave's plans had to go Dave's way as well. He needed a fence post moved and he told the neighbour on the right that he was going to move it so that it was easier to see when leaving the drive to get onto the road. The neighbour was a little taken by his direct approach which led to a bit of a fracas over putting fences up. Dave's arrogance takes over and he is like a bulldozer, nothing gets in his way.

We moved into our new house, building work going on all around us, power tools plugged in, walls pulled apart, the garden completely bulldozed, the drive completely bulldozed. Me and three little children, one of whom is still a baby, but it gave focus and it was manageable for a while. I did feel though that all the plans of this house being a project for Dave. I had now been taken over by the family and suddenly, my word, what little I had, had no importance. I was now being Mum and nodding in the right places, so as to keep the peace. Then the crunch came when we started to run out of money as the project was eating into our savings more than had been anticipated, in fact the concentration was going into the future extension instead of just getting the house right.

Work in general had become slow as well as the whole country was slipping into the recession and the pressure was starting to tell as Dave was not getting as much business. Dave's tempers although still tipping the scales occasionally had not been so bad but he refused to have much to do with Scarlett at all. Dave never changed a nappy, maybe once or twice with Olivia and by the time Scarlett came along there was even less contact. He would hold her occasionally when we had visitors to show willing but was all too quick to hand her back to me.

Time went on and we now found ourselves in the same situation but a different house. I was pussy footing around to make sure he didn't lose his temper and he was angrier than ever.

It was a night in February and I was upstairs putting the children to bed and I had forgotten to take the key out of the front door. Dave came home around 7pm and couldn't get his key in the keyhole. Instead of going to the side door, which he also had a key for, he starting banging and kicking the front door. He swore at the top of this voice, "Open this f**king door you stupid cow". I ran down the stairs. Scarlett was already asleep but I had to leave Olivia and Verity sat in bed as we were midway through their bedtime story. I opened the door and he pushed it really hard and almost threw me back. He was not pleased and he started to rant on to me about why the key was still in the door. I was scared but stayed as calm as I could. I tried to reason with him and get him to quieten down, as the children were trying to settle for bed but he continued to shout and swear at me. "You don't want me here. Is this your new trick hoping that I won't be able to get in?" and probably for the first time in a long time, he was right, I didn't. I didn't need my children hear him speak to me like this. It was not pleasant and they were very scared and so was I. He continued to rant, "I'm not going anywhere, this is my house! So, if you are thinking of getting rid of me, you've got another thing coming." Silent and shaking, I went back upstairs to finish the girls' routine and try to settle them. Olivia was very upset and asked why daddy was shouting. I reassured her that everything was okay and she knew that she had to go to sleep. Verity's reaction was to laugh, as she said, "Daddy sounds funny". It was her way of dealing with this frightening situation and perhaps she thought he was joking. She soon became aware that he was not. I managed to get the girls to sleep and we ate together whilst he told me about his day. Then I busied around doing what I needed to do for the following day. He sat in the lounge watching TV. I joined him for half an hour and then excused myself to go upstairs and give Scarlett her last feed of the night. I knew he would sit and watch TV until midnight and it gave me a chance to get into bed and fall asleep before he came up. That way we could avoid any more confrontation.

The frequency of him coming in angry was now almost every night and the disruption was always at bedtime for the children. The calm of the day had gone and the storm had arrived. I tried so hard to soften the blow, to make things better, to make things nice. I so desperately wanted our family to work but I was exhausted trying and I could no longer talk to him unless I just agreed with what he was saying, even if I didn't agree. I had become a glove puppet. I put on the smiles for the friends and relatives and showed him in a good light and all the while, behind the scenes, we were living in hell.

I spent many nights lying in bed, when he was asleep after hours of pestering me for sex, and I would cry quietly to myself and try to think of ways that this torture could end. Would I leave him; I was very scared; would he die of a heart attack?

Was it wrong to be thinking like this? Would he just have a car accident maybe? What did my future hold? All these questions were whizzing around in my head and I had no answers. I did not have enough calm time on my own to think things through. I was looking for the way out.

I was exhausted and I looked exhausted. Olivia had started her new school in the January term and I made friends very quickly with a few of the Mums, one of whom was an ex Health Visitor. She was absolutely heaven sent as she saw how tired I was and voluntarily started to come around and look after Scarlett and Verity for me whilst I had a sleep. And actually, I have a lot to thank this friend for as she gave me the strength to gather my thoughts and decide what I needed to do. I felt I was getting stronger until one fateful night. I will never forget her kindness.

Dave and I had had dinner together. He was quite adamant that I was not to eat with the children and that I had to eat with him because that is what he wanted. It was not what I wanted, eating at 8pm is not good for me, as I don't feel I digest my food properly before sleeping. We had cleared up the dishes and had settled down the watch the TV. I needed to tell Dave that we could not carry on some work at the house as money was running low and it would not get completed. I knew that I would have to be very diplomatic in my wording so as not to create his temper rising. I managed, I thought, to put the fact that money was running low very tactfully. I don't think I have ever seen him go into such a rage so quickly. His face reddened and it tightened like a bulldog. He stood up from the chair he was sitting at and in temper he threw the remote control in his hand. I was sitting on a sofa at the other end of the room. The remote control hit the inglenook fireplace and ricocheted off and hit me full on the head. I had searing heated pain in my head. I was shaking, I could feel my face tightening, my head was exploding and growing bigger and the pain was now throbbing. Dave's face was one of anger still.

His anger turned into fear, "Do you need to go to hospital?" He was childlike and shaking as he spoke.

"Dave, if I go to hospital and they ask me how this happened what do you think Social Services might say about it?" My mind was dazed and all I could think of in that moment, was that Social Services would take my children away if they knew what situation we were living in. The tiredness had dulled my ability to be logical. I didn't want my children being taken away from me. The pain was so bad and I needed to see what he had done to me. I ran upstairs and looked in the mirror. I couldn't believe what I was looking at. My face was unrecognisable. The lump on my head was the size of a grapefruit and my face was disfigured. I sobbed uncontrollably. I tried to put a cold compress on my head and take some Ibuprofen to ease the pain. I couldn't stop shaking. For the first time, ever, I glared at Dave with disgust. He had done this to me. He had hurt me beyond words.

He knew he had done wrong, "Do you want me to leave?" he was sheepish and falling over himself to try and help me. I moved away from him and my barrier had gone up.

"You are not leaving. What if I am concussed? What if one of the children needs me and I can't get to them?" I was now the force to be reckoned with. "You can sleep in the spare room until I know that I am okay and then you can move out!" He hung his head and moved into the spare room. I cried all night like I have never cried before, with pain and the knowledge that he had now physically hurt me.

He got up the following morning and entered the bedroom very hesitantly, "Are you going to tell anyone what happened last night?"

"I am not going to tell anyone what happened. Why would I, Dave?" I said sternly.

"Okay," he replied, "do you still want me to move out?"

"Yes, I don't think it would be a good idea for you to come back here tonight. I need time to think." I could not look at him and I certainly did not want him in the house with me or the girls.

He packed a bag and left. He went to stay with his parents for two nights.

After he left, I got myself up to look in the mirror, at the damage to my head. My face was no longer disfigured but the lump was still the size of an orange. My hair was very long so I carefully pulled it over my forehead so as to hide any evidence of the injury. I carried on with the children, getting Olivia up for school and Scarlett and Verity dressed and fed. The pain was unbelievable. My parents were arriving in two days and I needed everything to look normal before they arrived. My friend, Julie had come over to see me and I told her what had happened. She thought it was terrible. Then, later in the day, Dave's Mum came over to see me. They were anxious as to the situation with him staying with them. I showed her the lump on my head and told her how he had lost his temper. Her response was, "Well, he is under a lot of pressure with work at the minute!!!!"

It was the day of my Mum and Dad arriving. I had had very little contact with Dave. I enjoyed the peace and quiet and the girls had not asked any questions, as their routine had been maintained. However, I did not want them worrying about me so I rang Dave. "I'm going to let you move back in. My Mum and Dad are arriving and I do not want them worrying about me or the girls." I knew in my heart of hearts that if they knew what had gone on between us that they would not want Dave anywhere near me but how would I cope on my own? I didn't feel I could quite walk that path with three children who were very young. What I didn't realise was that the blood from the lump was now draining down into my eyes and by the time my Mum and Dad arrived later in the afternoon, I had one black eye and the following day, I had two massive black eyes. My parents were horrified, "he hasn't hit you has he?" my Mum asked inquisitively. "No, Mum, I told you, I hit my head on the fireplace whilst I was cleaning it out." I tried to laugh it off but I knew my Mum was not convinced. I told everyone, including the people at school that I had hit my head on the fireplace whilst cleaning it out. I don't think anyone really believed me. My parents were very concerned and I had excruciating headaches that were not getting any better, so they insisted that I go to the local hospital to get it checked out. Mum and Dad looked after the girls and I drove myself up to the local hospital. A lovely nurse examined me and asked me how I had incurred such a terrible injury. I told her the story that I had told everyone else but, I am sure, that she knew that I was not telling the truth. She advised me that the swelling would go but only when all the blood had drained away and she recommended that I have an x-ray to see if I had cracked my skull. I did not follow this through, as I did not want to be asked anymore questions, but I am sure that I did have a hairline crack.

Another friend of mine from school had guessed that my injury was not an accident but as she did not know me too well, had not questioned me as she did not feel it was her place.

Dave had moved back in but we had struggled to have a conversation and put on a front for my Mum and Dad. I had shut him out. The subject was never broached and he never attempted to apologise to me. If anyone brought up my black eyes he would tell them the story of the fireplace and even laugh it off. He actually believed what he was saying and was so convincing. It scared me so much. He was oblivious to what he had done and this story was enough that he could justify it in his own head that it was not his fault. A very dangerous place to be, for us all.

His temper was getting worse and he was now hitting out at the children, well when he was there. He was coming home later and later. He would not normally make an appearance before 8pm and he would be left in the morning around 6.30am. Saturdays, he would spend at his office, still leaving early morning and Sundays he would spend the day cleaning caravans, cars, mowing lawns or going to his Mums for Sunday roast and there was not a lot of time for the children or us as a family.

My brain had been in overdrive since the incident with the black eyes. This isn't how life was supposed to be. Where was the confident Jennifer, full of life and fun? I am intelligent and I don't need to put up with this behaviour. Enough was enough and I sought legal advice from a recommended legal aid solicitor about what my rights were in divorcing him. I listened intently and I knew that I would be okay but it felt scary and I wasn't sure I was brave enough or strong enough to move forward in this direction. In fact, it took another six months before I put the process in motion.

My Mum had witnessed him hitting Olivia and I was not aware of it. She was trying to slide down the bannister, like 5-year-old girls think they should and he caught her and told her off. She went to do it again and he smacked her hard several times. My Mum was horrified. I have a rule in the house that we do not smack or hit but we had the naughty spot. Dave was a rule unto himself and could not conform to what I was teaching them. My Mum never told me until our relationship was over and she was the one who comforted Olivia. Although, my Mum said that she never cried which was strange so I wonder how many occasions he had done that without me knowing.

I could no longer bear the outbursts. Our caravan holidays were a trial and a test of my ability to make it all go smoothly. Our final holiday together as a family was in the following March.

Both Olivia and Verity were school age and Scarlett was a toddler. We went to Slimbridge in Gloucestershire and it was a very pleasant site. We had decided one day to go off to the Forest of Dean. This part of the world is where I am from so I wanted the children to see some of the sites that I visited often as a child. We all got into the car and I fastened all the children in. Dave's parents led the way in their car. We were nearly at the Forest of Dean when Olivia announced she felt sick in the car. So, my reaction was concern and to find somewhere to pull over and Dave's reaction was to start cursing. Not very helpful. Children get car sickness all the time after all. We pulled into a garage at speed and halted suddenly. Olivia at this point was being sick everywhere. Dave was angry and started shouting at her. Then he started shouting at me, "It's all your fault. If you didn't let her eat chocolate then she wouldn't be sick." I was too concerned with Olivia to give him a response. She was crying and scared and needed comforting. Verity started to cry as well because Dave was shouting. We pulled over into the garage and I managed to get Olivia out of the car. Her clothes were covered with vomit so I stripped her down. We always carried picnic blankets so I wrapped her in a blanket and proceeded to get Verity out of her car seat so she could sit in the boot with Olivia. Olivia was a little cold so I wrapped her in another blanket. I then reassured Scarlett that everything was ok and left her in her car seat whilst I cleaned the mess with baby wipes and tissues. In the meantime, his Mum and Dad had turned around and pulled up in front of us. They got out and brought some spare blankets for the girls. I went to the back of the car with the spare blankets and Dave's Mum chatted to Scarlett. Dave had got out but was still shouting, "you need to stop these kids from eating rubbish. Look at the state of my car." He stomped up and down, waving his arms and ranting, his Dad trying to reason with him about children being car sick. They went back to their car to get some more wipes and some water.

I was staying calm for the children, "Can you please calm down as you are scaring the girls and it is not helping anyone." He raised his hand to me and I stood ready to take a blow. Both of the girls in the boot watched in horror as he pulled his hand down to strike me. Verity sobbed and he stopped himself before his hand hit me. He walked off towards his Mum and Dad at the front of the car who were totally unaware of what had just occurred. He was more worried about the state of the car, which I was cleaning, than the children. His Mum approached me and looked at me and I tried to hold back the tears but failed dismally. She placed a knowing hand on my shoulder and distracted the girls. Needless to say, he drove like an idiot all the way back to site and blamed everyone for spoiling his day!!!! I knew at this point that things needed to change and I needed to work out a way to change them. He was now starting to get physical. I had lied for him once and he had gotten away with it and now he was pushing the boundaries further. I now knew that if his Mum and Dad had not been close by that he would have hit me.

We got back from the holiday and everything was building up for the Royal Wedding. The girls were very excited and school were holding lots of wedding celebrations. It is lovely to see such a happy couple getting married. I would watch them on TV and think how lovely it must be to be with someone who absolutely adores you and would never hurt you. I know, like everyone else should, that we are only on this earth once and we need to make it work for us, not put up with suffering. I always tried to make out that there were other people in a worse situation, and there are, but in actual fact, there is nothing worse than being abused and unhappy.

Dave was badgering me about planning another caravan holiday and when we were going to book it. I did all the bookings for the whole family and I just couldn't do it but I couldn't tell him either and every day it became this dreaded fear that he would ask me as soon as he got home from work and sure enough he would. I clammed up and just said that I had not had enough time to look. That possibly was not a lie, as life is very busy with three children, school runs etc...

Chapter Eighteen

What's Love Got To Do With It?

Eventually about two weeks later I sat down to watch TV with Dave and he asked me the question about whether we were going on holiday. It was the day before the Royal Wedding so it was Spring.

I took a sharp intake of breath and said, "I don't think that there will be any more holidays, as I don't want us to stay together anymore. I want us to separate. We cannot live the way we are living".

He started to cry, "but I love you."

He always said that he loved me, it was the get out of jail free card (or so he thought) but it did not mean anything anymore. He had said it too many times followed by abuse of some sort.

This 6'2" man threw himself to the floor and lay there kicking his legs and banging his hands on the floor, crying and screaming. I was completely shocked and froze to the spot, watching and observing his behaviour.

He begged me not to end the relationship, "please don't end it, please, please. I beg you," but for the first time in a long time I stood strong and unemotional, there was nothing left to give him. He had taken everything he could have of me and I was empty. He got up off the floor and tried to kiss me and I baulked. At that moment, he repulsed me and all respect that I had had gone.

He stood up and he stormed off towards the front door, "I'm going to kill myself. That's it life isn't worth living. There's not point".

This scared me and I begged him, "please don't do this. We just need to talk".

He started to get angry and retorted, "Well, you've already decided what's going to happen so there is nothing to talk about".

I stood in silence, as he was right. He got into his van and wheel span out of the drive. I sent several texts to him to tell him to come back. He replied that he wasn't coming back and that he was going to Beachy Head to kill himself. He told me via his messages that he loved me and then went on to say that the insurance money would make sure that we were all taken care of. I was now very scared and felt completely responsible for this situation. I needed to sort it out! I told him, for the sake of getting him back to the house that I did love him but that we could not carry on living like we were. Eventually around 1am he returned home. I was exhausted, waiting to hear, possibly from the police. My nerves were completely on edge. He came up to bed with me and we tried to talk but nothing had changed for me. Then followed two weeks of what I would call emotional and mental torture.

Every night we tried to talk and he could not have a conversation with me. His temper rose and he would drive off and threaten to kill himself. I couldn't cope with his inability to reason and one night I snapped, "Dave, you need to sort yourself out. You have a problem and you need to deal with your temper". His head dropped to his feet, "yes, I know I do."

The next day, he booked an appointment with the doctors and asked if I would go with him. I agreed. The doctor was not our normal doctor but a locum. I sat with him whilst he cried and told the doctor that I was leaving him and that all he wanted to do was commit suicide. She prescribed him some anti-depressants. She moved her attention to me, "are you prepared to stay with him just to help him through this difficult time?" I must have seemed very cold to her, "no, it has not changed my mind and I am not sure I can be there for him". I had been through enough and so had the children. I couldn't have them witness anymore of his behaviour as it was very upsetting for them. Dave getting sympathy from the doctor was not going to make our situation any better. The doctor referred him to the Crisis team. They deal with mental health patients and make assessments on what sort of mental health issues they have. They arrived the next day. A lady and gentleman, Carol and Mike, and they needed to speak to us separately. They took Dave to the kitchen and sat with him to discuss what he was going through. They left him in the kitchen and came through to the lounge to sit with me and talked to me about what was happening in our relationship. They listened and then they asked a question which I found very difficult to answer, "has he been physical with you?" I was embarrassed as the true answer was yes, so I lied and said, "no," but I think they knew different. Carol then very kindly went on to say, "men who are mentally abusive normally turn physical". It felt as though she understood without having to say anything too much but it felt like my secret and I needed to keep it. She then said that she was not there to tell us what to do with our relationship. I sadly admitted to her that I could no longer put up with him and that it was not good for the children. She assured me that this was my decision and I must do what was best for the family. She then said that basically Dave was having what they called adult tantrums. To get what he wanted he stamped his feet, showed off, threw his toys out of the pram and got angry in the hope that people would give in to him. Basically, this is a trait of people who have been 'indulged'. They have never been stood up to. So, you could say that this was down to his parents. They would not and could not stand up to him and put him right and he had got away with it for so long and got what he thought he wanted that he carried on that way. It was normal behaviour for him as he had not been taught any different.

That night became the end of our relationship. I put the children to bed and we sat in the lounge again to discuss what we were going to do. He begged me not to end the relationship, "I'm doing everything I can to make things better. I'm even going to the doctors for you, as you say I have a problem."

"Dave you need to be going to the doctors for your own benefit, not for mine. You have a temper and you need to deal with it." I was struggling to understand how he was feeling.

"My temper is no worse than Graham's at work!" he stood his ground defiantly.

I looked at him with disbelief at his ignorance. He did not believe he had a problem. How could we solve anything if he didn't have any concept of what was really happening?

He threw himself down on the floor again and screamed and cried and kicked, just like a baby having a tantrum. I did not react, I sat and watched him in disgust that he thought that would change my mind. I really was an ice-maiden to these emotional threats. He got up and, low and behold, stopped crying straight away and left the room. I knew in my heart what he was going to do. I stayed very composed and waited for him to reappear. There he stood in the lounge with a 6" knife. I remember him telling me that he was going to end it and that this was it, once the knife hit his heart it would be over for me.

I stayed very calm and stood up, "give me the knife, Dave". He placed the blade at his chest. Again, I asked him, "give me the knife please, Dave".

He started to shake and I reached out, he pushed it against his chest and I grabbed the knife out of his hands, he let go and started to cry. He rushed off to the kitchen. I followed him and caught him trying to extract paracetamol and ibuprofen from their packets. It has to be said, even in the worst situations, I am very practical.

"What are you doing?" I had a calm voice.

"I'm going to kill myself," his voice was menacing and angry.

I reached for the packets, staying composed, "those tablets won't kill you, they will give you liver failure, but they won't kill you".

"If I kill myself, at least you can have the life insurance money," he seemed obsessed about money.

"Dave, you are under the doctor as you have admitted you are suicidal and no Insurance Company will pay out on that basis," I couldn't believe he was even thinking on this level.

"Oh, that just typical. I've stuffed up again. I can't do anything right!" He was really feeling sorry for himself.

I remained cool as a cucumber, I had to. I had three little girls upstairs unaware, I hoped, of what was taking place in their safe home.

Dave stormed off. He left the house and got in his van again and drove like a maniac. I phoned him, "Please come back. This is not going to solve anything." He ignored my messages, he ignored my calls. Then he rang me. All I could hear was him screaming and what sounded like the wheels on the van skidding and him saying, "I'm going to kill myself". He hung up and turned his phone off and I could not contact him for at least another hour. It was now 1am. I decided that I would wait for another quarter of an hour and then I would have to call the police. I did not have to. Just after 1am the telephone rang. I hesitantly picked up the receiver. It was the local hospital. Dave had admitted himself, saying that he was a danger to himself and they were keeping him in for observation and a consultant would assess his mental health. The lovely gentleman at the hospital asked me, bearing in mind that I had three young children, if I wanted Dave discharged to his home. I said that I did not want him back in the house as this posed a threat to the children and he needed to be discharged to his parents. He was discharged at 4.30am and he did go to his parents.

Dave rang me that morning and asked if he could come to the house. I told him that he could come and get some clothes but that he was not to stay. It was a warm day and Scarlett was at home with me and Olivia and Verity were at school. He turned up about 10am and as soon as he arrived, I exited the house via the back door and took Scarlett out to the trampoline in the back garden. This would at least allow him time to gather his bits without us having to face each other and avoid an atmosphere or confrontation in front of Scarlett. Scarlett and I were jumping up and down and the next thing I see is Dave at the kitchen windows (we had three windows). He opened every single one of them full force and wide open, so I could not shut them and then started to throw glass vases out of the windows. I stopped jumping and I could feel the fear inside me. I was trying to stay happy and smiley for Scarlett but was worried as to what he would do next. I then heard a bang (which must have been the front door) and his van leaving at high speed. I took a deep breath and looked at Scarlett. I walked towards the house almost in a daze, relieved that he had not approached us. I pushed and pushed with all my might and shut the windows. I may be small but I am quite strong. I managed to get all of them shut again. I took Scarlett inside and put her to bed for her afternoon sleep and then returned to the garden outside the windows and spent the next couple of hours clearing all the glass that had been broken, so that the girls would not cut themselves later. I remember sobbing, probably more in relief, that he had been and gone.

It was that day that I got a knock on the front door and Mandy, from next door was stood there. She knew from the way Dave had driven off that things were not right. I sobbed and asked her in and told her all that had gone on. From that day forward, she stood by my side. My Guardian Angel neighbour.

Throughout all of this, no one knew what had been happening. I had kept everything to myself. The girls had been going to school as normal and I remained my smiley, happy self, hiding my fear and unhappiness. I did connect and become very good friends with a lady, called Andrea, who was another angel sent to help me throughout all my court cases. She has a legal background and her advice and objective opinions were priceless. Andrea later confided in me that she had guessed what was happening but at the time was not in a place to question or even make accusations of what may or may not have been going on. We would spend many an afternoon in the school car park, me in shreds and trying to keep strong whilst she gave me words of advice and soothed the harshness of the legal letters that I received. Giving me another perspective and hope.

Dave did call me and ask if he could come and see the girls. I agreed as I would never deny him the opportunity to see them, they are his children after all, but he had to be aware that he would have to leave again. I told him that he would not be coming back to stay and that I would be present for their safety. He expressed his dissatisfaction with me for this but I could not risk the children getting hurt. The children knew something was going on but had not asked questions. His interaction with them in the past had been minimal anyway but every time he came to see the girls, he couldn't help himself from crying and wailing. One day, Verity thought this was highly amusing and said, "look at Daddy's face, it looks weird". I tried to smooth this over and said, "she's only four, she doesn't understand". He sobbed uncontrollably and turned and run off out of the house.

It was a week later and a lovely sunny Sunday morning. Dave appeared at the front door. It was 12pm and I was surprised to see him, as we had not planned for him to come over. He seemed aggravated. Olivia and Verity ran to the door and I had Scarlett in my arms.

"So, you want to separate, do you?" he had an aggressive tone and energy to him, "Well you will have to have a day without the children today," and with that he grabbed Scarlett out of my arms and pulled Verity along by her hand.

My heart started beating really quickly. What was he doing? He went to grab Olivia but she refused to go with him. He took the girls to his car. I followed him but tried not to panic, "What are you doing? Please don't take them? Where are you going?" he wouldn't look at me.

"I'm taking my children out for the day, because I can," he glared at me.

Verity and Scarlett were both unaware of what was happening and just got in the car as normal. He drove off with them. I could feel nothing but panic. He was in no fit state to be with the children on his own and who knows what would happen. Olivia just kept cuddling me and asking me if Verity and Scarlett would be ok. She was only five but she knew things were not right. I went inside and rang his Mum.

"Dave has taken the children," there was panic in my voice, "I don't know where he has taken them but he needs to bring them back."

"Don't worry, I'm sure they will be okay," she showed no concern whatsoever.

"Dave is a potential suicide case. He is under the doctor and actually, I don't trust what he might do with the children. I am very concerned and he should not be with them on his own," I could feel my voice and my heart racing.

"I just think you are overreacting. He will be fine with them," she was particularly blaze as if she knew he had planned to do this.

"If he does not have the children back by 2pm then I am going to call the police," I was firm with her and I meant it.

"I'll call him now and find out where he is and I will let you know," she now sounded concerned at the possible consequences of his actions.

She rang me back within five minutes and said that he was at a local National Trust park and that they were having lunch but she had asked him to return the children. I spent two hours pacing up and down and trying to amuse Olivia but we both were worried about Verity and Scarlett. He returned at 2pm on the dot so his Mum must have passed my message on. I have never felt such relief to see my cherubs back in my arms. Olivia ran inside with Verity and I held Scarlett in my arms.

"Please don't ever do that to me again," I said. He smiled and turned away to get in his car. He had enjoyed being so cruel.

By now I was not only dealing with him, I was having to deal with his parents as well. They would keep ringing me saying that he had stormed off and was going to kill himself. I told them that he would not do it and that they needed to wait and he would re-appear and he always did.

Then one day his Dad rang me, "Jennifer, it's Dave's Dad here."

"Hi," I said in anticipation of what was coming next.

"Look, this situation has gone on long enough and we are too old for this. We don't want Dave living with us in our house, "he hesitated, "he's your husband and you need to take him back."

"I'm really sorry you feel like that and if you really don't want him living with you, then you need to tell him that. I am not going to have him back here. He has done too much and I don't want him here." I was stronger now and I wasn't going to be pushed back into the situation we had been in.

"We can't do that to him, where would he go?" he was trying to get my sympathy.

"I understand what you are saying and I do feel for you but I have three young children and there is no way that I want someone in the house who is threatening suicide and holding knives to their chest. It isn't safe and the safety of my children is my priority." I was firm but being fare.

He mumbled something under his breath and then he hung up in disgust but it was all true. I felt very sad that his Mum and Dad could not bear having him live under their roof and hoped that I would never feel like that about one of my children.

Visits by Dave to see the children became more frequent. In fact, his interaction with them was more than they had ever had in their entire lives. I remained positive with him and he would say that he needed to come over and sort out finances but it was an excuse to see me. Initially, he carried on paying the mortgage and the bills.

It was the end of May. Dave had been gone about three weeks. He messaged me to say that he needed to come over that night to discuss how the bills were going to be paid. I was hesitant and I should have known better than to discuss things with him of an evening but I also knew that I wanted to know where I stood financially. I had put the girls to bed and Verity and Scarlett were fast asleep. Olivia had been very unsettled and had spent a couple of nights going to sleep in my bed but was settled. He came in and seemed reasonable for the first time in a long time. I was quite surprised. It appeared that he had accepted the fact that we were separating and divorcing and maybe we could now have a reasonable conversation. He seemed very level headed and had agreed to carry on paying the mortgage and bills but that we needed to sell the house. I agreed with him and said that I would instruct an Estate Agent.

Once our discussions had finished I asked him to leave, "I'm quite tired and I am glad we have been able to discuss things but I need to go to bed. I will message you when the Estate Agents have been around."

He smiled wryly at me, "I'm not leaving. It's my house and I'm not moving."

"Please Dave, for the sake of the children can you please leave quietly," my stomach turned. I knew it was too good to be true.

"I'm not leaving until you have sex with me," he sat steadfast.

I couldn't believe what I was hearing and I started to feel sick, "I am not having sex with you. We are no longer together and I would like you to leave."

"I know what you want, but I am not leaving, as it's not what I want," he voice was threatening and he leant back in the chair and folded his arms.

"Please leave. There is nothing for you here now." I beckoned him to the door but he was not moving.

I tried everything I could think of to persuade him to leave and he was far too big to drag to the door. He sat it out until 3am and I was so tired. I couldn't play this game anymore and I gave in to his demand, on the condition he left early so the children did not see him. I needed something to change for him to leave and, for the sake of the children, this was the only way he was going to leave. We went up to the bedroom and I felt dizzy and sick. I undressed and he undressed. I lay there and let him take me. He fell asleep and I cried quietly to myself. I could not sleep, I could feel nothing but shame. At 5am I woke him, "I need you to leave before the children wake up as it might confuse them." He said nothing but he dressed and left. I cried some more. I needed to shower to get rid of the smell of him. I turned on the hot water and stepped into the water. My body shook and I just let the water run down my face to wash away the tears and anything else it could wash away. I was disgusted and I would never let him near me again but I knew, having children with him, I was going to have to continue to have contact with this man. Something I didn't relish but I was prepared to do it for them.

His contact with the girls continued even though I could not bear to have him near me. He would come along to swimming most weeks and watch Olivia and Verity having lessons but it was very difficult as you could tell he was angry with me. We hardly spoke to each other and I struggled to look at him. One Tuesday night he came along to swimming, we watched the children and then took them home for MacDonald's. I had made a risotto and invited him back, as we needed to discuss finances once more and try and be adult about our breakup. He seemed in a reasonable mood but I was very wary of him after the last meeting. We ate and went into the lounge to talk. I sat away from him to keep a safe distance. I was very scared of him and I wasn't sure how he was going to be or how he was going to act. I announced that I had instructed my solicitor to go ahead with divorce proceedings. His reaction was instant. I have never seen him turn red so quickly. He rose up from the chair and started to scream at me, "what divorce?" I had been honest with him from the outset that this was what I wanted, a divorce. He lunged forward, grabbed my hand and took my engagement and wedding rings off. I sat still, in shock, not even sure what was happening. He stormed out of the lounge. He was angry. I stayed seated and thought that he was putting his shoes on to leave the house. I heard the stairgate go at the top of the stairs. All I could think about was the safety of the children. "Oh my god, where is he going? What is he doing? I need to get to the girls," rang the voice in my head. I ran around the house to the stairs at which point he was coming back down the stairs. I could hear Olivia awake. He reached the bottom of the stairs. I put my hand on the bannister to steady myself. I could feel my heart pumping. He put his shoes on and I thought he was going towards the front door. All of a sudden, he turned and his right fist came flying at me. He punched me in the chest and I reeled backwards. He turned and grabbed the front door handle, opened it and ran out, slamming it behind him. I picked myself up but I was winded. I lurched for the front door and locked it so he could not get in again and I went to the lounge to see where he was and instinct told me to pick up the phone on the way. He was in his van in front of the lounge window. I banged on the glass with the phone in my hand. "I'm going to ring the police," I said to myself quietly as the words could not come out due to fear. He drove off. I looked at the phone in my hand. He had hit me. He had punched me. I dialled 999. I asked for the police. I started to speak but my voice was crumbling with shock and tears. Eventually, the operator asked if I was who I was and tried to calm me. It was like talking pigeon English. "He hit me," was all I could manage to say whilst shaking and sobbing. They asked if it was my husband that had hit me. I said "yes". They asked if he was still in the house to which I replied "no". She told me that someone would be with me in five minutes. I text a very good friend of mine, Karen, from the school who lived locally, the message literally said, "he hit me" as it was all I could manage to type with my hand shaking uncontrollably and she arrived within two minutes. She did not know what had been going on and her daughter was a friend of Verity's. We had spent a lot of time together as the girls were friends. She was shocked to hear the story but happy to help out. I was hurt and crying. In the meantime, Olivia came downstairs to see what had happened. "Why are you crying mummy?" she asked. "Silly mummy. Daddy was a little annoyed and silly Mummy got upset". I pulled myself together, took a deep breath and used my hands to wipe away the tears and put her up to bed again in my bed, as she was feeling a little insecure since Daddy had left.

The police arrived a couple of minutes later, a lady and a male Officer. I was shaking and in a terrible state. They took a statement which took two hours. There were lots of questions asked and as my story unravelled it led to further questions. The male Police officer was absolutely horrified by my story and he actually said to me that he wasn't really supposed to pass judgement but that Dave sounded like a bully. In all honesty, he had hit the nail on the head, he was a bully. The police left after the statement had been completed and advised that they would contact me to let me know what action would be taken but that Dave would be arrested. They advised me to lock up and try and get some sleep. Karen made sure I was okay and then also left. I locked the door and went up to bed. My head was going over and over the events of the evening and I struggled to get some sleep. I text Julie, in case she was awake, to tell her he had hit me and was being arrested. She was awake and responded straight away, "I don't believe it. Silly man". At 11pm I got a message from Dave saying 'night x'. Then at 5am I got another one saying 'I love you'. At 5.15am four police officers turned up to arrest him.

The following morning, I rang my parents and told them what had happened before I got the girls up for school. They were devastated that so much had gone on and they did not know although, they knew things weren't right. They told me that I could go to them if I needed to. I said that I would think about it but that I needed to get the girls to school. I held it together for the children to get them up and into school. It was as if nothing has happened. They went in as normal and then, I went into the school office and asked to see the Headmistress. I had Scarlett with me and Karen, who had come to the house when the police had been called. When I got into her office I was in a terrible state. Karen amused Scarlett whilst I told the Headmistress what had happened. It is amazing how when you tell people what you are going through they all pull together and suddenly a whole new process starts. The headmistress rang social services who had already been advised by the doctors that there was a situation with Dave and the children were on their radar. With this incident it was a whole different ballgame. I was offered a refuge but I did not take it as I was trying to keep things as normal as possible for the girls. Although I wasn't under social services as a case, they were advising me of what steps to take next in order to keep the girls safety a priority. I just wanted to get the girls away from this situation and perhaps going to my parents was a good idea. The school half term was in two days. Social Services and the School agreed that it would be in our best interest to go away. I advised the Head that I would go home and pack and when the girls finished school I would drive them straight to my parents. The Headmistress contacted the local police as Dave had now been violent and they were already aware of the situation and had noted this information against our history marker on the property and at school, in case he turned up. (History Marker - this is information that the police keep when an incident has occurred and it may be possible that an urgent response is needed). The police also advised both the school and myself that if he turned up at any time I could call them and they would respond instantly.

Lorraine Butterfield

Karen knew I was still in shock and when we had finished in the school office, she invited me back for coffee. I needed to make sense of all that had happened. At 10am I received a phone call from the school to let me know that Olivia had gone up to her teacher and told her that whilst Daddy was upstairs he hit her. The school had also informed the police of this new information. I sobbed as I was in the house but unaware of what he had done and she had not told me. I then got a call from the police as they needed me to go to the school and examine her to see if she had bruises. The emotion took over and a choking sensation gathered in my throat whilst tears streamed down my face. I composed myself and went to the school and Olivia was pulled out of class. We were taken to a private room and I asked her where Daddy had hit her. She said it was her bottom. I examined her but there were no bruises. She said that he had hurt her but she had not cried, I pulled her towards me and hugged her tight fighting back the tears. This reinforced my belief that he had done this more than once to her. I let her go back to her classroom and left to ring the Police and advise them that she had no bruising.

Dave was held until 2pm that day but no charges were pressed as my chest did not bruise and Olivia had no bruises either, so they did not have enough evidence to hold him. I was devastated and now wondered what his next actions would be. I was so scared for me and the children. What would he do? How was he thinking? Would he come looking for me/us? The police advised me to change the locks on the house which I did straight away, so at least I could feel a little safer. They also advised that upon his release, they had advised him that he was not allowed near the house or us for the time being. I packed our bags. I must have checked and doubled checked we had everything. I felt panic creeping in and I needed to stay relaxed. I knew Dave didn't always do as he was told, even by the Police. I drove to the school early, ready to just take off. As soon as the girls came out I loaded them into the car and I did as I had planned to do and drove to my parents. The girls were very excited as they loved to visit their grandparents and even more excited that they didn't have to go to school the next day. I could feel the pressure easing, the further away we drove.

The break from our situation was a welcome relief. My Mum and Dad were very pleased to see us and see that we were safe. They now feared for our safety but made our stay as relaxing as possible. When we arrived, I had a missed call from the school. I rang them straight away and they advised that Dave had turned up at the school to see the children and that he had been asked to leave but they felt I should know. I was quaking in my shoes. I did not want to bring trouble to my Mum and Dad's door. I just hoped and prayed that he would not turn up. I kept my solicitor informed. I like to know that whatever I am doing is the right thing. I rang her to let her know where I was and why I had gone to my parents. I was exhausted from the emotional rollercoaster and she advised me that Dave was not to see the children at all and that he needed to stay away from the house for the time being so that he could cool his temper. I then rang the Police to advise them where I was just in case I needed their assistance in another County and they made a note of the incidents and placed a marker on my parents' address, so that instant response could be actioned. Dave had guessed where we were and did threaten to turn up.

I had to sit down and explain to the children that they would not be seeing Daddy for a while. They seemed fine about this, bearing in mind that they very rarely saw him anyway. Out of all the children, Olivia was the worst to react to the break-up. She cried and found going to sleep very difficult and seemed very angry, not with anyone in particular but just angry. I was glad to have support from my Mum and Dad.

The week seemed to fly past all too quickly and I found myself having to pack the car ready to return home and school. I didn't want to return home but I knew that staying with my Mum and Dad was not the answer and I was an adult and I needed to face this situation. I had also had some time to go running again. I had missed it so much, it brought me a little bit of calm during a highly anxious time, although the running was sporadic as I was too worried about leaving the children and felt I could only trust my Mum and Dad to look after the girls. Constantly in the back of my mind I wondered what his next move would be and knowing how unpredictable Dave was, was frightening.

Dave would constantly text and email me and I was legally advised that I should ignore all correspondence. As soon as we arrived back home I was bombarded with messages. Dave was now angry and his temper was taking over the grief. He started to make threats over text messages. He said that it was his house and that he would come and go as he pleased and that if I didn't let him in he would kick the door down. He told me one night over a message that he would come in the night and burn the house down with us all in. His excuse for this was that if he couldn't have us then no one could. I spent three months not sleeping, watching out of the window so as to protect the children from him. The police would pop by from time to time to make sure I was ok.

For contact to resume there was quite a bit of correspondence between solicitors. My solicitor came up with supervised contact at Dave's parents' house every other weekend between 10am-12pm. Supervision to be by his mother. This lasted a few weeks and then increased to 11am-3pm every other Saturday. Again, the contact to remain supervised. Unfortunately, Dave's mother took it upon herself to go shopping on one of these days, leaving Dave and the children unsupervised and of course, this information was fed back to me via the children. Children are so honest. The contact was stopped and my solicitor offered the opportunity of contact via a contact centre. Dave was not happy with this and decided to take the matter to court.

Chapter Nineteen

The First Court Order

Within four weeks I had received a very abusive solicitors' letter. In fact, I can honestly say it was not at all professional and repeated hearsay rather than fact. Sadly, I can confirm that my best friend, Julie, who had been coming over to talk to me was taking everything I had told her back to Dave with her own slant on events. I know that he had been using her as a shoulder to cry on and she obviously, had fallen for the sob story. He had then sat in the solicitor's office and spouted out the whole conversation and wanted it used in a letter but had manipulated the truth giving him ammunition to challenge all the things that happened. My solicitor advised me that Dave had spent 4 hours in the solicitor's office and the letter had cost him £1,000!! The letter outlined a proposal that I was to move out every other weekend so that he could move in and see the children. It was absolutely preposterous and as I had never received solicitor's letters before it felt very intimidating and I had to question my solicitor as to whether he would get away with such a proposal in court. My Solicitor just shrugged the letter off as very unprofessional and not a solution that a court would agree to. She also advised that if he should move back into the house, he would gain residency and therefore the children would be in his care, which was definitely not an option. My solicitor wrote back and made a suggestion of a contact centre for a starting point with a weekly phone call on a specific day so the children had a routine and she completely ignored all the tittle tattle that the other solicitor had spouted. My solicitor is to the point and factual, thankfully.

Whilst all this correspondence was flying about, I was now aware that my supposed best friend was informing Dave of all the details of the night of the assault, even down to the fact that Olivia had gone to school and advised school of her assault. He was now arming himself with excuses. An uneasy feeling when you no longer trust someone that you would have laid your life down for. I had felt uncomfortable the several occasions she had come over to see me. She constantly questioned what went on that night and then would question me again about what happened to Olivia and how it came about that we found out that she had been assaulted. My gut instinct was telling me that I didn't want her in my house and the day I read the solicitors letter, I decided that I could no longer trust this person and I felt extremely sad but I wasn't sure what I should do about it.

Her last visit to us was two days before Scarlett's birthday and I was at home. My Mum and Dad were with me and obviously, Scarlett, who was not quite two years old. My Mum and Dad were aware that I felt uneasy about Julie visiting and my Mum, who is very intuitive, also felt the same. They went upstairs to busy themselves and let me deal with the situation as I felt necessary. I saw her car arrive and took a sharp intake of breath. I smiled at Scarlett and announced that Aunty Julie had arrived. I let Julie in and we exchanged pleasantries. I then led her through to the kitchen to make coffee. We started to talk generally about Scarlett and how she was growing and suddenly, out of nowhere, I was being verbally abused by my best friend.

"How could you stop Dave from seeing his own children?" She raised her voice and her face was stern. "I cannot believe that he is not even allowed near his own home. What is the problem with you, Jennifer? I think it is disgusting the way you have treated him."

At this point I started to see red and I was shaking inside. I don't like confrontation but I wasn't going to put up with this line of questioning, especially from someone who was supposed to be my best friend, someone I trusted. Scarlett was extremely frightened and approached me and raised her arms to be picked up. She started to grip me around the neck and was crying.

I felt angry but stood my ground. I have never been so affronted in my life.

"This man has punched me, thrown things at me, assaulted Olivia, he has threatened suicide, held a knife to his chest and tried to take tablets, all whilst the children have been in the house. He is not fit to be anywhere near these children and you must be mad if you think I would put my children in that situation with him."

I then went on to say very calmly, "if I let him see my children and something happens to them then Social Services would have to question my ability as a mother to protect them and I am not prepared to put myself or my children in any harmful situations."

Julie calmed down, "what do you mean Social Services?"

"Social Services are involved and Dave cannot have his children without supervision and if he did, they would not be deemed to be safe," I held Scarlett close.

Julie seemed a little surprised by this new information. She quietened down and made some noises about not knowing that that was the situation. We made some small talk and then she left. When she had gone I was annoyed with myself for not asking her to leave when she raised her voice but I knew I was at a very low ebb in my life and I wasn't strong enough. My boundaries didn't exist and I needed to start building them. Before she left, she asked if I would like to go over to her house for a drink. I said I would see how I was feeling. Now she had gone, I thought about everything that had gone on and decided that our relationship had also come to an end certainly for the time being. I needed support at this point in my life and she was showing none of that. I could no longer have this person in my home. Knowing that I would crumble if I tried to do it face to face, I sent her a text message to very politely say, "It is very kind of you to invite me over but I am too tired tonight. I was sad when you came earlier as I feel that you cannot support me in my time of need and, therefore, it would be better if we did not have any contact for the time being. I do wish you well and hope things will change". It wasn't a horrible text message but it was straight and to the point and how I felt at that stage in the proceedings. She was doing me no favours with her visits and in fact it was dragging me down further and making me question myself about what I knew had happened. I felt a sense of a weight lifted once I had sent the message. I had no response from her.

As expected, my solicitor's response regarding the contact centre was met with disdain and there followed a letter advising that Dave had decided to take the matter further and a court hearing date had been set. I trembled inside at the thought of going to court. The battle was to begin and I wasn't sure I was ready to sit in Court and discuss our business.

Before we could attend court, we were asked to go to Mediation. This was arranged at the beginning of November. So, as required, we both attended a mediation session, just to see if we could work things out between ourselves. Karen offered to drive me and I was very grateful. I was to arrive half an hour before Dave and leave after him so that I was not in any danger. I arrived early, as requested, and I was directed upstairs. Dave arrived shortly afterwards. We sat in a room with a lady called Sarah. Sarah was the Mediator for the day. She asked us questions about our situation but Dave took over the conversation and started to rant on about how badly he was being treated. I sat and listened. Sarah turned her attention to me and every time she asked me a question, he interrupted. He eventually lost his temper and started to shout and be abusive. He was quite unreasonable and Sarah called time on the meeting. He was asked to leave the building. He seemed relieved to be leaving. I waited in the meeting room until he had gone. Sarah then asked if I would wait in reception for another half an hour before leaving, just as a safety precaution. I sat and waited the half an hour and then called Karen who was nearby to come and collect me. His behaviour was inexcusable to the point that it was mentioned on the report. We actually did not get very far with the mediation and no solutions could be agreed on. I am not sure how successful it really is in divorce or contact proceedings. Our case needed to go to Court.

It was the end of November and the day of the court hearing arrived and I think the whole of my family were nervous for me and I was quaking. My neighbour, Mandy, who has been a complete rock came with me. We drove and parked a little way from the court and then walked to try and calm me down. I am just so glad she came into my life. I couldn't have gone through all this without her. Courts these days are not quite the officious looking places they were. I walked into this very 1960s concrete block with lots of large windows and felt a little out of sorts. When you enter, you walk through double doors and then through an x-ray machine and your bags are searched by security guards. I asked at reception where we needed to be and was directed upstairs. There was another reception and I gave them my details. Due to my circumstances, I was not allowed to wait in the waiting room with Dave and I was directed to a side room, where my Barrister would come to meet me and discuss the proceedings.

Before the hearing each party gets to put forward what their proposals are. Dave had requested every other weekend and me to move out and had also requested that the children be introduced to his new girlfriend, Tracey. I was aware that he had started dating again as he had plastered it all over a social networking site of them on holiday in our caravan, at a very famous nightclub in Essex and basically galivanting all over the country. I found this extraordinary behaviour from a man who had said that he loved me and wanted me back. I was even receiving love letters from him to that nature whilst he was at the beginning of his relationship with his new girlfriend. I had prepared myself quite well for the first hearing and had done a little research on google about his new lady friend. I needed to protect my children and I needed to know, for their safety, who this person was. I had this gut instinct about her and a fiery determination to discover who she was and got to page 14 of the google search and up popped what I had been looking for. She was a very attractive blonde lady with short hair and rather large. The newspaper article had linked this woman to being part of a criminal fraternity and had listed several criminal convictions against her. It seemed that her whole family in one form or another had links in one way or another to criminal activity. It all seemed a little like EastEnders. I had printed off this information and on the morning of the hearing and had taken it along with me. My proposition for contact at a contact centre was put in front of him and his solicitor to read. Whilst in the side room with my Barrister and Mandy looking through Dave's proposition and discussing the case, we heard an insistent knocking at the door and in burst the solicitor who represented Dave. She was almost hopping from one foot to another and anxious to talk to my Barrister. My Barrister excused herself and left the room only to re-enter five minutes later and ask if I had the print out of the criminal offences that I had found against his girlfriend. I gladly handed over the print out and smiled, as I had realised at this point he was totally unaware of her criminal background, but I was.

I remained composed although I could feel a headache approaching. The whole time in the room with the Barrister we were trying to come up with a solution to contact that would be acceptable to me and also that a judge would be happy to confirm as suitable and just. My instinct was initially to go to contact centre, although not ideal, this would give the children a chance to see their Dad and I would feel they were safe and protected. I recommended fully supervised and notes would be taken by the supervisor at the centre and a report could be done to see how his behaviour was with the children. I was advised that the times had to increase from 1 hour to 2 hours and it could not be a permanent solution so an alternative form of contact should be considered after contact centre ceases. Therefore, it was recommended by my Barrister that a neutral ground be considered where we meet and I drop off the children and come back to pick them up, knowing they are within a public place and he would have to be supervised by his mother. This would be for only 3 hours. Then the contact would move to grandma's house and she would supervise contact between 10am and 7pm two alternate Saturdays. I would drop off and pick them up. After that period, we would return to court to see how the contact was proceeding. Dave was not happy but his alternative was not even a sensible suggestion. Even the judge agreed that, as he had not even been a hands-on Dad, looking after three children is a task in itself but could cause concern with no experience and regardless of what he thought, he would require assistance to look after them. So, that was the start of the contact again with provision for a phone call from Daddy every Wednesday evening at 6pm. A routine so the children knew he would be ringing. It was also considered that due to the fact that his new relationship was in the very early stages, he needed to build a relationship with his children first before introducing a new person to them. It was also agreed that due to Dave's temper he would have to attend a Living without Violence course.

I was learning very quickly that when you go to court enough, that the Barristers in these cases are very laid back and take everything in their stride but I suppose they see these situations most days. It can be very frustrating learning how the system works.

Underlying attending court was the fact that I was having to deal with distressed children who, in their eyes, felt their whole world had been turned upside down. Olivia was particularly wired at this point. She was very aware of what had gone on and very aware that Mummy had been very scared. She constantly would go around the house checking that windows and doors were shut and locked. All through the summer months I couldn't even have a window cracked opened otherwise she would scream and cry and shake with fear. I was scared of Dave and, as I mentioned before, there were three months where I hardly slept keeping watch to make sure we all stayed safe. I am a very peace loving and level-headed person naturally and I was aware that any level of distress that I might be feeling, I needed to conceal it and try to relax. I was fully aware that I didn't want my children to pick up on any stressful vibrations.

As the head of the family, and in fairness, that had always been my role, I showed nothing but compusure, happiness and control. The children went to school as normal and at no point were they late. I had moments with Olivia when we would be in the car park at school and she would be screaming and crying and refusing to get out of the car. She even managed to climb over the rear seats of our seven-seater car and hide in the boot and I have had to physically lift her whilst managing to get Verity into school and carry a baby. The physical and mental strength has been paramount and the school would just take her off me, sometimes at the gate, sometimes in the reception and march her off to her classroom. They would always ring me later to confirm she had calmed down and usually it was very quickly. It was exhausting and distressing for me but I knew we had to keep going and it would get better. Poor little Verity, she would just wander into school and not make a fuss, possibly because there was no opportunity for her to struggle and she isn't unlike me, in that she is very logical and level headed and very accepting of what goes before. I think Scarlett found it all very amusing but was too young to comment or understand fully.

Apart from the daily stress of getting into school, I was dealing with night-time stresses as well. Olivia was finding it difficult to settle. I have always had a routine with the children. Bath and then bed with a story. It never changed with whatever we were going through. I would spend about an hour in the garden with them every night as well. We would play obstacle course games where I would set out hoops and balls and we would race each other up and down the garden and I would run with Scarlett, my youngest, she would be almost flying as we tried to beat the others. Olivia had to always win and then she would tease Verity about the fact that she was slower. But it meant that I was getting some quality time with them. Sometimes we would just all get on the trampoline together and I would sing nursery rhymes with them and we would all fall over or I would stand over them and play this game where they all lie under my legs and I sing, 'Sailing' by Rod Stewart and I bounce them all around. This caused great amusement and laughter and at the end of the day, laughter is a great medicine and for a little while in all our lives we forgot about the seriousness of the situation we were in.

Bedtime was very traumatic especially for Olivia. I would race them all upstairs and they would undress and a bath would be run and they would all jump in followed by hair wash and teeth and then they would be allowed to play for five minutes so they had an opportunity for them to discuss any worries with me. They would sometimes ask me questions about their Daddy and I would answer them as best as I could. Always in the back of my mind aware that things you say can be so influential and you have to remain objective. Not just for my sake, but for the sake of the children. At the end of day, no matter what goes on between two adults the children cannot be brought into the argument. Unfortunately, my husband, as he was, is like a lot of supposed to be adults and was not sensitive to protecting the children from this harsh situation.

I would dry all the girls one at a time and put their pyjamas on. All three of them would have a bedtime drink, usually soya milk. Scarlett would be the first to go to sleep and the other two would be allowed to be in their room and play quietly whilst I was dealing with her. Scarlett was only 2 years old and would have her story, I would walk away and she would be asleep. Then to the two other monkeys who were sharing a room and were very different. Verity would have a story and would be quite content to lie down, as long as I was nearby, but Olivia was not. This was obviously very disruptive to Verity and so, of course, they would end up both being disturbed at night. I would have screaming and crying from Olivia and I would put Olivia back to bed and she would come out of the room again, wanting to get into my bed. Olivia wanted to sleep with me and I would not let her. I did initially when Dave left the family home but, I wanted her and needed her to sleep in her own bed. I believe it makes them stronger, more independent and makes them face their fears and not run away from them. Not only that but in the day-time I was putting on my metal armour, being strong for me and them and at night time sometimes I needed my space where I could take the armour off, be me and cry if I needed. She would physically fight me and I would have to be very careful how I restrained her as, regardless of her age (6) she was determined and strong. I remained calm and returned her to her room. It would set Verity off and she would cry and then both of them would be crying and Olivia would be fighting me. She would continue until she was so exhausted that she would collapse into my arms and I would cuddle her whilst she sobbed and eventually she would give in and go to sleep. At the same time, having to reassure and cuddle Verity. They would ask me night after night if I was going to leave them and, again, all I could do was reassure them that I was going nowhere and show them that I was always there for them. It is so painful to see your children insecure and tears running down their cheeks, scared for what the next day may bring.

Night after night this continued for months and months. I remained composed and level. The disruptions would be worse just before or after contact and not only was I dealing with the children's fears but I was dealing with the damage that was being caused by adults who should know better. I hear it so many times and have witnessed how detrimental comments can cascade into dramas in a child's mind. Thoughtlessness and immaturity.

I started to write a diary quite early into the separation. Olivia's behaviour was of considerable concern and it was recommended that maybe a children's counsellor would be able to assist me in dealing with the situation that we found ourselves in. The diary in itself was to become my way of dealing with the daily struggles and also an excellent record of events that could help me recall incidents for the purpose of the court hearings.

'My first Diary Entry:

19/08/2011 – I have started a diary to log how I am feeling and the things that happen to us as a family on a day-to-day basis. Olivia's behaviour is of particular concern as she is being spiteful to Verity and Scarlett. She is biting, hitting, pushing – all bullish behaviour. I stay calm with her but it is very difficult when you feel she may harm someone. I have spoken with the Counsellor about my concerns and she is coming to introduce herself on the 25th. Her behaviour worsens on the day of the phone call from Daddy and the days she sees him. I have reassured her that I love her and her sisters and I am always going to be there for her.'

Olivia's behaviour concerned me as I questioned whether she has her father's tendencies. I knew she had a heart of gold and of course, I realised deep down that it was a reaction and her only way to express herself was in this manner.

Every day in my diary I have written about how I have expressed to Olivia how much I love her and her sisters and how much her sisters love her. I know this repeated pattern of reassurance is a great way to re-programme the mind. If you hear something enough you start to believe it and I am sure at this point in her life she felt that nobody loved her and her world was crashing down around her ears. I just wanted her to hear what I was saying and know it was true.

The diary was a way for me to express myself too a I had not confided in too many people. I needed an outlet and this was the safest way and gave me a chance to reflect and put things into perspective. It felt very cathartic to write it all down.

Diary Entry 12/11/2011 –

I have never bad-mouthed Dave and I remained impartial at every stage. His actions and the actions of his parents I have found inexplicable. Not so much on the initial contact, as this was carried out in a contact centre, but when things moved out of contact centre. I have to say that the contact centre situation was a false environment and being supervised enabled Dave to be on his best behaviour and not a true representation of his real personality. Whilst we went through this procedure, I met a lot of fathers/mothers whose other halves have used this system to be on their best behaviour enabling the contact with their children to come out of a contact centre situation and then they can revert to behaving like children themselves. Unfortunately, in a lot of cases, this is not funny and it is after all the welfare of the children that needs to be considered. I have spent many a night mulling over how this can be allowed to continue but, in a supervised situation, these men (and women) are fooling everyone.

I would turn up at the contact centre and I always had someone with me. Generally, it was my Mum or my neighbour and very good friend, Mandy. The waiting room was plain but had a few toys in whilst we waited so at least the children could play until their Dad arrived. Dave would be directed to the room where he could be with the girls. A member of the supervision team at the contact centre would come into the room and take the children upstairs with them to a playroom for them to spend two hours with their Dad. I could wait in the waiting room if I liked but I chose to leave and go and have a coffee, as a distraction, so as not to try and worry. The girls actually enjoyed that time with him. I think it was because it was in a room with loads of toys and he had to play with them, there was no choice. This was something that they never had a lot of with him. It was a known fact that he would work on a Saturday and he was having to take time to be with them. He would occasionally do things with them but he wasn't particularly hands on so this one on one time with him they could at last get to see him in a different light. But, like I said, this was a temporary situation and not real life. These contact centres do not really highlight any potential threats as you find that the people that need to use them play to the fact that they are being supervised and for an hour or two can put on a very good act.

I returned to the centre to the waiting room and the children would be returned to me. Dave left first and I waited a few minutes to make sure that he had left and was not waiting for me. It was all very organised and safety was penultimate.

In no time at all the contact had moved out of the centre and into a soft play area. The children loved to go to this particular soft play. It was very big and lots to do. Again, I turned up first and waited in the car park, I had Mandy or my Mum with me and I handed over the children at the entrance to the soft play. This was interesting as it was the first time we had really had contact directly. Dave's Mum handled the hand-over and we exchanged pleasantries. I waited to make sure that he would take them into the play area. He had both his mother and father with him. I gave a rundown of how the children were and if any of them were under the weather or any misdemeanours had occurred. Dave's Dad completely ignored me and headed on into the soft play so as to avoid any conversation. The children picked up on this straight away and when they were reunited with me three hours later, the girls mentioned it to me. They told me that they had noticed grandad had been rude and not spoken to me, even when I had spoken to him. Children are very quick to pick up on these atmospheres.

The children enjoyed their time at the soft play the first couple of times but Olivia kept asking why I couldn't come with them and why I had to go. It was obviously a source of distress for her. It then started to come to light that grandad had not been saying nice things about me to the girls and in their presence and, also about their father. The children were feeling uncomfortable with this situation and told me. The girls' loyalties lay with me, which I see as normal, as I have always been their main carer. I was the person who they look to when they are ill or hurt and I am the one that settles them to sleep at night and there when they wake in the morning. Why would any adult do this to children? It all felt very uncomfortable and unacceptable. They love me unconditionally as I do them.

Very early on in our separation, their father met Tracey and he had moved in with her. I was a little relieved as the pressure was off me. His text messages were less and I no longer had to worry about him begging me to reunite. His relationship was his prime importance and his argument in the many court appearances that we made. It seemed that the welfare of the children had disappeared and that meeting someone new was the answer to all his contact prayers.

I attended court eight times in this very long court process for contact. Every occasion was distressing and I totally feel for anyone who is currently or will shortly be entering the court room for this purpose. Writing my diaries for my own personal sanity had proved to be a bit of a godsend when it came to the court process, as I had written dates of events and reactions of the children which could be used to provide the counsellors and social services with useful information in order to assist us. But more importantly, my diary was keeping me level headed and providing me with a way to cope with all that was happening in my life. Every night it seemed my head was full of a series of events and every night I could spill the ink onto the page. The scenes in my head now on paper and no longer playing out over and over in my mind.

January arrived and so did the second Court hearing. This court case was quite a significant one in the whole process. This return to court was three months after the last hearing to review how the contact was progressing. The main word here is progress as the courts do like to push the contact on, so as to get it out of the court room.

I arrived at the court with my friend, Mandy, who drove. We proceeded through the double doors and through the x-ray scanning machine before being directed up the stairs and back to the court room where all my hearings were to take place. My stomach knotted and the feeling of sickness and anxiety were all I knew at this point. We were directed into a side room where my Barrister met us and discussed what the forward plan was for contact. I really detested these meetings. My brain went into overload trying to think of a way to maintain contact but keep the girls safe. When you want to protect your children the last thing you want to do is put them into the care of someone you don't trust and especially extend that time frame.

My Barrister was very understanding about the way I was feeling but advised me that the court would now be looking to bring the contact out of contact centres and short soft play meetings and let him have them at his home. As Dave was living with his new girlfriend and her background was not particularly very salubrious, I needed to make sure the children were safe. I also knew that the children were looking for stability not to have someone else thrown into the equation. Therefore, I agreed that contact could take place at the grandparent's house (the children were familiar with these surroundings) and that his mother would have to supervise all contact to ensure safety and help with the children's needs and as Scarlett was only two, she would need extra supervision and attention.

Dave had again put in his proposal that he wished for his new partner to meet the children. I had said that I thought this was inappropriate and stressed that I felt that it was too soon. They already had so much to get used to.

The Judge on this case was known to be impartial and very fair. However, I was dismayed at his decision to allow the children to stay overnight. Remember, we have gone from contact centres and three hours contact to two full Saturdays and then to overnight stays!!! It was agreed that I would drop off the children at 5.30pm on a Friday and they would return the children at 6pm on the Saturday night. The judge also advised Dave that he needed to consider what car seats he had available as I had handed over the drop off to him on the condition that he showed responsibility and provided his own car seats. He did also make it clear that Dave was not capable, having never done it, of looking after three little girls on his own and his mother supervising was for his own good. He then went on to comment on the fact that Dave's new partner needed to meet the children, and I needed to get over it, however not at the moment but maybe at the next court hearing!!! I was flabbergasted and very upset at his attitude and insult. The only reason I did not want this woman near my children was that Dave needed to build his relationship with the children and I didn't need her influence at this point. At the end of the day, I wasn't saying never, I was saying not at the moment. I needed to trust him with the children first before that was even considered. I also felt his mother was taking a lot of the load off him, which meant he wasn't fulfilling his role as a father, as his mother was doing it for him. He then went on to assure me that no harm would come to my children whilst they were with him. They were, as we call them, 'famous last words'. The next court hearing was set for another three months, again to monitor progress.

I was not happy with the Judge's decision for the children to stay overnight or his insult.

It also turned out that grandma did not have enough beds to accommodate all the children. The girls didn't like to stay because they were sleeping in original cot beds that were not big enough for them and Scarlett was sleeping in a double bed which she did not like. I suggested that maybe they invest in bunk beds and then Scarlett could have a cot bed but they refused to do this. Knowing how Scarlett felt I bought a full-sized bed with money I had saved from an endowment that I had and I gave the cot bed, mattress and covers and spare covers all to their grandmother to help contact to proceed more smoothly and give Scarlett her own bed. It just seemed very inappropriate to have a two year old child in a double bed, it must have felt very insecure for her.

The first contact after this hearing was interesting. It was at Grandmas and I dropped them off but I was met with hostility. I was met at the garden gate and was not allowed to go any further. Dave's mother opened the gate for the girls and then closed it as soon as the girls had passed through. Making it very clear that I was going no further onto their property. I noticed that his girlfriend's car was parked in their drive and I then had to ask if she was at the house. I was advised that she wasn't and Dave had borrowed her car. I was then asked if Dave could borrow a car seat for one of the children as he did not have his own. My car seats were Isofix, which meant they clipped into my car seats, and upon examining his car it was decided that they would not fit in and therefore he could not borrow one of mine. I advised him that he would need to sort this out in order to transport the girls when he returned them home on the Saturday. It was the strangest feeling being without my babies and I really couldn't relax. My Mum and Dad had arrived to visit me so they could be around for me. They knew that I would find it hard to be without my girls. The following morning, I got up and went for a run just to relax me and process all my thoughts. I wanted to use my time positively and this was the best way I knew how. Once I had had a shower and lunch, time started to tick by and it was almost time for the girls to be reunited with me. When he did return the girls, I discovered that he decided to bring the children home to me in his father's car with no seat for Verity, who was five and needed a booster seat and only a sit-on booster for Scarlett, who was two!!! Totally illegal and very irresponsible. So, again, I had to address this with him and text him asking that he provide a seat for Scarlett as she needed to be fully supported and Verity should be on a booster too. Although, his attitude was that he needed to borrow the seat from me. I said that I didn't want to do that in case I had to pick them up in an emergency or should one of us forget to transfer the seat. He agreed he would sort something out.

On the morning of the second contact, I text and asked if he had arranged to get a seat for the car for Scarlett. His text read, "I'm not going to waste my money to get a car seat and I don't see why I should." I therefore refused to send them to contact until he had sorted a seat out. He was very angry with me and refused to sort the seat so I stood my ground, which took a lot of guts for me, as I would have normally given in. Knowing that he drove like a maniac most of the time, I was not happy for the girls to be transported without the correct seat. A few hours later he sent me a text to say that he had sourced a booster for Scarlett. He had wasted a day of contact with his children because he was being awkward and stubborn.

Within six weeks of the overnight stays starting (so basically, only two contacts) Olivia was returned to me on a Saturday night looking very white. As soon as she stepped out of the car I could see she was unwell. I asked her if she was okay and she said that she felt ill. I felt her head and she had a searing temperature. I asked her grandmother if she had been okay. She said that Olivia had complained of a headache but that she was fine. I asked if they had given her medicine. They said that they did not have any medicine and they did not see a need to buy any. The children came inside. Olivia wanted to go to bed. I took her temperature it was 41 degrees. I put the light on to give her medicine and she cried and asked me to turn it off as she couldn't bear the light. I rang NHS direct and within 5 minutes an ambulance was racing Olivia and I to the hospital. Luckily, my Mum and Dad were staying with me so they could stay with Verity and Scarlett. Obviously, there was a concern that she had meningitis. She was rushed to A and E and put on a stronger dose of ibuprofen to get the temperature down. It took four hours and eventually, her temperature dropped. She was compos mentis and could talk again. The panic over, we were sent home. My neighbour, Mandy turned up to be with me and took us home. The doctors diagnosed severe tonsillitis and that if she had been given medication at an earlier stage, she would never have got to quite the severe state she was in. I cannot tell you the distress that this caused me. The fact that they would not buy some medicine for a little girl who was poorly was beyond me. My mind couldn't comprehend what was going on in their heads.

Trying to communicate with Dave was virtually impossible and it appeared that the only way I could convey a message to him was via my solicitor. I advised my solicitor of the situation and she sent quite a terse letter to remind Dave and his family that whilst the children were in their care it is their responsibility to be able to provide medical care and car seats. There was also a dispute with Dave about the girls' clothes. I would pack the girls with all their clothes that they needed and more for a night and Scarlett would have extra clothes, just in case of accidents. Then whilst they were with him he would be texting me asking me why I hadn't provided wellies or shoes or trainers. I would tell him to go and buy them some if what I provided wasn't sufficient. At this point he was not paying any bills and I was surviving off savings and goodwill of my parents to provide us with food. He was going out to shows and London for the day and clubbing but still expected me to provide for all the children's needs. That all sounds very bitter but to be fair I couldn't understand why he would think like that and his parents as well. He could not have a reasonable conversation with me about anything. Through a solicitors' letter, I suggested that maybe they could provide some clothes/shoes for the children to be kept at the grandparents so it felt more like a home from home for them. He was quite disgruntled at this by his solicitor's response but his mother did take them shopping and she bought them some clothes and wellies. I could tell that they didn't like being told but none of his family were even trying to listen to me.

All of these things seem probably nit-picking but actually, all of these things are important to make sure that trust is built and that the best interest of the children are met. It is very wearing dealing with someone who argues over every little point and will only take notice once a solicitor's letter is issued.

Whilst all these things were trying to sort themselves out my intuition was working overtime. I was worried he was planning something behind my back. For some reason, I decided to go on a club website that we used to book our caravan holidays through, just to check our account. There I found that Dave had made a booking for ten days to take the children away in a few weeks with him and his girlfriend and her son. I just couldn't understand where this man was coming from. Was it me? Was he delusional? Was he planning to take them without my permission? I didn't know the answers to these questions. He hadn't even got full contact with them and introducing his other half was out of the question at that point and yet he was blatantly forging ahead to book a holiday for them all. They weren't even really enjoying staying one night and ten days away from their main carer was unthinkable at that point. It is hard enough for a mother who has a good relationship with their ex but not under the current circumstances and the lack of trust that I had in him at that point, this was unthinkable. I contacted the solicitor and she sent an email to address the matter appropriately.

It was quite heart wrenching taking them to contact, trying to stay positive. I would take my Mum or Mandy with me, for safety reasons, as Dave was still very angry with me and I could not hide my fear, even for the sake of the children. Olivia would not want to go but they would go and kiss me goodbye. There would normally be tears from Verity and she would wet the bed the night before and during her stay.

On their return, they would tell me what they had been doing and a lot of the time, Scarlett had been left out of the equation or had been left to play on her own. I found all this very hard to deal with but remained upbeat and encouraging for their sake.

The next event in the contact has to be the most painful and upsetting moment a mother can go through. I also appreciate that there will be people out there that have experienced much worse and I can only offer my sympathies. For me this was very traumatic.

It was the weekend of Olivia and Verity's birthday. With only three days between their birthdays a joint celebration was planned. A friend of mine had a printing company and had made a huge banner for the house. We planned to have balloons everywhere and a joint party on the Sunday with all their friends from school, 44 children in total.

The girls didn't really want to go to contact on this particular weekend with it being Verity's birthday on the Friday and Olivia's on the Monday. I told the girls that they would have fun and they would be receiving lots of presents from other members of the family and getting another party. It softened the angst. I made the most of the Friday with Verity before school giving her presents and singing 'Happy Birthday' to her. After school, I made sure that we had extra presents to give her and cards that arrived in the post that day. My parents were staying so they made a fuss of her as well. We even had an extra cake so she could blow out her candles before they all departed.

During the day, I packed all their clothes, including lovely party dresses, as apparently, the grandparents wanted to do a little family party at their house. I felt a little sad that they weren't going to be with me but I knew it was only one night and it would give me the time to decorate the house and make their cakes ready for their big birthday party on the Sunday.

I dropped the girls at their grandma's house and their Dad was there but was very off with me. I was never allowed to get beyond the garden gate and handover was very awkward. He would not even try to be polite to me in front of the children. Their aunt was also there with her two boys but she did not make an appearance.

I spent all of Saturday morning baking cakes, icing the cakes and decorating the house. I always bake all of the girls a special birthday cakes, every year – it's a done deal and every year I am challenged by the type of cake they may like. My friend with the banner arrived and there was a hive of activity with banners being raised and balloons being hung. My neighbours, Mandy and her husband, Paul, came out and helped and we had such a lovely day. At 3.55pm my lovely day turned into a whole sequence of events that I never want to go through again. Dave's Mum called me to say that Scarlett had hurt her knee and all she wanted was me and was inconsolable, but it wasn't serious enough to take her to hospital. In the background, I could hear her screaming. The screaming was the worst I have ever heard and I knew my baby was in excruciating pain.

"Bring them home now," I said.

"Ok, well I think it's best as she doesn't want anyone else but you," his mum replied almost uncaring.

I put the phone down. My stomach was churning; I was starting to panic. Maybe I should have gone to get her. I tried to calm my nerves, they only lived 15 minutes away and they will be here soon. I waited and I clock watched, where were they? Twenty-five minutes had gone by. I asked my Mum if I should go and get Scarlett. However, if I went now, I may pass them in the car and more time would be wasted. I paced up and down, watching out of the window. I knew in my heart of hearts that this was not just a matter of a mummy cuddle that she would need. I walked to the end of the drive looking for their car coming towards the house. No sign. Mandy came out as she saw me pacing up and down. She tried to relax me and reassure me that everything would be ok. She came back into the house with me and my parents. At 4.55pm they arrived, an hour later. Grandma apologised and said that they needed to collect all the girls' things up first before they came to me!!!! Seriously!! Dave got out of the car complaining that Scarlett had been a nightmare and all she wanted was me. I grabbed her from the back seat and she turned to me sobbing, "mummy, I need a doctor," she was two years old!! Her left leg was limp and she couldn't stand up.

His mother talked at me, "I don't think there's too much wrong with her. She wouldn't take any medicine from me so she must be okay."

I was stunned, as I could see she was in pain and she couldn't stand on her leg. The other girls got out of the car subdued. Olivia mentioned that Scarlett had not stopped screaming. I ushered them into the house and their grandmother and father unashamedly drove away.

I let my Dad have Olivia and Verity and I put Scarlett in my car and I took her along with my Mum to the local Accident and Emergency hospital 45 minutes away.

We arrived at 5.50pm. Scarlett was given medicine straight away by the triage nurse and then I was asked for the circumstances leading up to the event and how it had happened. I was unclear so I rang Dave's mother. She advised that she had Scarlett on her hip to take her over to see the lambs in the field across the road from their house, she had slipped on the wet ground and had fallen on her! I asked what time this was and she could not give me a time but advised it was around lunch. All I could think about was Scarlett screaming and crying in pain. We had X-rays carried out but they could not see any issues. Scarlett was still crying in pain and eventually she was seen by a consultant at 8pm. He could not see anything wrong with her x-rays but was very concerned when he tried to get her to stand and she couldn't. My Mum pointed out to him about her floppy left foot. He removed her shoe and sock and her ankle was so swollen. He sent her for further X-rays and discovered her tibia and fibula were completely snapped at ankle level. I was upset and the realisation of what had actually happened to this little girl distressed me. It takes quite something to break the bones of a two-year-old.

Scarlett was sent to get her leg plastered and at this point she was still sobbing, it was now 9.30pm and I cried with her as I couldn't hold it back anymore, it was heart-breaking. I then wiped my tears and composed myself. Her leg was set in plaster but they needed the consultant to confirm that it was set correctly. The consultant attended about 10pm and advised that it needed to done again. So, they removed the plaster and started again, only leading to more distress for Scarlett. Again, it was not correct and they removed and re-plastered the whole leg up to her thigh/hip. At this point we were advised that Scarlett was going to be placed on a ward. The consultant felt that she may need an operation and pins placed in her ankle to help the repair. It was midnight now and at last Scarlett was starting to calm down. The ward staff made me a bed next to Scarlett and I called my brother to come and collect my Mum so she could be with my Dad and the two girls. My brother came into the ward room and he struggled to hold himself together, as Scarlett was still very upset. He had to leave the room as she was crying, he could see how much pain she was in and it had made him cry. It was a very distressing time but I knew that I needed to remain composed.

I had kept Scarlett's Dad and my brother constantly updated with what was going on, as well as messaging friends to get the word out that the party for Olivia and Verity would not be going ahead. I was overwhelmed with messages of love from friends who had found out where we were. When Scarlett eventually settled in the early hours of the morning I was approached by a lovely staff nurse who asked how Scarlett had broken her leg. She felt that the situation was a little suspicious and advised that if her Dad had taken her to hospital Social Services would have been brought in; as she was in a contact situation and not with her primary carer. Questions had started to whizz around in my head. If the walk was at lunchtime that means that there must have been a considerable delay from the moment of the accident to them contacting me. Why would you wait that long? Why would you fall on a child and not take them to hospital?

My car was in the hospital car park and early the next morning a very good friend of mine, Karen messaged me and asked if I wanted the car taken home so as to avoid extortionate car parking fees. I agreed and Karen and her partner, Jack, popped in to see Scarlett then took my car keys and delivered it home for me. At this point I was still waiting to hear from the Consultant as to whether Scarlett would be taken down to surgery for pins to be placed in her leg. The Consultant was very good and he visited quite early in the morning to advise that, due to Scarlett's age, they felt that the bones would heal without having to perform surgery. He did feel however that they would like to keep her in one more night to observe her and to ensure her leg did not swell as the cast went all the way up to the top of her thigh. This was such a huge relief for me. As soon as I had this information to hand, I rang my Mum and Dad to let them know. I then messaged Dave to let him know. Unfortunately, with her father it started a whole barrage of questioning and accusations that we were not really in hospital because my car was at home. He had obviously been watching the house and had seen that my car was now back. I felt quite sickened at this accusation and threatened that he was watching the house. I got a text message from Dave that said that I must have over-dramatized Scarlett's leg because I was at home. I advised him that I was still at the hospital and staying another night. I couldn't believe how callous he could be. This poor little girl was in so much pain and he's playing games. I might add, that at no point during her stay in hospital over the two days did he attempt to come to the hospital or ask to see her or phone to see how she was. The fact that he could not grasp how serious the injury was that Scarlett had incurred and now, he was trying to say that I had lied about staying in hospital and the operation begs belief. My brain was struggling to take any more on board and the possibility that we were being observed was frightening.

For a long time, I had realised that he had been watching the house. I don't know how he did it. I'm not sure if he had cameras set up or he was driving by but I had several incidents where he would text me when a friend was there to say that he knew they were with me. Vicky came one night and we hadn't had much contact for a while. She arrived in her new car, so he wouldn't have known it was her, and within half an hour of her being at the house he messaged me to say that he knew she was visiting. He even sent me a text once that said he knew my Mum and Dad were staying and he wanted to know how much rent they were going to be paying him. I had to try and ignore all of these silly, pathetic game playing tactics. I may have played it down but inside it felt very uncomfortable and I didn't like it, but I was trying to show that it didn't bother me. It put my brain on high alert. Every time I came or went from the house, I found myself scanning the area to see if I could see anyone watching without trying to get too neurotic about it.

The same evening, I was approached by a member of the nursing staff who advised me that my husband was on the phone and was asking questions about Scarlett. Because of our situation, they would not give him any information without my permission. So, not only did he not believe me, he was checking with the hospital to see if we were still there. It didn't feel as though he was concerned with how she was. The nursing staff asked if I wanted him to be advised of Scarlett's situation and I told them that I was quite happy for them to impart any information they felt necessary. They went back and advised him that the operation had been decided against and Scarlett was having a second night in hospital under observation. I cannot fault the staff on the ward in the hospital; they were absolutely super.

The girls wanted to come and see Scarlett and my brother very kindly picked them up with my Mum to bring them in. Although, in hindsight, it wasn't the best idea as Olivia got extremely upset about Scarlett being in hospital and was almost distraught at seeing the cast on her leg. Then she didn't want to go home without us. However, I wanted to see them and also wanted them to know that Scarlett was going to be fine. I had to do a lot of cuddles and reassurance that we would be home the following day, as it was Olivia's Birthday.

It was a very uncomfortable stay at the hospital, not because of the hospitality but the put-up beds are never the same as your own and I think for two nights I must have watched Scarlett all night with one eye open, in case she needed me. She was also being dosed up with ibuprofen and paracetamol on a regular basis to reduce the pain.

The following morning, quite early, the Consultant visited to advise that we could go home and that we would have a follow up appointment in four weeks; sooner if need be; to see how Scarlett was healing. I was given instructions on pain relief and we were allowed to leave. He advised that her plaster would need to have a top layer put on to protect it. We were wheeled down to a side room where a purple plaster outer layer was applied to Scarlett's leg. My brother came to the hospital to pick us up. Scarlett was very uncomfortable travelling as she was in a five-harness booster seat and the plaster kept pinching the top of her leg, so we had to prop her leg up and support it as well as we could to get her in the seat. A full leg cast is actually very heavy. I was relieved we were coming home and Scarlett was no longer screaming in pain.

My Mum had brought my diary for me to the hospital and during the quiet times when Scarlett could finally get some comatosed sleep, I sat and I wrote. It got all that was in my head on paper again and then I could let the information go and prepare for the next phase. It was helping me to release some of my emotions. I was extremely tired so some of my entries were short but healing nevertheless. Reading them back gave me some clarity of the series of events.

Diary Entry

22/4/2012 – Consultant advised at 8am that no operation but Scarlett would need to stay one more night and be re-plastered Monday. Jan, Mum, Dad, girls, Mike, Becky (his wife) and Layla (their daughter) have all visited. Dave nor his mum and dad did not even ask to visit.

23/4/2012 - Scarlett got re-plastered and we went home after lunch. Mike came to pick us up. Had a Birthday celebration for Olivia but in her own words, "my Birthday has been spoilt". The next few days have been a blur. Scarlett in pain screaming in the night and very clingy. The girls seem traumatised and also very clingy.

We arrived home to lots of hugs and kisses. The girls were so pleased to have Mummy and their sister home. I had made two humungous cakes and now seemed an appropriate moment to do candles and cake cutting and some Birthday singing.

Still lots of questions had been whizzing around in my head; why did they wait so long? why take boots off and put shoes on?

Whilst we were having cake and tea Olivia decided to tell us that she was glad Scarlett was ok now, "Scarlett screamed when she hurt her leg and I heard her leg crack when grandma fell over. It was a horrible noise."

"Really," I said curiously, "what happened then, Olivia?"

"I asked Grandma if Scarlett had broken her leg and Grandma said that I was being silly." There was a short pause and she continued, "Daddy lost his temper and he was swearing."

I think the whole room went silent.

She continued, "Grandma went back to their house with Scarlett and we went with Daddy to go and look at the lambs. Then when we got back to the house, Scarlett was lying on the sofa crying really hard and didn't want to take medicine but was crying out for you, mummy."

"Oh, was she Olivia," I felt a sadness in my voice.

"Yes, then Daddy smacked her to stop her crying. She wouldn't stop crying."

I think at that point I could feel my blood boiling.

"and then what, Olivia?" I was intrigued by the events that had taken place.

"Well, grandma took clothes off as they were very muddy and then she put them in the washing machine and dried them so that Scarlett had her clothes on that you sent to go back home in. Daddy got angry because Scarlett would not stop crying and he rang Tracey. Then he started swearing *a lot,* so grandma told me and Verity to go up to the bedroom and shut the door."

"Why did grandma put you in the bedroom?" I was now fuming but trying not to show how I felt.

"Well, we were crying as well, so grandma thought we would be better in the bedroom." Olivia then distracted herself with a toy and the conversation tailed off.

I'm not sure if Olivia and Verity were locked in or just in the bedroom but to this day, Olivia struggles to go anywhere where she may have to lock a door or have it shut. Apparently, all Scarlett did was cry and call out for me and eventually she slept (that would be the shock kicking in), her grandmother had told me this on the handover, then she woke again and starting the screaming again which is when they rang me. I think I could have been physically sick at that point. I was stunned but I had to remain composed for the children.

There would have been a delay of approximately two and a half to three hours before they contacted me. It was also made aware to me that if Dave had taken Scarlett to hospital social services would have been called in straight away but if I took her she is no longer in his care and they don't get called in!!! I believe this is the reason they did not take her to hospital but instead let her suffer. My little baby was in pain and this woman, who was supposed to a be a responsible adult supervising contact had fallen on Scarlett and did not have the intelligence to take her to the local hospital. All I can say is the room was in stunned silence.

Then the telephone rang. I answered it to be told that it was a representative of CAFCASS (The Children and Family Court Advisory and Support Service). CAFCASS are brought in when there is child protection issue and have to assess whether or not contact is appropriate or safe or in the child/children's best interest. They look after the welfare of children who are involved in family court. I was quite shocked to hear who was on the other end of the phone but I listened carefully. They had been advised of Scarlett's situation and were not happy about the circumstances in which the accident occurred and were very keen to get to the bottom of how it happened and why her father did not take her straight to hospital himself. Neither was I, having heard what Olivia had to tell us. The directive from CAFCASS was that Scarlett was not to be in her father's care until an investigation was carried out into the accident and the circumstances surrounding it and further instructions would be given by the Court. I took the information on board. When I put the phone down I turned and looked at my Mum.

"What was that all about, Jennifer?" she said inquisitively.

"It's being investigated," I was still digesting the information. My intuition had been rumbling and this confirmed everything that I had questioned.

"What? Scarlett?" my Mum said in a hushed whisper.

"Yes, Mum," my Dad looked at me concerned but said nothing.

Today was about Olivia and Verity. We needed to make sure they had a lovely birthday. I turned my attention back to them. We carried on with our day just enjoying being all together, playing and eating cake. Scarlett sat on the sofa, propped up with cushions and enjoyed being fussed over by the girls.

CAFCASS had instructed that a full investigation (Section 47 Referral) of the case be done. Therefore, a social worker was appointed to take details from everyone involved. The social worker was a lovely young lady and the girls took to her straight away. Her report was non-conclusive I might add, as Dave was more interested in running me down than discussing the issue. I believe she found him quite difficult and unreasonable to deal with. The report was supposed to be provided for the next court hearing but it was delayed. Upon the eve of the third court hearing no report had appeared and therefore this made a very difficult situation for the Judge.

Now I also need to tell you at this point. That my disgust at the last Judge meant that I had written to the Ombudsman about him complaining about his attitude towards me and the fact that he assured me that none of my children would come to harm. This meant that whilst the complaint was being looked into he had to be removed from my case. Which I was very happy about. The next Court Hearing was interesting.

Life was just spiralling for Jennifer. How was this fun? What was coming next? Why was this all happening to a happy-go-lucky, loving, friendly girl?

Chapter Twenty

Another Hearing

Along with everything else that was occurring, thrown into the equation was a letter, written by Julie, expressing her very strong opinion about myself following my text to her. She also had her opinion on what had happened the day of Scarlett's accident (of which she was not present). A letter which she decided she would send to my Mum and Dad, my Dad who was of poor health, and my brother, Mike. She had also enclosed a copy of a letter from CAFCASS which advised that they would be investigating the accident with Scarlett. Mike, who is a high-powered businessman was infuriated by this letter, reacted and actually picked up the phone and called her. She did not answer but he left her a message to say that she needed to get both sides of the story before she started making accusations and he told her to leave my Mum and Dad alone as my Dad is of poor health and does not need her interfering. I'm not one for reacting to these things but on this occasion, I felt 'Good on him'.

The letter referred to how Dave had made our home secure and how he had improved it to make life more comfortable. It also mentioned the fact that she knew how unhappy I was in the marriage and that I had sought legal advice, which she was party to. She inferred that the children required love from both parents, which was never questioned by myself, but that we needed to show a harmonious front for their benefit! Julie then went on to talk about our last meeting and how my text message had cut her off completely and had apparently said that I wanted no further contact. Her letter stated that she felt she had to remain impartial and keep a distance so as not to upset anyone but had been glad to be invited to Dave's parents to see the girls. She had addressed this letter to people who already knew everything that was going on and not just from a one-sided perspective. She went on to say that she had read the CAFCASS communication and felt very sad that people were being accused when Scarlett had only had an accident and received minor fractures!!! She then went on to refer to the fact that Dave had spent all his money on legal fees and felt that this was such a pointless exercise and that I was on a quest to destroy him and I was ripping the girls away from their other family and that was unforgiveable. She spoke in the letter as though my family were unaware of the circumstances. It felt very condescending, very one-sided and actually it was not her place to comment.

I was truly upset by this intervention and my diary entry read:

Today I had a very upsetting phone call from Mike. He has told me that both he and my parents have received a letter from Julie. He was absolutely disgusted at the accusations that have been made and infuriated by the nature of the letter. So much so that he has rung her to put her straight. I felt sick and shaky and very sad that she could do such a thing. My Mum, Dad and brother have been through everything with me and are fully aware of what has been happening. The thing that upset me the most was that she referred to Scarlett's leg and said that she had only fractured it!! Two complete breaks are not fractures. This has to be ignorance at the highest level. What was she trying to achieve?

I presented the letter to my barrister. I felt that the letter actually showed that her sympathies lay with the other party. I was upset as this was my friend of fifteen years. My other concern was that she was copying and sending out a letter from CAFCASS to other parties and the letter was addressed to Dave. Any information on the children is confidential and, therefore, there could be serious consequences to her actions. A lot of judgements were made in this letter, which I found interesting, bearing in mind that there had been no contact since before Scarlett's birthday, over ten months ago.

During this period, I had also received correspondence from Dave via my solicitor that he would now be representing himself. He had declared in his email that he had spent over £19,000 on solicitors' fees and could no longer carry on paying legal fees. There were interesting times to come.

The day of the hearing arrived and the Judge was not impressed with all that had happened and in fact, advised Dave that the correspondence relating to the children was not for him to share with all and sundry. He then said that my brother should not have done what he did and the third parties need to stay out of the equation. Because the CAFCASS report could not be presented the only contact the Judge could authorise was that Dave could visit the house for half an hour on a Saturday morning, from 10am until 10.30am, before taking the girls away for the day but they would have to be returned by 7pm as he could not grant overnight contact until the report was in. He also advised that I would need someone present in the house with me whilst contact was taking place for my own safety. This was a huge thing for me as I had not let Dave into the house since he had assaulted me. He then advised that another hearing would not be reconvened until after the cast had been removed, also providing time for Scarlett to recover, so in eight weeks. His telephone contact was moved to a Friday between 5.30pm and 6pm due to the fact that it was disrupting the girls and their school work and he wasn't always ringing.

Underlying just the basic need for contact to continue, the incidents that I was dealing with and the safety of all of this, was the fact that I was receiving no income. I was dealing with the CSA (Child Support Agency – for those of you unaware of who they are) every day. Their job was to assess how much Dave would need to pay me in maintenance. I can honestly say, in my case, because my husband was self-employed, they had no power to enforce anything. He would show he wasn't making a profit and they would say, "he can't pay, his business isn't earning him any money". I had a counsellor visiting every week to check that we were all okay and the girls were having counselling in school to help them. I held regular meetings with the school and there were phone calls backwards and forwards between social services and CAFCASS. Scarlett was recovering well and there were regular visits and check-ups at the hospital which were never particularly quick.

Due to the lack of money coming into the house, I couldn't afford to hold onto the family car. We had an Audi Q7 and it was super but very thirsty and very expensive to run. I was putting £98 a fortnight in fuel in the tank. It was due its service, it needed four new tyres and the tyres alone were going to cost me £1000. There was no way I could carry on trying to run this vehicle. I contacted the garage I bought it from and they agreed they would do a straight forward swap for me. They had a new smaller car which was very economical to run. This in itself turned out to be a saga. I had to prove that the Audi was owned by myself. When I turned up at the garage to do the deal, I had to provide paperwork to say that I had permission to sell the car. They insisted on ringing Dave and that caused all sorts of issues. He was telling them that I couldn't sell it. He wanted to buy the car from me and he wanted my private plate off the car as well. I didn't want to accept his offer. At the end of the day, we had verbally agreed in our many conversations about finance that he keep the caravan and I have the car for the children. His offer was for only £9,000 and I knew the car was worth more than that. After a lot of telephone conversations and me speaking to my solicitor, a lot of tears and four hours later, the deal was done, as they had ascertained that the car was registered to me and he could not stop me selling it. Another battle over. He did make everything as difficult as possible. The private plate he agreed to buy from the garage and they arranged that. But it was a strange request as the number plate was something I chose for my 40th Birthday, so you would think, as he wasn't very keen on me at this point, he would not want it. Anyway, each to his own, who am I to question his thinking at this point.

The next few weeks were difficult. With assistance from either my Mum or Mandy, Dave and his Mum would come to the house on days of contact and see Scarlett. However, it was really weird as the interaction between Scarlett and her Dad would be very small and he spent most of his time, along with his mother talking to the two eldest girls.

These half hours in the house were the longest hours of my life. Scarlett, to be fair, was very upbeat. She is a lesson to us all of how someone can bounce back. She carried on playing in her own little world and it was me that amused her whilst her Dad and grandma visited.

It was after the second one of these contacts that I felt disturbed the most. Olivia and Verity had returned from their grandparents with their Dad and grandma. They came in and gave Scarlett a big hug as they were not used to being apart on the weekends. Olivia then went on to tell me about her day with Daddy and I smiled and listened intently, as Olivia is quite funny when she is explaining things and you have keep up with her train of thought and explanation as she tends to go off on tangents. My smiles turned to shock though when she started to explain that she had been shown a video of Scarlett.

"What video of Scarlett, honey," my heart sank into my stomach.

"Daddy showed us a video of Scarlett when she was crying," her expression was so innocent as she continued, "the day of her accident when she broke her leg."

I was stunned into disbelief and a wave of emotion came over me, tears rolling down my cheeks, "Daddy videoed Scarlett when she was screaming in pain, Olivia. The day she broke her leg?"

"Yes, Mummy," completely unaware of the implications of what she had just told me.

I couldn't believe her Dad could do such a thing. Why would you video a child in pain but not have the common sense to take her to hospital and why, oh why, would you then show the video to your two eldest children? This was all beyond me. I was disgusted, my stomach turned. I wrote down everything that had been said later that evening and the following Monday I rang and spoke to CAFCASS and social services. They both made a note of what had occurred but both informed me that if they approached my husband he would obviously deny that he had done any such thing on his phone and he would delete it to make sure that there was no evidence. This is when you start to learn that children are pure and innocent and couldn't make these things up if they tried but their word means very little. My view of this man that I had married and lived with for all those years was becoming more and more obscured.

Why had this all happened? What had I learned from the events over the past few months? It had certainly tested my ability to remain calm in a storm but how had we even gone down this path? The happy-go-lucky Jennifer had had it all; the cars, the cottage in the country, a great job, beautiful children, a great best friend. This had all changed and she was now in the middle of a whirlwind of events that escalated beyond anything she had ever experienced or known. She knew she was strong, a good mum, positive, intelligent and balanced in her view. This situation was certainly testing all of these for her. There was something more and it was keeping her safe. She knew that the universe somehow was working in her favour and she trusted it. She had to, there was no other choice than to travel the path and see where it led.

Chapter Twenty-One

Be Strong and Carry On

Life settled down again for a couple of weeks until the next contact. Every contact was bizarre as Dave would use it as an opportunity to collect items from the house. When I asked my solicitor about this she told me to stop giving him these things as this will be sorted when the house was sold. I gave him LPs/DVDs and other things that he asked for and then told him that contact was not an opportunity to reclaim these items. Within this four-month period other little things were coming to light. Dave had requested a change of contact on one of the weekends due to him having an operation. He had told the girls that he was having a mole removed. My solicitor then asked for evidence of the operation in order to be able to change the contact. It was also Easter weekend and I believe that he had really booked to go away on holiday. I wasn't being awkward but due to there being a court order in place, apparently, it is normal to ask for an appointment confirmation and then contact days can be changed accordingly. This evidence was never provided. It came to light later on that he had been into hospital and spent £2,500 on a vasectomy reversal (the evidence being a new born baby to him and his new wife later that year).

The house had been on the market from the time that the separation occurred but we had had very little interest with a recession in full swing, houses were not selling very quickly. I was now responsible for all the bills, including the mortgage and I was very worried about how long I could continue to maintain payments. I spent a lot of time keeping the house tidy, keeping the garden dug over and lawns mowed. Little by little the price was reduced. There would be a spurt of interest and then it would be sporadic shows of interest. I was very panicked as the only income I had was tax credits, child support and initially I was getting some mortgage relief. Every month I would ring Santander Bank to ask if Dave had paid the mortgage and every month I got the same response that he hadn't and that they didn't mind who the money came from as we were both jointly liable for the debt. I had savings, an endowment from when I had owned a flat and some premium bonds that I had bought after selling my flat. I cashed everything in and bit by bit used it to pay the mortgage and keep the house going. I had asked Dave several times if he would be contributing, as did my solicitor and was advise that he couldn't afford to. In actual fact, he sent me a text message saying 'I'm not paying the mortgage. I'd rather you be repossessed than contribute towards you staying in the house'. He still didn't understand that this was his children's' home. A very sad moment when a parent cannot see that actually this wasn't about me, this was about them. He was so wrapped up in his anger towards me that he could not see the damage he was doing. Every message he sent I could feel the energy of his anger and resentment.

The fifth hearing was in the July and due to the Section 47 and Section 7 report not being carried out by social services the hearing had to be adjourned. We attended Court as normal and went through all the procedures of pre-court meetings with my Barrister. The hearing was being heard by a Judge who had been at a previous hearing with us. Dave sat alone. The Judge addressed the issues with contact and all that had happened with Scarlett. He turned to Dave to ask him some basic questions about his contact and Dave showed his true colours. His aggression was plain to see and he started to answer the Judge back. He had no representation at this hearing and thought that he could bully his way through it. The Judge turned on him and told him that he was showing signs of behaviour that correlated to the court reports that I had presented to them and that this wasn't showing him in a good light. He was advised that he needed to conduct himself in an appropriate way whilst in court. The sixth hearing was to be in the October to give Social Services time to collect the information they would need and present to the court an assessment of the risk that the children were under during their time in contact. In the meantime, the contact would remain the same.

All of the hearings so far in the proceedings had insisted that due to the fact that there had been several incidents during contact, that Dave was not to introduce his girlfriend into the equation. The contact was an opportunity for him to bond with the girls and this hadn't really happened.

A week after the last hearing the girls went to contact, Scarlett stayed at home with me. Upon their return, they were always excited to see me and I believe that they had a good time as I know their grandmother always did lovely things with them. Olivia is very chatty and always has a lot to say. On this particular occasion, she happened to mention that Daddy had got them to speak to his girlfriend on the phone and that whilst they had been at grandmas they got to meet her son who was staying there for the day. All I could do was sigh with pity. Yet again, he could not behave himself. I was also a little sad for the girls as this contact day was about them and not Daddy looking after someone else's child. This contact was forbidden and a solicitors' letter was sent. For me, the saddest part is the fact that at no point was the court hearings or contact about seeing the girls, it was about him getting his own way, at whatever cost and not considering anyone else's feelings in the process. I sometimes wonder how I came out the other end but I did and it is about staying mentally strong and letting people help you. I had spent six years of my life supporting this man in any way I could, emotionally, financially and spiritually. I had done everything I could to keep our relationship together and it wasn't enough. Even providing him with the most beautiful, intelligent, loving children wasn't enough. I realised that you cannot be the only one to give in a relationship. The more I gave, the more he expected but he wasn't prepared to give in return, at any cost.

Lorraine Butterfield

Behind the scenes, I had constant contact with the CSA still and I was writing letters to and receiving letters from the Ombudsman regarding the Judge who had granted overnight contact. He had assured me that no harm would come to my children whilst they were with their father and he was wrong. No one person has the right to make that judgement. I had meetings with solicitors, counsellors, school and social services. Not to mention the disruption the family had every time contact took place. The bed wetting, the stories they came home with, the fact that Daddy was asking them to keep secrets about the new car he was having or the things he was saying about me. He even sent out an electrician to the house because we had a problem with the lights and then sent me a bill for the repair. I sent the bill back to his electrician and wrote to his Mum and Dad to make them aware that he was not paying any bills and that with all the outgoings that I had, I was not in a position to pay any more bills. I never heard another word.

Many a person would have crumbled but I marched on. I have to say I had a very small but very select group of friends who stood by me the whole of the time. You have to trust people during these very stressful periods however hard it may be. My friend Andrea was also another very good friend and throughout the court process, being a legal beagle herself, gave me many valuable bits of information, advised me when things got nasty on how to react (or not react in most cases). I have been very blessed that these people came and stood by my side and I believe they are all earth angels that were sent to guide and help me through this very tough period in my life. I can never thank them enough for everything that they did because life became a little tougher.

Because we were selling the house and I knew that I would have to downsize I had started to sort out the house. Things I would need and things I would not take with me. I used some of the money I had cashed in to buy a sofa that would fit in a smaller house and psychologically it was to make me feel better. I felt I needed furniture that was mine and that I didn't owe Dave anything and he could have all that he wanted. I wrapped up his leather sofas very carefully and placed them in the oak garage outside making sure that they were well protected and then I sorted other things and boxed them so that if we had to move quickly I wouldn't have it all to take on in one go.

During the next contact, the girls had told Daddy all about the new sofa. It took about ten minutes of them being with him when he started to text me about having his old sofas. The legal stance is that until the house is sold none of the items within the house are to be removed. Also, due to the fact that he was very unpleasant to me and could not be trusted to behave appropriately, it was deemed that he should not set foot upon the premises unless it was to drop off during contact or related to contact in any way. I told him that he could have his sofas when the house had been sold and he would have his opportunity to collect any of the contents of the house that will be agreed to when we get to that point. He must have spent all morning texting me. This was supposed to be his time with his children and with the very little time that he had I felt extremely sad that all he could think about was items of furniture. I wondered how the children were and what his mood must have been like, then I worried in case he was taking out his mood on them. Not one contact went by when I didn't worry about the moods he got into and how this was affecting our children. It's not healthy for one to be so obsessed about possessions.

Dave, being Dave, couldn't let this matter lie. By the following week, he was threatening to come to the house for everything that he wanted. I tried to tell him that he could not do this. I then got a text late one night to say that he would be turning up the following morning at 9.30am to pick up his items. I spoke with Mandy next door and she said that her and her husband, would make sure they were around for me. I then managed to get hold of my solicitor on her personal mobile number and she advised me that I needed to contact the police as he had been told that he was not allowed onto the property without my permission. I dialled the local police. They are always so helpful and I explained the situation to them. By having a history marker on the property, they were fully aware of the incidents that had taken place at the property. They advised me that once the two eldest girls were at school I was to come back with Scarlett and close all the curtains making sure all the windows and doors were locked and go upstairs on the landing. I am presuming this is due to the fact that if anything were thrown through the windows we would not be in danger. They advised me that he was not to set foot in the house. They would send a police presence whilst he collected his items from the garage. I was advised to call them as soon as he arrived at the house.

The following morning, I remember feeling very nervous and on edge. I got the girls ready as I did every morning but there was a different feel in the air today, one of apprehension and fear. During the time that we had split up I had developed shaky hands and had been diagnosed with Raynaud's disease, along with losing lots of weight. I dropped the girls to school and drove back home. I remember my stomach just constantly churning over. Scarlett was sat in the back, smiling. She always has a smile on her face. She is my little crystal child. I arrived back at the house and Mandy came out to me. We went inside and did as we had been told; shut the windows and doors, ensuring that all were locked and shut the curtains. We headed upstairs, telephone in my hand and from the landing I could already hear somebody pulling onto the drive. I quickly went to the bedroom window to glance out and caught sight of Dave's truck and his father's car on the drive and five men (some of whom worked with him and one who was his parents' neighbour). It felt very intimidating. Moving back to the landing I dialled the local police who advised they were sending a car out and they would be attending shortly. Scarlett at this time thought we were playing a game of hide and seek with her. She found this quite amusing but I am sure that she would have picked up on the tense energy that surrounded us all at that point.

Dave approached the house and knocked the door. Mandy, who I thought was very brave, went downstairs and opened the door to him. He went to put his foot in the door, "why are you opening my front door to my house?"

Very gently Mandy spoke to Dave, "don't be silly, Dave, you know you are not to enter the house."

His reaction was to scoff at the remark. He removed his foot and Mandy shut the door and retreated back to the landing to be by my side.

"Thank you," I whispered to her.

Mandy smiled reassuringly, "you're welcome my love. He won't get in here with me around."

At that point, apparently, he called the police as well to get him access to the house. Within five minutes there were two police cars and four policemen in attendance. Mandy peered through the bedroom window to see what was going on. In the meantime, the men that he had brought with him had started to load the sofas and other packed bits in the garage onto the lorry. Mandy came back to the landing to update me. We sat in silence and listened for activity. Then we heard some talking on the driveway and eventually there was another knock at the door. Mandy descended the stairs and looked through the spyglass in the door. This time it was one of the policemen. He was actually one of the policemen who had attended the house several times to check on me and make sure we were safe.

He came in, "your husband says that he wants to come in as he has some personal belongings that he wishes to retrieve. How would you feel about this?"

"Ok, but where do I stand? As he has not entered the house since assaulting me and it feels a bit uncomfortable." I felt very nervous and the officer could tell I felt uncomfortable.

"Look, we will walk around with him whilst he collects his personal belongings. Just give me a list of everything he cannot take and we will make sure it is safe. We wouldn't want him causing any criminal damage."

"Ok," I said hesitantly.

"Can you get to your neighbour's house via the back way?"

"No," I said.

Mandy stepped in, "I can take her to my house via the front, if you will walk with us?"

"Brilliant. Thank you for your co-operation," and he really meant it.

He then clarified with me what he couldn't take from the house. I advised that all the furniture in the house was to remain so the children didn't notice any difference along with the TV, DVD player and Humax box and all the bedroom furniture was to remain. At that point, I wasn't even sure that he had any of his personal possessions remaining in the house. Over the several periods of contact from the house I had given him all of his items. Having agreed to this I was escorted by the policeman and Mandy to her house. Mandy at this point was very clever and so as to not upset Scarlett she carried her very purposefully on her left hip to the end of the drive, so that all Scarlett could see was me and Mandy's house and at the end of the drive she changed hip. Again, all Scarlett could see was me and the house. Scarlett was completely oblivious to all the men on the drive and the fact her Daddy was there and was very excited as

Mandy had a dog, called Rosie, and it meant she could have a stroke. Scarlett was, and still is, dog mad.

The policeman then left me there and went back to the house, escorting Dave around the premises.

Half an hour later the policeman knocked at Mandy's door, he came in, "How are you?" he knew I was a little shaken by events.

"I'm okay thank you. Did he get everything that he needed?" I was curious as to what was so important to retrieve.

"Well, the only things he took were a box of old telephones, a flask and a cool box and the small TV off the bedroom wall. In my opinion he did this to intimidate you and that he was showing his bullish behaviour, sadly."

I nodded in agreement but I am sure he really wasn't able to voice that opinion however, it reassured me that I wasn't the only one who felt this way.

During that time, Dave and his men left the premises and the police advised him that now he had all that he required he was not to set foot back on the premises. Another incident over and time to try and get some normality back. I breathed a sigh of relief, even more grateful for the support I was getting along the way.

When you have so many incidents happen in a successive period a lot of it becomes a blur and I am certain there were other events that I have not diarised due to lack of time or lack of sleep or both.

The next court hearing took place several weeks after Scarlett's incident. However, due to the CAFCASS report still not being presented or actioned, the court requested that the contact remain the same and a hearing was postponed for a further few weeks. In fact, the following hearing was the same, as not all the evidence had been gathered to be presented to court, so yet again it was adjourned. This had been going on since the summer.

Chapter Twenty-Two

Social Services Reports

The following weeks that passed consisted of the social worker interviewing all parties involved with contact. Therefore, my Mum, Dad, myself, Olivia, Verity and Scarlett, along with Dave's Mum and Dad and himself. Dave, apparently, was very difficult to interview as he constantly wanted to throw mud in my direction. A theme that he carried through in contact with the children.

Over the whole two-year period of this divorce I had received various correspondence from Dave via solicitors. Some of which I found quite extraordinary. Letters advising that the reason he didn't call was because he was on holiday and had a bad signal or other excuses along those lines. Most of the changes of contacts that were requested were due to him going on holiday. He openly admitted that this is what he was doing which was very hurtful as we had no income from him whatsoever but he was able to holiday. I received letters to the house from Audi finance advising of the finance on a new Audi Q7 and the amounts. Some quite unbelievable information was falling into my hands. But I always believe this information was for a reason and it really does give you a different perspective on how a person is; not that I would judge anyone; but how different people's priorities are. My first amount of maintenance came because I escalated a complaint to the CSA and raised awareness with my local MP who then escalated to a senior MP. Bailiffs were sent in and my first payment of £1,200 was gratefully received and helped pay the mortgage. By this time, Dave had managed to work his accounts so he showed no profit and his assessment by CSA had gone down from £650 a month to £72 a month to £0. I rang the CSA and argued that even people on benefits pay and it was agreed that he would pay £5 per week - a total of £21.75 per month. I received £20 a month so he couldn't even pay that in full. He still owed £700 back pay. It made me sad that this was how he felt we should be treated.

I then attended court for the Financial Hearing. This was held in the same Court room as the contact hearings. This was to be a straight forward court appearance where both parties agreed the split of the house proceeds and any other financial business, e.g. pensions. Our pensions nulled each other out so there was nothing further to do there. Dave at this point still had my engagement and wedding rings which he would show to the girls and on several occasions, Olivia would ask him to return them to me. It was made clear in this hearing that the rings belonged to me and needed to be returned. He agreed to return them to my solicitor but on the condition that I never sold them and kept them for the girls. This made me giggle as this had been a condition that I had placed in my will so that the girls would get my rings upon my death and this was my wish, nothing to do with him. I agreed as this had always been my intention. The split of the house was interesting though. Because Dave had not paid any maintenance, mortgage or bills for over a year it was taken into account and it was considered that the split would be 26% to Dave and 74% to me. This is very rare and I believe doesn't happen very often, if at all. The judge agreed that this was a fair split and Dave was not happy. But he did return my rings to my solicitor and I still have them to this day. I have cleared the energy of the rings as they may have been carrying some bad vibrational energy with them.

Our financial split was agreed and it was now just the contact that we needed to agree on. I was getting stronger the longer we were apart and slowly I was becoming me again, the Jennifer I loved and the Jennifer I missed. I was operating in hyper alert mode, as so many things had happened that I still had that fight or flight energy with me. The running was helping me to release this energy and process all that was happening but I was still very alert at all times. The next hearing was to be the final one and it was going to change everything.

Chapter Twenty-Three

Final Hearing & Family Group Conference

The final hearing came around and social services were present to give their outcome of the Section 47 report and their concluding advice as to how contact could proceed. The judge on this particular hearing was the Judge who I had originally complained about to the Ombudsman. Although my complaint had been escalated to the Ombudsman, they found my complaint inconclusive, therefore he was allowed to preside. There was also no conclusive evidence of neglect as far as social services were concerned with regard to Scarlett's accident. However, it was felt that contact needed to proceed slowly and a relationship between the girls and their father was going to take time and effort on Dave's part to ensure that this was positive and happy contact. Dave was advised that the contact would not change and that the Court hearings would now stop but that social services would provide a service called Group Family Conference. This was agreed to and a final order was made. Scarlett would see her father for an hour supervised by Grandma and Grandad and Olivia and Verity would see him for the day and then return home at 7pm. The contact would be able to increase and develop by going along the process of a Family Group Conference, where all parties could meet and decide how best to take things forward. Then something really unprofessional happened and I really couldn't believe my ears. The Judge felt he couldn't just leave it there, he proceeded to tell the whole court how he didn't understand why I had made a complaint about him, which is why he had been removed from all of the previous court hearings. I actually had to question the intelligence of this man. Dave started to pipe up with comments about the fact that he knew something was up. I ignored both of them and said nothing, no reaction on my face. My complaint was felt important enough to elevate it to the highest level and, as far as I was concerned, I had been through enough abuse with Dave and I was not going to take it from a Judge. Funnily enough a few years later I heard that before the court hearings started Dave had had a meeting with a Judge!

The house eventually sold and, on the day that the completion took place, I had not a penny left of savings. It was my intention to stay local but a property came up a few miles away and it was perfect for what we needed and by the sea and I decided to move us to a different area for a fresh start. So, our new life began with a little bit of distance between me and Dave. It was a breath of fresh air for me. The girls changed their school to one just across the road from the house and Scarlett got a nursery space for two afternoons a week. The new school were advised of our family situation.

Although we had to rent a house to start with in our new town, it had given me time to think about what I wanted to do.

I did feel safe in this new house. The distance it gave me from Dave was a breath of fresh air. I could go to bed at night and sleep and I started to get my strength back. I had been so depleted of energy and so hypervigilant that I hadn't been able to relax. My brain was working on overdrive and my body on adrenaline and it struggled to learn how to relax but I was getting there. When the girls went to school, I would bake and play with Scarlett and when Scarlett went to nursery I used the time to run. My lovely running that would allow me time to relax and process.

One day whilst I was running, I decided that I needed to study and a book-keeping course seemed perfect as I was good with figures and it was something that would allow me to earn some money from home once I was qualified. It also gave me a positive focus. I also at this point was offered an opportunity back in Financial Services, sourcing mortgages for an adviser. I jumped at the chance as the potential earnings were good. My only restriction was the fact that I had Scarlett at home and she was only 3 and I could only get her a nursery space for two afternoons a week. I couldn't give the job the time it needed as Scarlett needed me more and believe me it needed lots of time to source a mortgage and in fact, took a lot of research as so many of the mortgage lenders had changed their criteria since my previous experience in financial services. The person I worked for was very demanding and the way he spoke to me triggered me big style as it just rang of Dave and the way he spoke to me. He really wanted me to work around the clock and I couldn't give it that amount of commitment. There were still things to be sorted with the children's contact. I decided that I couldn't work for him and in a very short period of time I told him so. It was a huge relief to me and although it could have earned me a lot of money the pressure was immense and I had to juggle too many other things at that point. My life had changed since those carefree single days, where time would not have been an issue. My children were now my priority and they needed me more than ever with everything that had happened between me and their Dad.

I started to do my book-keeping course and have quality time with the children to get them adjusted to new schools, nursery and friends. Everyone at the school was lovely and I felt more relaxed but I wasn't sure that I was living somewhere I wanted to be. I missed my friends and the countryside and was craving to be back there. The girls however settled really quickly and they loved being by the sea and in town. This was all a new experience for them and they were enjoying it. We settled into a new routine and things felt more relaxed, although I knew there were still contact issues to sort out.

A Family Group Conference Mediator was brought into the new school to meet Olivia and Verity, her name was Martine. She was being brought in to smooth issues with the contact and make it run more smoothly. She contacted me first by telephone to confirm it was alright for her to visit and interview the girls in school. The girls had already been interviewed by many people during the last 18 months and I advised that I would be happy for her to interview them but as she didn't want me to be present I insisted that a representative of the school was in attendance at the interview. I am so glad that I insisted on this as what transpired was disgraceful behaviour for someone entrusted to deal with children. The morning of the interview I went into the school and confirmed that someone from the school would be able to sit in with the Conference Mediator. The Office Administrator confirmed that someone from school would be present. I asked that if no one was available then the interview was not to take place. They confirmed to me that this would be the situation. When Olivia and Verity came out of school they were very distressed. I got the children home and sat them at the breakfast bar in the kitchen.

Verity burst into tears and started to apologise to me, "I'm so sorry Mummy. They made me agree to it."

"It's okay, Verity. What on earth has happened," I felt my stomach turning and a little shocked at how she had come out of school.

"The lady we saw today made me agree to meeting Daddy's girlfriend and son and I don't want to." Verity was shaking and sobbing.

I could not believe what I was hearing. I rang the school straight away and asked if I could speak with the person who attended the meeting. The school rang me back and said that the teaching assistant had actually spoken to the Head about the conduct during the meeting and was very concerned. The teaching assistant also confirmed that she would be happy to put down in writing what actually happened during the meeting. The letter I received from school was of great concern. This lady had led the children into a conversation and had insisted several times that they should meet Dave's girlfriend and her son, Tom. I am so grateful to the attending teaching assistant who wrote a letter outlining the content of the meeting. She pointed out how frightened Verity was and was shaking during the meeting and sobbing. I thanked the school very much for their concern of how this adult was trying to coerce two young, frightened children into doing something they did not feel comfortable doing. The purpose of the meeting was not for that but to work out how the girls could build a better relationship with their father.

I immediately contacted the Manager in charge of the Conference Mediator and advised that I would be making a formal complaint about her behaviour and that she would be not allowed anywhere near my children along with anyone else who was behaving in such a way. This is a professional body who are employed to step into court disputes and deal with children who are already in a very stressful situation and I really couldn't believe their actions. They were using this opportunity to twist the girls' arms into meeting Tracey. Not the purpose of this exercise.

Needless to say, an apology was offered and she was removed off the case.

I had lost faith in the system and I wasn't sure how these meetings would benefit any of us, if this was the way that things were being dealt with but I did agree to a Family Group Conference. The meetings were held nearby to where we lived which did not please Dave at all. He didn't like the thought of having to travel and made his opinion known. The Conference organiser advised that the meetings had to take place near the children, so that I was nearby should they need me. The meeting consisted of the Family Group Conference Mediator, Hattie, the social worker, myself, my brother Mike, Dave and his Mum and Dad and for some strange reason, he chose to have Julie there. For me that said it all. My best friend of 15 years sat by his side. Mike and I had discussed a plan of how this contact could move forward, as I was aware that it needed to move forward. The meeting was very hard going and Dave was stuck playing the same record about the past and me. It was very easy to see that he had not moved on at all. The conference leader tried to sway the meeting so that things could move forward. Nothing major was agreed at this meeting, so we carried on contact as agreed in Court and another meeting was arranged.

The second meeting was more interesting a few weeks later. It was December and the same people were asked to attend only this time Julie was not present. Dave was already in a mood when he entered the room and I could feel his energy. Mike sat next to me and we gave each other that knowing look. I was asked by the Conference Mediator to stand at the front of the room and write down on a white board what I wanted to achieve with the contact and how things should move forward. I was heckled by Dave who was very negative. The girls had started dancing locally on a Saturday morning and they loved it and they were making new friends. I felt that contact should not affect their dancing and suggested that he attended to let them take part and it would show that he was taking an interest in their hobbies. He advised that he didn't want to be coming to where we lived to pick his children up as it was too far to travel and he certainly felt that he shouldn't have to do what they wanted to do. He wanted to do what he wanted to do with his children. Actually, that would be nothing then, as he never really interacted with them and his mother took on most of the activities. I was quite saddened at his attitude. He seemed to want to fight over every little thing. The conference leader actually took him to task over this comment and advised that it would help him build a relationship with his children if they were doing something they like to do. He then continued to reel off lists of negative information that he didn't want to be doing. "Why should I spend money on them," was one of the comments he made and "why should I spend money on petrol to get to see them". I felt my heart sink; this man was paying very little for his children and still begrudged them the smallest things. Again, the conference leader took him to task, as did the social worker. At this point he stood up and went bright red, he clenched his fists, his demeanour was threatening, he threw his chair out of the way and came storming towards me. I sat very still and I felt myself hold my breath. He brushed past me and went outside. I could feel Mike shaking and so was I. I really thought he was going to strike out at someone in the room. It was obvious he was furious but managed to control hitting out as other people were present. The comment from the social worker was that she thought he was going to hit someone and felt scared. We sat in silence for several minutes. Mike looked at me reassuringly and asked me if I was okay. I nodded as I couldn't speak, I was still reacting to his anger. He re-entered the room a few minutes later and composed himself enough to get to the end of the meeting. He did agree to go to the dancing with the girls and let them do their activities but it was obvious that he was not happy about this.

The contact was not very long lived, in fact only lasted six months. Sometimes the contact did not happen and he would call to cancel either on the day or the night before and it never progressed on from the day contact. It also came to light that during his time with his children he was having stand up verbal fights with Verity about me. He was advising them that I was trying to stop contact and Verity was telling him exactly what I had told them, which was that "I was happy for them to go to contact as long as they are happy." There were so many things that went on. Days that got changed due to his holidays or very often they would spend the day with grandma because Daddy was watching the Grand Prix. The girls would tell me stories of him running me down and the way it was told, it was obvious that an adult had said these things. Olivia was so scared when these conversations or arguments arose that she would hide behind curtains.

A couple of weeks before Scarlett's 4th Birthday in the June I received a phone call from Dave. It was to be his final phone call to advise that he was no longer going to have contact if he could not have the contact a normal father has. He swore at me and was verbally abusive. I didn't rise to the bait. I remained calm as I listened and when he finally stopped I said that I thought it was very sad that he felt the way he felt and that this would be his choice. He said that he didn't have a choice and he wanted contact to stop. I later discovered that in the August he remarried and a couple of months later they had their first child. I feel that he used the contact situation with the children as his scapegoat.

Scarlett's birthday arrived and there was no contact from Dave. On the day of her birthday, his mother and father brought presents from them, Dave and his sister. Dave was not present and his mother would not stay, even though she was invited in. She stood at the door and handed the bags of presents over. I was very saddened by this action as it was Scarlett's birthday. The girls rushed to the door to greet her and were disappointed that she would not come into the house. That was the end of the contact from all members of the family. Dave and his mother sent birthday cards to the girls but nothing more.

When the contact stopped I emailed social services straight away. They rang Dave and tried to get him to change his mind on two occasions but he was not for swaying. The social worker came to see the children twice more to make sure they were happy and settled. The children were then removed from Child Protection register, as they no longer had contact with their father which was considered possibly unsafe. I reacted internally at this moment and it suddenly hit me how serious the events in our lives had been. It took me a few seconds to regain my concentration. It was a huge relief to come off the register and I felt we could now get on with our lives. I did spend a long time pondering what everything had been about. Why had he taken us to Court so many times? Was it just that he wanted the girls or was it about getting his own way? Was it to prove a point maybe? It felt as though I had been on a rollercoaster and it had suddenly stopped and I could now get off.

We stayed living by the sea for a few months and I decided that I wanted to go back to countryside and the friends that I knew so well. I found a property for rent right in the village, not far from where we had lived before and we were on the move again.

I had great expectations when I moved back and actually it felt quite flat. It is amazing how quickly things change and this is how it felt on our return. The children's friends did not accept them back as I had hoped and in fact, Olivia and Verity went through a period of bullying, not just verbal but Verity was being hit and kicked to the point where she was bruised. She did not say anything to me for a long time but I knew things were not right as she would come home from school and was screaming, tetchy and struggled to interact with us. Eventually, after asking her about some bruising on her legs, she told me what had been going on and then Olivia also opened up and told me that the children had said that they were odd because they did not have a Dad.

I went directly to the school and expressed my concerns and, possibly my perception at the time, I felt as though I was wasting their time as they had not witnessed anything.

Within a year I was heading back down to the coast where the children said that they felt happy. Although finding a property was impossible. I travelled backwards and forwards every day, a 40 mile round trip for six months. I have to say the children welcomed them back with open arms and they have a very good selection of friends still to this day.

I had also managed to secure myself a little job doing book-keeping. Quite the coincidence really. A friend of mine who I knew from working at the telecoms company had advertised for a book-keeper as he had started up a local business and so we met up and hey presto I had myself a little job. It was at this point also that I had started to date which was a very scary prospect. I was starting to get my life back together. I was Jennifer, bubbly, excitable, fun, loving, happy and carefree, not quite with the sporty car and lifestyle but we had a comfortable life and I was very grateful for all that we had. Dating was different this time round. I had children and I felt guilty if I had to go out for the night and the only people I trusted to look after the girls were my Mum and Dad. I still felt I needed to protect them and I was still hypervigilant. I wasn't even sure if I could cope with having a new relationship and having the family. This was all new territory for me and I have learned so much by being brave enough to give it a go.

Chapter Twenty-Four

The Start of A New Romance

It had been almost two years since my marriage had broken up. One day whilst sat doing my book-keeping, I decided that it was time to get myself back in the dating game. I went onto an online dating website and registered my details. At first it felt exciting and within an hour of me joining I had been inundated with messages. Most of whom I politely declined. Believe me when I say that it is something I would never ever do again. I did go on a few dates but actually wondered why I went on these dates. I'm a great believer in my time is precious and why waste a good evening out on someone you may never see again. However, some people meet their forever partner this way and who am I to judge. It's just not something I would do again. I found looking through the profiles a bit tedious.

Anyway, my friend Debbie persuaded me that I needed to make it more fun. I needed to look at things from a different perspective and relax and enjoy it. One night after a few Proseccos we decided to go through a few profiles on the internet and comment on their photos. I remember there were quite a few men who like to pose with their car or boat and we were making comments such as, "nice boat!!" Very childish I know but it made us laugh. I told the one guy he reminded me of a famous actor and he decided to take up the conversation. By the end of the night I had agreed to meet up with him for coffee.

I met him in a local coffee shop in the July and a friend waited with me in the café. I had become a little wary of where I meet people and I wanted to feel safe and people to know where I was and whom I was with. When he turned up he was a little taken aback to see someone sat with me.

"Hi, you must be Jennifer?" he said a little nervously.

"Yes, I am and you must be Patrick?" I smiled at him.

"I'm just warming your seat for you," said my friend with a giggle.

He nervously twitched, "I'm going to get a drink. Would you like one?"

"Hot chocolate, please," as I indicated to my friend to leave, trying not to giggle myself.

He went over to order a drink and my friend disappeared whispering "good luck," under her breathe. He wasn't quite sure how to take this behaviour but I'll give him his due, he stayed.

He was a little untidy and I like my men to be smart but he went on to say that he had come out of work to meet and as he worked on cars, I gave him the benefit of the doubt. My intuition said, "no, boring, not my cup of tea and a bit scruffy". Don't ever ignore your intuition. He talked about the company he ran mainly and it wasn't my cup of tea but I listened politely. He seemed a little unsure of himself and guarded in what he said. The most amusing part of the coffee date was my friend waving to us as we were sat in the window, trying to show me what she had just purchased in a clothes sale. So, I called her in to talk to us and break the monotony and then I drank my hot chocolate and the flight mode kicked in and I just wanted to leave. I made my excuses and left. But Patrick was to become a very important part of my life.

He messaged me about an hour later to say that my photo had not done me justice and it would be lovely to meet again and maybe I would like to attend a gig he was playing at. What??? He plays in a band!! He hadn't told me that. I suddenly had images of me at the tender age of 19 idolising Jon Bon Jovi, throwing myself at him at a gig in the NEC, Birmingham. Oh, well, if he plays in a band that makes him so much more interesting, doesn't it and he was a drummer (strong, silent type)!!! The gig was the following week in the next town in one of the pubs and I went on my own all dressed up in one of my swing dresses. I got to the bar and he appeared next to me. He was pleasantly surprised I was there and even more surprised I was on my own. He bought me a drink and then took me upstairs to the room where the rest of the band were and introduced me. He then introduced me to a couple of people who would look after me whilst he played. He came across as very caring and considerate. The gig was fantastic and I was introduced to the wife of the lead guitarist in the band. She was really lovely and we got on extremely well. So well in fact that we are very close friends to this day and has introduced me to a network of lovely, caring Mums who do fitness together. We are a very close-knit community and so supportive.

The relationship grew as we started to see more of each other. He introduced me to his many friends/associates that he either played badminton with or had a connection with the band. He not only ran a small business but had a music studio which he rented out and his flat was above the studio. Our relationship moved on very quickly as getting time away from the children was difficult for me as I didn't trust just anyone to babysit. Very often Patrick would come over for dinner or visit us on a Sunday and we would all go for a walk together. He also had an older Alsatian dog, which was great for Scarlett as she adores dogs and she became very attached to her. The girls thought it was great fun on a Sunday as we would visit the studio and they would get a chance to sing into the microphones and have a go on the drums.

With him living in one town and me in another it was quite a trek all the time to see each other and he was visiting more frequently and then after two months started staying over a lot.

I was preparing to move to the coast but we hadn't yet found a property and I was still travelling backwards and forwards doing my forty-mile round trip to get the girls to school. We decided to live together once I had moved house and the easiest thing to do was for him to move in with me because I had the children and the space and he only had a one bedroom flat over his music studios. This had caused a bit of a problem with my Mum. She felt things were moving too quickly and she made her feelings known through temper and it had become very heated. She told me that I was thrusting Patrick down the girls' throats and I was harming them. She felt he couldn't be trusted and had a roving eye but I was not prepared to listen. At that point, I had asked her and my Dad to leave. I felt that it was time for me to get on with my life. My Mum and Dad left under a cloud, which I felt very sad about. But I needed to live my life.

I was doing a bit of book-keeping for a local company but it wasn't really my thing. I was bored with sitting working with figures. Patrick offered me the chance to set up a business with him but I would run it. So, we decided to set up a business together as an aside to his main business, selling online. I designed the website and did all the work and used his workshop as the delivery centre. I also lent him a lot of money to support his business. Things were slow to grow but I learned so much. I had never set up a website before and it was great to learn something new.

I eventually managed to find a property to rent in the centre of the town where the girls were at school in the September. On the day we moved I had a removal company do most of the work and a couple of my friends in the town I was moving to came along to make sure there was parking for the three lorries that transported our furniture and bits and pieces. The girls were at school, which made it easier to get on and move. By 12.30pm all the furniture and boxes had been moved into the new home and it was an opportunity for me to get beds set up ready for when the girls arrived home from school. Patrick didn't arrive until 4.30pm. I was excited to see him and thought he might stay and help me unpack. He said that he had to go to a friend's Birthday meal and that he couldn't let her down. I felt a little deflated and I was tired. The days leading up to the move I had worked day and night to pack and get ready and all I wanted was a little moral support whilst I unpacked and sorted out our personal belongings. He ordered me a take-out and then he disappeared. The girls were excited to go to bed and were all asleep quite early and I carried on unpacking and organising. The sooner it was done, the better and then it would feel like home.

Patrick would finish work at 4.30pm and visit his flat first and do some catching up and arrive with me around 7pm to eat. I let this go for a while as I felt he may need his own space and it gave me quality time with my girls. He'd never had children and had never really lived with anyone so it carried on for another six months. He had lots of ex-girlfriends, most of whom followed him round with the band. The alarm bells should have been ringing and actually it was chiming big and loud but I was not listening. I would turn up at a gig and he would struggle to acknowledge me. He would not approach me and say, "hello" when I arrived or "goodbye" at the end of the night. He would say that lots of the fans had come to see him and he had to give his attention to them. I always said that I wasn't asking for his full attention just an acknowledgement that I was there and with him. At the end of the day, they weren't the Rolling Stones, just a local band doing cover versions of songs. I just felt that he was lacking some basic life skills. When we were together one on one we got on extremely well and enjoyed each other's company.

My girls seemed to like him and things were ticking along well but…. and it's a big BUT, my gut feelings were telling me things weren't right. He wasn't paying anything towards the rent or food, even though I had asked for a contribution. He had offered to pay half towards the girls Christmas presents and that never happened either. At that point, talking about money had become uncomfortable. Neither of us wanted to broach the subject of money. Possibly because we have a belief system that likes us to be polite and not to ask for things.

Our Christmas together was lovely. The girls had a lovely time and it felt at last as though we were a family. The best surprise was the fact he had bought me a Pandora bracelet. It was beautiful and meant the world to me. His face even lit up when I opened it. It was the best Christmas since my break up and it felt special. He admitted that he'd never bought anyone something so expensive so I felt truly honoured that he felt I was worth it. It's a shame that I didn't realise at the time that I was worth it and I didn't need someone else to buy me gifts for that to be the case. My Mum and Dad had accepted the fact that we were together and had now moved in together so had been to visit several times.

This person did do something for me though that I hadn't done for a long time. I was living again, going to gigs, enjoying some freedom. I loved it and he introduced me to Jive dancing. I was laughing and having fun. It gave me some balance in my life. I wasn't only a mother, I was Jennifer, a person who needed other things for me. It became another passion of mine. I love Modern Jive. However, this was the start of the end for our relationship.

Dancing was every Monday evening and as I needed a babysitter and it wasn't cheap, the compromise was that we went every other week. I found a lovely lady who I could trust completely and she happened to be a childminder as well, perfect. I was a little nervous as I wasn't sure what to expect. Not like me, as I have never really thought about things, I normally just do them. This meant a lot to me as it was something we were doing together. We walked into this hall and we were made very welcome. My partner knew a lot of the people as he had been dancing many years. There were approximately 20-30 people in the room. We formed two lines with our partners and then the instructor would show us the move we needed to do, which we copied and the ladies would then move one round to the next gentleman dancer to practice the move. When the lesson had finished, it was into freestyle which meant you could pick who you wanted to dance with. Obviously at first my partner danced with me and then I got asked to dance by the other gentlemen there. It was a very different concept for me. As lots of the ladies would ask Patrick to dance and I'd be sat watching and feeling a little uncomfortable. You do get used to the fact that it is just dancing and the more people you can dance with the better you become. We got talking to another couple who danced and they seemed very pleasant to start with. Then one week (me being psychic and not thinking) the woman turned up on her own and we were talking and she mentioned her hands were cold. Without thinking I said, "cold hands, warm heart because we have cried many tears" and with that she burst into tears. Wow, I felt awful. It transpired that she and her partner had split up as he did not want commitment and marriage. I apologised and Patrick glared at me as though I'd done it on purpose. After that, this woman decided that at every moment she could she would corner my partner and talk to him about her split. It became very uncomfortable and I was becoming more and more insecure about the liaison and her actual real intentions. I mentioned it to Patrick several times and how uncomfortable it felt. He could not see my point of view. Enough was enough, I had to tell him how I was feeling. We had been dancing and were just getting into bed and I broached the subject.

"Why does this girl keep cornering you to chat?" I was trying to act as cool as a cucumber.

"She just needs a friend to talk to." He sighed impatiently at me.

"Why hasn't she got any female friends to talk to? That's what I do when I need to talk," I felt almost exasperated at his lack of understanding from my point of view.

"She needs a male perspective," was his response, "and she is my friend. Anyway, she says that she doesn't have any real female friends".

"She's not a friend, Patrick, you've only got to know her through dancing with me and she's certainly not my friend. She's just an acquaintance. Doesn't it say a lot about her if she hasn't got any female friends?" I could feel myself getting upset.

"Oh, so you're saying that I can't make new friends now, are you?" he attitude was very catty.

"I'm not saying that at all but she never includes me in these conversations and it feels as though you are having a private relationship behind my back." I could see him baulk.

"So, now you're saying I'm cheating on you?" he was started to get annoyed with me and I could feel his temper rising.

"I'm not saying that. I'm saying I don't feel comfortable with this situation and I would like you to respect how I am feeling. I am your girlfriend at the end of the day," I could feel my emotions rising and I was trying not to cry.

"Well you can just f**k off as I am not putting up with this behaviour," and he grabbed his clothes to leave.

"Please don't leave," I begged him to stay. "I'm sorry, I won't mention it again."

"I'm with you and that should be enough," he climbed back into bed and went to sleep. I lay there crying, unable to get across how I really felt about the situation and I now felt I could say no more.

I bit my lip and didn't mention the situation but it was eating me up inside. My weight had dropped considerably and I was feeling more insecure than ever. New Year's Eve arrived and he was gigging at a pub and I was at home with the girls. I had been to sleep and then woke up. I always struggled to sleep knowing he was out and was happy when he was home safely. I was just trolling through Facebook, waiting for him to come home, I happened to see the girl from dancing had friended Patrick on Facebook (Facebook can be such a nightmare) but she had not friended me, which I felt was a little odd. So, me being me, I friended her. I think I was trying to make a point of seeing that she had friended him. Patrick got home in the early hours of the morning and I was awake,

"Are you okay?" he said tiredly, "that girl friended me on Facebook. You know the one from dancing. Did she friend you too?"

He had mentioned straight away and I was a little suspicious about his motive, "I friended her, as I had seen she had friended you."

"She messaged me too," his voice was hesitant.

"Why was she was messaging you?" I wrinkled my face as I was trying to make sense of this situation.

"I'm just helping her out. She wants to talk to somebody who understands her." He seemed very proud of himself.

"Patrick, she is not a friend just someone we had met at dancing and I don't think it is appropriate. I would not approach a couple and keep chatting to the man and have private conversations. It's not right." I was fighting a losing battle with my point of view.

This disagreement just hung in the background constantly and made things very uncomfortable. It made our relationship very unstable and we could not agree to agree and made me feel very insecure to the point that I didn't trust him or what was going on. My gut feeling was telling me her intentions were not good ones. This woman was messaging him every day and little did I know, was turning up at his workplace and having coffee with him at his flat (this all came to light later). Instead of reassuring me, all that happened was he would rub it in about the female friends that he had and how many of them he was messaging. My self-esteem was plummeting and Patrick couldn't see this. He started to hide his phone from sight and turned it on to silent. He would disappear into the toilet of an evening and take his phone with him. I knew he was looking at his messages but felt very sad that he could not be honest with me. It was tearing me apart inside but I felt I could not say anymore. I didn't want him to leave me. I thought I felt secure with him but actually I was feeling more insecure as every day passed. He really didn't understand me and he didn't want to listen to what I had to say.

A few weeks later it was my birthday and we went for a meal together. We had booked a pub in the middle of the countryside which I had never eaten at before. We arrived and there were not many people in the restaurant. We sat down by the log fire that was burning and it was all very romantic but he couldn't look at me or wasn't even interested in anything I had to say. It was very uncomfortable and a very telling sign that things were not right. I felt very sad and my heart sank as I realised that this person didn't care as much about me as I cared about them. We tried to talk to each other but it was stilted conversation. I managed to start talking about cars, his passion and the atmosphere lightened. I love my birthday and the shine had been taken away. Even his birthday card to me said, 'To Jennifer..... Love and Stuff, Patrick' and it felt half-hearted. A couple of days later I couldn't take anymore. I felt totally let down, deflated, destroyed. I ended the relationship and asked him to move out. It was one of my saddest birthdays ever.   He was gutted when I asked him to leave and he did cry. I think he thought a lot more of me than he let on but that I will never really know for sure. But it was a very painful separation as I had lent him money and we had to keep in touch in order to separate the business off and sort a few things out. Keeping in touch just kept opening the wound.   He did repay my money, for which I am very grateful for. He dated someone very quickly after we separated, about a week after, and several different people since. I have seen him from time to time and I did try to talk to him to see if we could rekindle our relationship, not knowing that he was already dating someone else. I was very upset. Possibly because he was the first proper relationship after the divorce and I think I was hanging all my expectations on this being 'the one'. He was never the one and my instinct told me that the first time I met him but I was trying to make him the one. I fell in love with the image of a drummer, not the person. So many people do this. They make excuses for their partners/husbands/wives' behaviour just so not to be alone. It is ok to be on your own/single. In fact, it is better to be on your own than in a relationship which is unhappy or you can't be who you want to be. I was in this trap of feeling that I needed to be with someone and I wanted this person to make everything right. My perspective now realises that only YOU can make everything alright nobody else.

After this relationship finished, I became a bit of a talking point at the school, but I was unaware of it and it was fuelled by a close friend at the time. I had confided in a couple of friends about my life and what had been happening.   The school gates can be a very judgemental place, where people with nothing better to do stand and talk.   I walked in on a group conversation one day,

"Did you know what had happened with Jennifer?" one lady said to the group.

They were all huddled together and I was stood behind them, "Yeah, well she couldn't trust him and she's asked him to leave. Mind you he wasn't very nice to her whenever we were out."

"I think she was a bit of a fool to let him treat her like that," then they all realised that I was stood behind them.

"Oh hi, how are you?" there was an embarrassed silence.

"I'm fine," I turned and walked away. It was about me! I was mortified and very hurt that I was the subject of local gossip. I learnt a very important lesson about trusting people and who not to trust and developed my self-awareness again about keeping my distance from people who live off drama instead of living their own lives. Not only that, but to keep my business, my business. A very important lesson for us all. If people really care about you, they will not judge you and talk about you behind your back, they will pick up the phone and find out if you are ok and help you out if you are not.

One person did notice how upset I was and approached me. She noticed that I wore running gear to the school a lot and asked if I would like to join a gym group who did Boxercise and fitness. I agreed to go along with her and low and behold, guess who was running the classes? The guitarist's wife, Kelly, who I had met at one of the gigs with Patrick. I felt so sad after this relationship ended and it took me a long time to come to terms with what had happened. I didn't know what I was going to do for a career and I needed to start earning some money. In the meantime, I decided that getting fit again would be a good start. The classes were fun and the people even funnier. They raised my spirits and we all got on very well. My running had become important again and I entered races, something I hadn't done for a long, long time. Fun runs, half marathons, obstacle course runs. Life was back on track and I was feeling great and looking fit. I was even persuaded to enter the London Marathon, even though I had always said I would never do a marathon. Kelly offered to run it for me if I did get in and didn't want to do it. I had at last found a group of like-minded people to connect with, laugh with and exercise with. It was all the things I loved doing and we were close and could talk or not talk, whatever you wanted and people respected that. It was so lovely after being locked into dysfunctional monogamous relationships.

Life was fun and I had also started dancing again at a local venue rather than the same dance class as Patrick. I had missed being with people and had missed doing something for me. My life was fun again. Fun was so important to me and exercising was my passion and outlet for any stresses in my life. The old Jennifer was back but matured and evolved. Knowing that I wanted to be a good example to her children. It was so important to get this balance right so that everyone was happy.

It was all very well having fun and exercising but I really needed to focus and decide what career opportunities were available to me. I sat for some time and thought about what I loved to do. Then life did what it always does and presented me the opportunity to learn and grow. Sometimes when you sit long enough you get a moment of clarity.

Chapter Twenty-Five

My Spiritual Revival

The next nine months I was on my own but during this time I decided that I needed to start a new business and I had toyed with this idea and that idea. I never really knew what I wanted to be or what I wanted to do. My Mum for years had told me that I needed to tap into my psychic and healing abilities. I finally stopped fighting myself and I took my Reiki levels 1 and 2, the most amazing energy healing therapy. I had always had healing hands but had denied it for so long. My Reiki course had been very profound and by doing the reiki I found my situation becoming calmer and I felt myself moving away from people and situations that were not good for me. In turn I had started to connect with other like-minded friends. Spiritual people who understood me and what I did. It was during the early part of my new business that I really connected to a lovely lady and friend called Lucy. Lucy is a Londoner with Irish connections and has a wicked sense of humour but very humanitarian, sensitive and has good boundaries. Not only that but she is a very good business woman and mother. Lucy and I got talking one day and she started to tell me about some of the therapies that she had studied such as NLP (Neuro Linguistic Programming) and Emotional Freedom Technique (EFT) and Matrix Re-imprinting. She knew that I had been struggling with the break up from Patrick and volunteered to do some EFT (Tapping) with me to release my emotions that I had been holding. I couldn't believe how quickly I was letting go of the anger, sadness, frustrations that I had built up. It made such an impression on me that I found an EFT course locally and signed up. These undeniably wonderful therapies have helped me tap into the unconscious level of why I do things and why I was repeating unhealthy patterns. I have never looked back. I advertised locally and on Facebook and I steadily built up a client base from home. The therapies never cease to amaze me at how much people get out of them and how they change people's lives for the better. How I have changed. This whole new world has opened up to me and I have evolved who I am as a person and who I want to be. I might add that it is a constantly changing process and learning journey but I now feel that I am on the right path. I have taken quite a few diversions in life but these have been created by me and when I look back I always had a choice. Everybody has a choice.

The Reiki has maintained my balance, and when I feel that my Chakras (energy centres) are out of balance and I don't feel myself, the Reiki will rebalance me.

When I say, "don't give up", I do mean it. The Emotional Freedom Technique and Matrix Re-imprinting that I do is tapping into the subconscious to change all those limiting negative beliefs that I had about myself. You know; those voices in my head that told me that I couldn't do something, that I wasn't good enough, that I don't deserve success/love/money. Whatever that belief was, it had come from an event or a trauma or a memory created a very long time ago which I had reinforced in order to believe it. At the end of the day we are all energy and what you send out comes back to you. Therefore, if you believe one of these negative belief systems that is what you will create. By doing the EFT, it taught me to claim what I had created and change it. It is one of the most powerful tools that I have ever used in my therapies and I have seen wonderful transformations in people, that includes myself.

The voices in my head were attracting men who did not know my worth and the reason for this was that I did not know my worth myself. Although my life has been a mixture of many experiences, I have never met a man who would adore me and knew how much I was worth. This was because I did not love me. Every time I met someone, I moulded myself to who I thought they wanted me to be instead of being me. I have hidden my spiritual side for so long. I spent months working on many, many childhood memories. Some of the memories were small memories but had implanted a belief system in me, things such as, not speaking up to say what I thought, having to please other people, other people are more important. I am sure that you understand now how I became a people pleaser with no voice. But I did have a voice and I do love myself and I have had to deal with these things in order to change the vibration that I send out and attract what it is that I would like in my life. The next part of my story was a very amazing time of my life but it was also very sad. It came into my life for a reason, which I know for sure. A very hard lesson was coming to me.

At last I found my true calling. I am bright, bubbly, life is amazing, I am surrounded by the most wonderful people; healers, fitness friends, dance friends and long term old friends. I am building a business and finally I feel me. I am doing school fetes and psychic venues and promoting my business anyway that I can and generally, loving life. I am Jennifer, the Jennifer I am meant to be but I was about to repeat a pattern subconsciously. The Universe was checking to see if I had learned.

Chapter Twenty-Six

My Soulmate

It was June and it was the summer school fete, I had a stall promoting my Reiki and EFT. The children were running around with their friends and I was chatting to all the people that came along to see what I was promoting. There was a tombola, food stalls, lucky dips, a few fairground rides and lots of people. The police were there showing children around the police cars and to chat to the children. The fire brigade also attended the fete so that the children could climb on and off the fire engine and explore what it was like to be a firefighter. One of the firefighters noticed me and approached me at my table. I recognised his face from my Jive dancing class. I had started dancing at a new venue closer to home and I had seen him several times but never really taken any notice of him, as I had my head in the clouds and I was not really in a place where I was looking for a relationship. He chatted to me for quite some time and then I ran off as Olivia and Verity were performing in the talent show. I came back to my stall and he reappeared to chat some more. I did notice him sneakily take a business card off my table and a wry smile crept across my face. His name was Sam Fisher. He then bid me adieu and we parted company. My Mum and Dad were attending the fete on this particular day and a friend of mine had commented on what an active interest he had taken in me. My Mum was not too keen on him, she felt he was too full of himself. My Mum is very quick to judge.

The following five months were a mixture of synchronicities and coincidental meetings. It seemed every time I went to the local shop I would bump into him. The weirdest thing of all is I would ask the angels to show me when my soulmate was going to appear and sure as eggs are eggs, this man would come into my field. Friends of mine would tease me that he was the one and I always denied it and said that he wasn't. I had at this point been involved with the fitness Mums that I mentioned earlier in my story and through them I had really got back into my fitness and running. I had just found out that I had a ballot spot in the London Marathon and I was over the moon. The odds of getting a space in the ballot is incredible as 250,000 people apply and only 10,000 get a space. I was truly blessed and on a high. I wasn't sure that I really wanted to be in a relationship and I really didn't think Sam was for me.

Eventually in the October, Sam asked me to attend a party with him that we had both been invited to. We exchanged a few text messages beforehand about a present for the host. Sam had offered to buy champagne, that impressed me as I love a glass of champagne. We had exchanged some jokey messages regarding the Champagne. The party was for a mutual acquaintance from Jive and he would drive, so I agreed to go with him. He picked me up from my house and complimented me on my dress. He then presented me with a bottle of champagne. I was a little overwhelmed and a felt a little tingle inside of me. He had obviously taken note that I liked Champagne. We chatted extensively in the car and giggled a lot. We arrived and sat together at the venue; a village hall with lively music and people dancing and something very weird happened for me. I felt very safe with him, very protected. He sat right next to me and kept putting his arm around the back of my chair. We got up and danced a few times. He wanted to sit and talk with me and we found out that we had so much in common. He had three children, although they were older, so he could relate to all the things I talked to him about with my three girls. He was a cyclist and with me being a runner, we had a common fitness interest. He was very excited that I had a marathon place and wanted to help me with my training. We seemed to like a lot of the same music. He was into his heavy metal, which I was. He had suddenly become a lot more interesting to me. He was very smiley and smart and well spoken. He had manners and was very approachable. He would help anyone who needed help. He'd had been married for 19 years before they divorced and one relationship after that. We danced and laughed and it was a very lovely romantic evening. I I let my guard down and the evening ended in us kissing. It had been noted by everyone in the room the chemistry between us.

That was the start of a very beautiful romance. This man did not want to change me or hurt me or belittle me. We laughed, we trusted each other. There was no doubt in my mind that at last I had met "the one". We were so connected in every way and yet I had been pushing him away. To me he was perfect.

One day we decided to go to the cinema together, it was the new James Bond movie. He was so excited we were together. Everything we did together was exciting and fun. The cinema is on a complex and his Mum happened to be working out in the local gym. He was so desperate for me to meet her that we wandered into the reception area and asked if she was there. They said that she was but that she would be in the middle of the workout. We seemed to have to giggles the whole time. We left and went to the cinema and afterwards he drove me to her house and introduced us. We got on like a house on fire and her words to me were, "if you ever split up I would like to keep you as a friend". Everything was wonderful and when a man introduces you to his Mum, you know that things are serious. We spent many times with his Mum and her sister and meeting up with other members of the family. We all got on very well but my girls were not so happy always to be doing these things. They just wanted to be at home. Olivia and Verity particularly were not very keen on Sam. They felt he was trying to take me away from them.

Because of his shifts and the flexibility of my work we could meet in the day time and go for walks and meals and I would spend a lot of time at his house. We were very blessed to have time to develop our relationship without having the children involved. He would pick me up every other Tuesday to go dancing and we would dance and laugh. Sam was a beginner but was improving all the time and we would spend time going over moves we had learnt that week. We had friends who had a tandem and we would borrow this and go on epic bike rides together across the local countryside. It was blissful. He would text me all the time and we trusted each other implicitly. If I put a run or a cycle on Strava (activity app for runners/cyclists) he would comment every time with words of praise and kudos (thumbs up) and I would return the appreciation. If we weren't together of an evening or morning, he would message to say "good morning" or "good night". We had little nicknames for each other, he was honey pot or sometimes 'sweetpea' and I was honey bee. He was keen to assist with my marathon training and would impart pieces of good nutritional information or training practices.

Sam was desperate to meet my children and be a part of our family lives. I insisted that I wanted to wait until after Christmas, just to give our relationship time to develop. He agreed but he would still occasionally turn up at my door at 9pm and have some shopping in a bag for me, just as an excuse to see me or turn up in a place he knew we were going to be just to say, "hello". I was very flattered by all the attention but felt he was trying to push the boundaries of what I wanted. I still wanted to protect my children and I didn't want to rush anything and get hurt. I made it very clear to him from the outset that I wanted a relationship where we would end up living together as a family and he agreed that he was looking for his life partner and wanted the same things.

I wanted to introduce Sam to my Mum and Dad first. Just before Christmas I invited him around to my house for tea and cake and to meet them. It seemed to go very well. Although, after the event, my Mum told me that she was not very keen on him. She felt he had too much to say about himself and was very full of himself and my Dad was also very unsure. He didn't feel he would be the type to commit but could not give me a reason for why he felt this way. I was a little upset at this as to me he was generous and friendly and everything I like in a person.

After Christmas, he came and met the girls who were a little wary of him. Then he became a regular visitor and eventually started to do activities with us, such as cycling as a family and going on holidays together. We would combine going on holiday with visiting his children living in Devon and everyone got along so well.

On my birthday he baked me a cake and brought it round and my present was a Garmin watch that would give me my pace of running and monitor my heart rate, just what I needed to run a Marathon. It was another awesome gift and I loved it. I was glowing and my shine was back and my birthday was happy once again.

As time went on, he would stay on his four days off but go back home for his shift days. I was glad when his shifts ended safely and he was very flattered by the fact that I cared about him and he would always tell me that the only other person who had worried about him had been his Mum. Every day he would tell me how I had changed his world for the better, how different I was to other people that he had dated and how I made him feel good about himself for the first time ever. I would glow as he made me feel the same. Very often he would make a comment about how he was going to fit all my furniture into his house; my furniture is rather large and there was a feeling of permanence about this relationship which I loved. He would help me with the girls if I needed them picked up or watched/amused whilst I had clients. He virtually had stepped into the father role. My focus had moved fully to us as a couple and running, cycling and life had become more important than my business.

The day of the London Marathon came and I had been training very hard and I was very nervous but excited. I was running for my friend Lucy's local children's charity and had raised £325. My nickname is Quirky Bird, a name that originated from me not being able to put my real name on Facebook for a few years whilst Dave and I went through our divorce and that is how I became known with all the fitness Mums. A friend of mine was a printer and put my name on my t-shirt for the race. The girls were staying at home and my Mum and Dad had come to stay with them. Sam and I drove to Brighton and parked at the fire station to get the train to London. It was an early train, arriving in Blackheath at 8.30am. He wished me luck and we parted company there and had agreed at the end of the race I would meet him at the coffee shop at Embankment underground station. The marathon is definitely a test of someone's physical and mental abilities. It is one of the hardest but most rewarding things I have ever done. I had been very consistent with my training as I knew I wanted to run this race not walk it. Kelly had run London several times and had given me some very valuable advice on nutrition and training. I waited around the toilet area and made sure I had my banana and jam sandwich ready to eat before I ran. I sat on the ground and bumped into a girl who I chatted to for a while. It turned out she had not trained for the marathon, had not had breakfast and was carrying a selfie stick with her. I could not comprehend how you could enter the marathon and not train for it but I am sure lots of people do. We had to go to the designated cages that we had been given either blue, green or red. It was very noisy and I had not been used to the noise after spending hours running the South Downs but it was very encouraging. It is a humbling experience to run next to some very amazing people. I hit the very famous psychological wall at 22 miles and I remember seeing lots of people starting to walk, the noise was now distracting and I wanted it to stop. My mental strength took over and I told myself that I had got this far and walking was not an option. My legs were still strong and I was going to run it. I turned the corner at admiralty arch and I knew I was on the final stretch. People were grouping and walking and I remember parting the waves of people with my hands and shouting out, "I'm coming through". The last 850 metres were the longest part of my race. I could see Buckingham Palace but really didn't take it in I was looking for the finish line. It was there I could see it. I ran over the line and burst into tears. I had done it, I had run the marathon and I was having a medal put over my head. I stopped my Garmin watch - 4 hours and 32 minutes. I was ecstatic. My goal had been between 4 hours 30 minutes and 5 hours. I was directed to have my picture taken and then to collect my goody bag with my London Marathon T-shirt. I picked up my bag that I had dropped at the beginning of the race and changed clothes and drank my soya drink and had some food. I then got myself up and walked to meet Sam. It took Sam another half an hour to get to me due to trying to get through the crowds and I was so pleased to see him, as I hadn't managed to spot him on the run round. He had a pot of pasta for me to eat and we sat in the park whilst I told him all about my race. I then rang the girls to tell them I had finished and then posted the obligatory photo on Facebook for all to see. It was a very proud moment indeed and Sam was a very proud, loving and caring partner. We got home and the girls wanted to see my medal. The next day I took the girls to school and when I got back I carried on as normal. However, the second day I felt very dizzy and ill so I stayed in bed and Sam came and took the girls to school. I soon realised that I hadn't really had any salt and needed to eat some to correct my body imbalance. I felt super douper after my second packet of crisps. I am still so proud of this achievement. I did it, I ran the marathon. If you set your mind to something you can achieve everything. Sam was very proud of me too.

Things were starting to change and I noticed very early on that he found it difficult to pay for things. More often than not, if we stopped for a coffee and cake on a bike ride he would have forgotten his wallet or didn't have any money so I would pay. If we went on holiday I generally paid for the accommodation and the fuel and food supplies whilst we were away. I always excused it though as I felt it was for my girls so I needed to pay. I told him on numerous occasions that I loved him and his response was always the same, "thank you". It made my heart sink.

One Spring day we were stood in Sam's garden and I was helping him to sort out the borders and make it pretty. We had been dating six months. Six months of bliss and fun together. He made a passing comment about our relationship but I felt an underlying tone to his comment. It felt uncomfortable and I needed to address it.

"Sam," I paused before I spoke. I had learned to think twice before I said too much, "where is our relationship going?"

His eyes almost popped out of his head, "What do you mean?"

"Well we've been together a little while now, how do you see our future together?"

"I don't really know," he looked uncomfortable.

I felt uncomfortable, "do you see us living together eventually?"

"I'm not sure. I'm not sure how I feel about you." Things then changed. His face changed and I could see the fear in his eyes. "It isn't something that I was considering."

I burst into tears at his reaction, "so why are we together? I don't understand."

He grabbed me and held me, "I love being with you and you are everything I have been looking for all my life but I don't know if I can consider living together. I don't even know if I love you." My heart hit my stomach, the bombshell had been dropped. I couldn't comprehend what he was saying to me.

"If you don't love me, maybe we should end our relationship now because I know that I love you," I was putting my heart on a platter to him.

"I don't want to end our relationship but if you feel you do then you must go with what you feel," his eyes filled with tears.

"No, I don't want it to end. I love you," he seemed shocked at this news and yet I had told him recently that this was how I felt.

We hugged the tightest hug I ever had and agreed to stay together. I needed to leave to do the school run. I felt weird. I felt removed from all that was going on. I was hurting and I didn't want to believe what he had just said to me but we were still together so that was good!

His whole demeanour changed towards me. His text messages changed. He no longer referred to me as 'honey bee' and the love in his messages no longer existed, even putting kisses at the end of the messages stopped for a while. He was retreating and frightened and I couldn't believe it. I felt as though a knife had been stabbed into my heart and then someone was turning the blade, my throat closed with the emotion that I felt. For two weeks' we talked, I am very good at talking and being a therapist, I found myself having to use my skills about his fear. I pleaded with him to work with this relationship as it was so lovely. He would turn up talk and then almost run away. Then one day I had had enough of him running in fear. I confronted him "Sam, stop running and start acting like a responsible adult." It shocked him out of his state and we started all over again.

It took a few weeks for us to get back to where we were but we did get there. My motto on these things is that if it's good, it's worth fighting for. It was good, we had never had a cross word or argument and everything was lovely. But things had changed and his messages were a lot more cautious. His fear of commitment really was showing. Then one day he surprised me; he told me that he was going to buy me a bike and he needed to stop being tight with money and treat me. Then we could enjoy riding together. He asked me what type of bicycle I would like. Sam rode a road bike and me, being very competitive, decided that that is what I would like too. We drove around Sussex to find a bike that I liked and, in the end, I decided that the first bike I tried was the one. No sooner had I said the words than he was on the computer ordering the bike for me and hey presto I was getting some goodies to go along with it. I was so excited. I even got some cleats (proper clip in pedals) and cycling shoes. We did many rides out together. They were very enjoyable and fast. I love the speed of racing down a hill with the wind rushing past your face and feeling free.

In between riding bicycles and running and dancing, I was seeing my clients and helping Sam with his garden. He wasn't that interested in his garden but I love having my hands in the soil. I volunteered to help him sort it out and so we took the task on together, ripping up bushes and weeding borders. We would then sit on the grass and he would have cooked us lunch and we would sit and smile at each other in appreciation of all that we do for one another. He would then tell me how amazing I was. Then he would laugh at me as he would make cups and cups of tea and for some reason, I would never fully drink them. It became a little bit of a joke between us. His neighbours were lovely people, Colin and Mary. Very often, when I was at Sam's house, they would make us a cup of coffee and pass it over the fence or pop around and help us with deciding what was a weed and what was not. They would bring around plants and help us plant them. Very beautiful people and Sam would help them out when they needed it. In fact, they became very close to me and my girls. They would complement me on what a positive effect I had had on Sam and how lovely it was to see him happy.

We were growing together or so it seemed, and our friends were becoming mutual friends and we were getting invited out for meals as a couple. We had got over our blip earlier in the year and it did feel wonderful. Everyone was commenting on how happy Sam was and what a lovely effect I was having on him. They would admire how lovely our relationship was and it was.

The turning point for me and, although I did not acknowledge it at the time, was a wedding we were invited to attend. It was a beautiful wedding. The groom knew Sam and I had met his bride when we had been invited to a meal one evening. We got along like a house on fire as we are both runners and run together still. The wedding was one of those beautiful occasions where the bride and groom are so in love and so meant to be together. When I turned up at Sam's house to go to the wedding I had had my hair done and I was wearing a new dress. I have to admit I looked gorgeous and I could tell Sam was in absolute awe of me. Sam and I had a wonderful time but I do feel at that point, he looked at this event and realised that I would want to get married one day and he couldn't do it.

The wedding was amazing, the evening was incredible, we danced the night away. I got to meet some of his cycling friends that he talked about all the time. We even got to stay out the night together and not have the children with us, which we had never done. For me, this evening was precious. When we did get to go to our beds Sam turned over to go to sleep and once again, I felt my heart sink into my stomach. I was feeling loved up and passionate and he was tired. It's only when I look back that I realise the cracks were starting to show on his part.

We carried on for another two months, going on holidays, doing things with the children but I knew this man had changed and was backing off again with his emotions, as he didn't want to get hurt. But it was me who was hurting. We had a discussion about love and the fact that he would never tell me he loved me and it led to him saying that he could never give me commitment.

"Do you love me?" I asked Sam.

"I don't know. I love being with you and you make me feel incredible. We laugh and we have fun but I don't think I know what love is." He lowered his head to look at his feet.

"You knew from the beginning that I only wanted to get into a relationship if we both wanted the same things. You told me that you wanted me as a life partner and you told me that you wanted to live together." I had my therapist head on so as to not connect with the emotion I was feeling.

"If I told you how I felt, I'm scared you will want more and I'm not prepared to give you any more. I don't want to live with someone. I just want to carry on the way we are." He folded his arms and stood defiantly.

"Then we cannot continue. It is over. I want more and you can't give me more. That isn't going to work for me. I love you and I want to give you everything." Floods of tears fell.

He started to cry, "I'm so sorry. Jennifer, I'm so sorry. What have I done. You are the loveliest person I know. Why have I done this to you."

"I don't know but please leave," I pushed Sam away and he nodded in acknowledgement of my request and left.

I put the kettle on to make a cup of tea and I shook as I made it. I looked at it but my throat would not let me drink. I needed to cry.

I knew he loved me from the look in his eye, the things that he did for me and the card that he sent me at Valentine's Day. It had the most beautiful words but for him to physically say these things to me, he couldn't do it.

I waited a couple of weeks to adjust to the situation before telling my girls. Sam and I were still meeting and talking. I hoped he would change his mind and admit his feelings but nothing changed and every time he walked away it got more difficult.

You see Sam's belief system was running along the lines of I've been hurt and married and it didn't work so it won't work again. He may beg to differ. I saw in him this stubbornness. He very often would comment that when he got married, he got married for life, regardless of whether he was happy or not. Which is a huge statement to make and actually tells you a lot about a person. It was a warning bell and I ignored it. There is a belief that once was enough and they will never marry again, unless of course they do the therapy work to get beyond that point. At the end of the day, you have to want to change and he didn't want to change, regardless of whether I was the love of his life or not. And that, for me, was the sad part. His previous relationships had also been very fiery and there had been lots of arguments. I don't argue, so for Sam this was something completely different. He hadn't been used to a mature relationship. He had built a barrier and he didn't know how to pull it down and learn to give of himself to another. But I forgive him and we were not meant to be together in this lifetime but it was wonderful while it lasted.

Although I had attracted a lovely relationship, it was not quite complete as commitment and love is a biggie in my book. I deserve that and so do my children. Heart-broken I let him go but it hurt like crazy. He has tried to be friends with me but that doesn't work for me. My heart wasn't ready to just be friends.

We kept in touch for three months after we split up and he would still pop round and we would cycle together or go out for a meal but I wanted us to be back together and he couldn't decide how he felt, other than he loved being with me and had told me on several occasions how he never stopped thinking about me and he missed me. It just gave me false hope that things would work out and eventually at Christmas we had a close encounter and almost slept together until he told me that there would be nothing but sex. I asked him to leave as I had more dignity than that. When I got his Christmas presents and cards my heart sank. His card said, "To Jennifer... Thank you for all you have done for me this year.. Sam". I cried as it was so cold and heartless. He made me feel as though I had been his therapist not his girlfriend and I suddenly realised that this man had not an ounce of feeling about me or how I might be feeling and it was all about him. Him keeping in touch was to appease his guilt of how he had led me down the garden path with no intention of ever committing.

He started to post photos on Instagram on Christmas Day and I commented on one of his photos as he had been for a run. Something he told me that he would never do, he replied to me in a private message to say that he had no bike and at that point I knew that he was either seeing someone else or there was someone else he was interested in. I Knew, my gut feeling told me and at that point I cut all ties, deleted his number and decided it was time to get on with my life. I was right and, on my Birthday, I found out that he was dating someone else. Someone with a similar background to me but as I said to the person who told me, "she will never be me". It cut me like a knife but you know I sent him a message to say that I had been told about his new girlfriend and I wished him well and although it took him all day to reply and thank me, he never returned the sentiment and to me that spoke volumes. I also found out that he had bought her a bike like my bike and he was taking her dancing. It felt as though he had found someone to replace me and was trying to make her me. As I said before, "no one will ever be me". Out of this experience came my realisation that I need to love me and not change for anyone. My commitment is to me and my children. Olivia and Verity were not too upset that Sam and I had separated as they were not very keen on him but Scarlett had become quite attached to Sam and he had taken her under his wing, particularly with the cycling and she loved to cycle with him, so she missed him greatly.

A few months later I received a message from Sam. Sam's neighbours who had been so lovely to me had kept in touch. Sam was messaging to tell me that Colin, his neighbour, had been taken to hospital and was very ill. I immediately asked if I could visit and the following day took myself off to Brighton to visit him. It was a little awkward as I had decided to cut ties with Sam and Colin and Mary knew how hurt I was. I know that Mary particularly was very disappointed with the whole situation and surprised he had even moved on to another relationship but who are we to judge. Colin had been taken to Oncology Ward and when I saw him he had lost the use of his legs. It was all very sudden as he had really had no symptoms and if he had, he never let on. We talked for a while about the girls and, I told them that Scarlett had wanted to come and see him but I felt it was better that she did not. Scarlett had given me an amethyst to give to Colin to help him heal. He was very overwhelmed by this and held onto the crystal. Mary decided that she needed to leave and I offered her a lift home. She took herself off to prepare for the journey home and I had a few minutes with Colin alone. I told him how much I missed seeing them and at that point he burst into tears and so did I. We held each other and I knew that would be the last time I would see him. A few days later his sister in law messaged me to say that he was terminal and was being moved to a hospice. I was driving to Eastbourne at the time. I pulled over and cried my eyes out. A day or so later Sam text me to tell me the same. He was quite insistent that I visited but I said that I felt at this point it was time for me to step back from the equation. I feel in these final moments it is time for family and very close friends.

I knew Sam viewed Colin as a father figure and I felt that I needed to step out for my own protection. It was pulling me back into his matrix and I wasn't sure I could cope with that especially knowing Sam was with someone else and Colin and Mary felt awkward about it. Even introducing me to their relatives they stumbled over their words as they weren't quite sure how to introduce me. It's just a generation thing but I knew they felt uneasy. I stepped back and within 8 weeks I received a message from his sister in law to tell me that he had passed away, preceded by a message from Sam. I asked Sam to let me know when the funeral was and I would attend. He agreed that he would. A week or so later, I was talking to a lady in a local shop who was also a neighbour of Colin and Mary's and she told me when the funeral was. Two days later I saw Sam on his bike and he waved. Two minutes later I got a text from him telling me the funeral details. I just thanked him.

The funeral was a lovely occasion and I attended for Colin and Mary and whilst in church I asked for strength as I was still heartbroken but healing. Colin had been a firefighter and I knew it would be a fire brigade funeral and Sam would be a pallbearer. I sat with a friend and it was one of the most beautiful personal funerals I have ever been to. We then went to the local club for the wake. I wrote in his Book of Remembrance and had a coffee and chatted to some of the neighbours that I had got to know. Mary entered the room with her family a little later as they had attended the burial. She approached me and hugged me and then told me the most precious thing anyone could have told me. She said that whilst she was sorting out some of Colin's things, she had opened a drawer with all his special keepsakes and, in the drawer, was Scarlett's amethyst that she had given to him at the hospital. Mary said that to her it was a sign that Colin was saying that it was special as he had held it every day until he died and with that she had decided that the amethyst should be buried with him in his coffin. Oh flipping heck I sobbed like a baby. What a beautiful thing to do and say. My friend already knew about this and had been waiting for Mary to tell me. I felt very honoured that it had meant so much. I pulled myself together and apologised to Mary who was holding it together very well. I don't think the reality of it had really hit home. Sam then walked into the room and my friend nudged me. He didn't approach me and I felt it was silly not to speak so I approached him to say "hello". He picked me up with such gusto my feet left the floor and kissed me and told me how lovely it was to see me. He commented on my hair and how lovely I looked. He then introduced me to the people he had been talking to (ex-neighbours) who said that they recognised me and I just said that it was lovely to meet them again. I turned around and Sam was looking at his feet. He had shut down. I'm not sure if it was the realisation of what he had lost but I touched his back and said "goodbye" to him and he never looked up, as though he couldn't say goodbye. That was the last time I saw him and for me, it was my closure. He was with someone else and I had moved on. My heart will always have a place for him but it will never open up to him again.

I asked myself so many questions about what this relationship had been about. Why were we together so long? Why could he not tell me how he felt? Why jump in with both feet if he was scared of commitment? Why is this happening to me again? Was it me?

My lesson was to listen. To listen to what people are really saying when they speak. It's that unspoken word that is so important. The Universe wants me to love me first, to respect my needs and commit to me. Only then will I be at a place to bring in the right person. You don't have to stay stuck.

Although It took me a long time to come back to fun loving Jennifer, I did. I worked on what had happened, I cried, I reflected, I did EFT work and Reiki. I took time to heal the wounds as I knew I didn't want to repeat this cycle. I do the things that make me happy and no one can ever take that away.

I can laugh again and be me again. My girls are the centre of my world. I focused my attention back on my business and built it up again. Time and therapies were the healer for me. It was a hard lesson to learn.

Chapter Twenty-Six

Home at Last

Don't ever give up hope. You don't have to repeat the patterns of having abusive relationships. I knew that my self-esteem had taken a battering and needed to be restored. Sam may not have wanted commitment but he did want all the other things I wanted and I know there is somebody out there with the same attributes that will want commitment. It is all about being precise about what you do want and not lowering your standards, knowing your self-worth. Neither Sam, Patrick, Dave, Matthew or Finlay were bad people. Just broken people who have not healed their past and are living denying themselves the ability to fully love and I just wanted to make them 'the one'. For me, Jennifer Smith, it was a lesson in really listening to what people are saying to me and not hearing what I want them to say.

Finlay was afraid of commitment and showing affection but when we met life was about living and exploring and it was all very exciting. It masked the underlying commitment phobia in him and I was prepared to go along with it because I loved him and because I wanted to live the life we were living, not knowing what was around the corner. It's only when life became real and normal that the cracks started to show. I was prepared to carry on in a one-sided relationship until my self-worth could not take any more and I realised that it was not acceptable or what I really wanted.

Matthew was loving and giving but deep down he didn't want commitment either. The warning bells were there with regards to his background. He had married and walked away from his child, although he had married again he had not addressed what had happened or why. He wanted to have someone by his side but not someone who wanted children. If only I had read the messages and considered his past relationships but I didn't and I had to learn a lesson again. He had overwhelmed me with attention and I was ignoring the little signs that said that things were wrong. I had suffered a certain amount of mental abuse towards the end of this relationship and I had allowed it to happen.

Dave was slightly different, he liked the idea of family and commitment and he desperately wanted somebody by his side but he couldn't cope with what came with family life. He hadn't grown up himself and yet he portrayed an image of maturity and professionalism. This gave a different impression of him but it was not a true reflection. Because we had children I was prepared to make it work at all costs and keep up the appearance of the perfect family. The relationship was very draining and damaging mentally and physically. The longer I stayed the worse it got. I was the one giving and trying to make it work. Another lesson in having balance in a relationship and learning not to take the abuse.

Patrick came along at a point in my life where the thought of dating was scary. He showed interest in me which felt flattering and I certainly wasn't interested but I was overriding my intuition as the attention took over. It felt exciting to be living again after having been at home with the children and it was lovely to share family times with someone. Again, it was another person who thought he wanted all the commitment of a family relationship but when it boiled down to it, it was another person who didn't want commitment and couldn't give me what I was giving them. Again, another mentally abusive relationship and very damaging to my self-worth.

When I look back at the last relationship, I had to ask myself, "what was it about the commitment that Sam mirrored in me". Everything we send out we get back, remember! I realised that all along I had said that my children are my responsibility and I don't expect anyone else to take care of them. In actual fact, my children are part of me and we come as one, so anyone who wants to take me on will have to take responsibility for us all. I was sending out this message that I was available as me and not sending out the message that we are a family. Although he acknowledged we were a family I never made him responsible for them.

With all my relationships they have been one-sided. They all loved the image of me but none of them were able to give me what I really wanted. There was almost a pretence at the beginning of each relationship to capture me. The heady days that you get when you first meet someone. The emotions take over and the reality of it all can be so different. I wanted to be a people pleaser and the perfect little partner, prepared to love unconditionally. The unconditional bit being to my detriment. Once they realised that I was their partner they no longer felt the need to try. It said a lot about my self-worth and the level of unacceptable behaviour that the lovely bubbly Jennifer was prepared to accept. It also pointed out that I didn't love myself enough. I loved myself when I wasn't with someone but as soon as another influence came into my life, my self love went out of the window, just to be accepted.

Although my last relationship was lovely, it ended for a reason. I know that there is somebody out there ten times better who will adore me and won't think twice about the commitment. I'm writing it down for the universe to see and trusting that it will be delivered. The therapies have been invaluable in examining what messages I have sent out with regard to all of my past relationships and it has enabled me to evolve into the person I am today. The beliefs from my childhood have played a major part in how I have evolved. I have always struggled in asking for what I need, perhaps because of being told as a child to be seen and not heard and that you must always do as you are told. It's very interesting how these beliefs rollercoaster into bigger issues and you end up being a chameleon and not a leading star.

At the end of the day, life is for living and I believe that none of us are here to suffer or live in pain. We are here to make a difference but also to be happy and love our lives. What is your passion? What makes you happy? Have you forgotten? Then it's time to reconnect to that. What beliefs are stopping you from the life that you want to achieve. Claim your life, your mess, your situation and create a better one. There is always a choice. Jennifer had a choice.

I was at the school gate and a lady asked me about my running. I told her that I had run 10 miles and she asked me how I had time to do all the things I do. My answer is I made a choice. I made a choice to be happy; happy with who I am, happy in the things I do, happy to just be.

I'm not saying everything is hunkey dorey at this point there have been lots of things I have had to deal with. Particularly the eldest two children. Olivia has struggled to go to sleep since the divorce and still to this day it takes her time to unwind but she is now a beautiful young lady, very balanced, happy and cheerful and she loves her home and going to secondary school has been the making of her. Her reports are superb. Olivia is quiet and mild and loving but has an inner strength. Verity went through a period of having the e-coli UTI and it has taken two years for it to clear her system. She is very sensitive, deep, extremely intelligent and has excelled at school. Scarlett is Scarlett, she has such a lovely nature and is loving and caring but very demanding at times. She is definitely older than her years or likes to think she is. They are all very beautiful children and intuitive and all showing signs of their psychic abilities. Olivia is dreaming about things that happen the following day and Scarlett sees angels when I do my reiki. Verity writes her manifesting lists and sends it out there to the Universe. It has been a bumpy ride, especially when I started to date again but it's about living your life the best you can be. That's all anyone can be is the best version of themselves.

These amazing therapies have been the turning point in my life and I know that they have helped thousands of people all over the world. The power of the mind is amazing and the realisation that we are energy and connected is mind blowing. We all transmit a vibration and it is up to us as an individual to decide what we want to transmit. It is your choice. Make that choice, don't compromise. Be best version of you.

Jennifer Smith had many life lessons before she could come to this realisation. But how life changed and she doesn't have to put up with unacceptable behaviour. Jennifer is now a fun-loving Mum and living a life she enjoys knowing that good things are happening and love is all around her. What will the next chapter bring? Who knows but it will be so much better than what went before.

We are all looking to be supported, accepted and unconditionally loved. Remember that all of these things you have to acknowledge in yourself first. The perfect relationship is within you and is you.

Don't ask me what is right or wrong
I only have one answer,
If life is full of love, laughter and song
And the steps we take are lighter,
Then you have won.

The End

Lorraine Butterfield runs her own business based in Seaford, East Sussex. Working with people locally and all over the country and world to help them to heal the past using EFT/Matrix Re-imprinting and Reiki.

To connect with Lorraine visit her website:

www.lorrainebutterfield.co.uk

www.facebook.com/LorraineButterfield

For a tarot card reading with Lorraine:

www.facebook.com/lorrainebutterfield69

Printed in Great Britain
by Amazon